CALIFORNIA'S
Channel Islands

CALIFORNIA'S
Channel Islands
A HISTORY

FREDERIC CAIRE CHILES

University of Oklahoma Press : Norman

Chapter 5, "Santa Cruz Island," is a condensed version of
Justinian Caire and Santa Cruz Island: The Rise and Fall of a California Dynasty (2011)
and published courtesy of the University of Oklahoma Press.

Library of Congress Cataloging-in-Publication Data
Chiles, Frederic Caire, 1947–
    California's Channel Islands : a history / Frederic Caire Chiles.
      pages cm.
    Includes bibliographical references and index.
    ISBN 978-0-8061-4687-4 (pbk. : alk. paper) 1. Channel Islands (Calif.)—
History. 2. Channel Islands (Calif.)—Description and travel. 3. Natural
history—California—Channel Islands. I. Title.
    F868.S232C54 2015
    979.4′91—dc23
                        2014025636

The paper in this book meets the guidelines for permanence and durability
of the Committee on Production Guidelines for Book Longevity
of the Council on Library Resources, Inc. ∞

1 2 3 4 5 6 7 8 9 10

Contents

Illustrations

Maps

Preface

L ike nowhere else on the planet. These are the Channel Islands of California, a home of biodiversity unrivaled anywhere on earth. Not only
that, they provide a window into the complex geology, natural history, and
human history of this part of the world, going back to the first probing of
humans into the unpopulated continent we now call the Americas.

I learned of the Channel Islands at my mother's knee, filtered through
a golden haze of reminiscence of her childhood and young adulthood
when her family owned the largest of the chain, Santa Cruz Island. For her
Oakland-based family, which ran the Santa Cruz Island Company from its
San Francisco headquarters, these were years of gracious living on the island,
mostly in the summers. Her story was dominated by a bold French-emigré
entrepreneur who built a California rancho in the old grand style. The narrative included the stalwart men and women who carried on his legacy and
the colorful ranch hands who worked in this island kingdom.

The fact that there were other islands in the chain or that they had been
inhabited since the first epoch of human existence on the continent was
purely incidental to the main story. It was not until I began researching my
book on the history of Santa Cruz Island (*Justinian Caire and Santa Cruz
Island*) that the depth and breadth of the human and natural history of these
islands was revealed to me. It was an eye-opener that piqued my curiosity
and made me resolve to find out more about the other islands and their flora,
fauna, and human history. It set me on a journey of discovery that took in the
prehistory of the indigenous peoples, who called the islands home for at least
thirteen millennia, and the history starting with the Spanish exploration

in the sixteenth century and culminating in the period in the nineteenth century in which my great-grandfather came into possession of Santa Cruz Island. As interesting as its history is, that of Santa Cruz is only one strand of a complex tapestry of nine histories—first, the thousands of years of the most complex forager society of North America, and then the individual stories of each of the eight islands in the modern period. With the establishment of the Channel Islands National Park in 1980 and the accessibility of six of the islands to the public, it seemed to me that the time was ripe for a book that would combine the latest strands of research into the natural history, island ecology, and historical human endeavor to tell the full story of California's Channel Islands.

Acknowledgments

Because this book is a collection of nine histories, one for the indigenous prehistoric population, and one for each of the islands, I have relied on the help of a number of collaborators who have profound knowledge and experience relating to one or more of the islands of the chain. California's Channel Islands have been the object of study for a large number of scientists and researchers whose work has yielded valuable insights encompassing the past millennia of this part of California and on which I have relied heavily. Chief among those to whom I am indebted is Lyndal Laughrin, director, Santa Cruz Island Reserve, UC Santa Barbara Reserve System, whose knowledge of the fauna, flora, and human history of these islands has been invaluable, and who has been openhanded with his time and kind in his judgments of my attempts to understand the various aspects of island ecology and diversity. Mike Glassow has also given generously of his time and advice on the prehistory of these islands, as has John Johnson of the Santa Barbara Museum of Natural History. I am also grateful to Lynn Gamble for her encouragement of this work, and I thank Professor Brian Fagan for the inspiration to imagine the daily life of the Chumash islanders. Betsy Lester Roberti gave a constructive and encouraging reading to the chapter involving her family. Tim Vail was helpful and supportive in his reading of the chapter on Santa Rosa Island. My family, the Caire descendants, provided their usual invaluable level of support in recounting the story of Santa Cruz Island, particularly my sister Mary B. Brock. Ann Huston, Chief, Cultural Resources of the Channel Islands National Park, was a key advisor on the writing of the history of the five islands within the park, San Miguel,

Santa Rosa, Santa Cruz, Anacapa, and Santa Barbara. Dewey Livingstone's unpublished historic resource study of the Channel Islands, written for the National Park Service, was an excellent source. Geoff Rusak of the Wrigley family provided important insights and assistance in helping me understand Santa Catalina Island, and the curator of the Santa Catalina Museum, John Boraggina, was also very obliging. Steven Schwartz of the Environmental Division of the Naval Air Weapons Station, Point Mugu, was very supportive and encouraging in matters relating to San Nicolas Island, and Dr. Andy Yatsko, senior archaeologist and Region Southwest archaeologist for the Naval Facilities Engineering Command Southwest in San Diego, contributed his kind encouragement and knowledge to an understanding of San Clemente Island. Always in the background, providing her unrivalled knowledge of the islands, was Marla Daily of the Santa Cruz Island Foundation.

Beyond these experts on California's Channel Islands, I owe a debt to many others who encouraged me, notably Professor Richard Oglesby, my mentor and advisor. I also owe a debt to the staffs of the libraries of the Society of California Pioneers and the California Historical Society as well as to the anonymous readers of the University of Oklahoma Press for their comments on the manuscript. The press's Kathleen Kelly was encouraging and supportive in getting my ideas to the printed page.

I am hugely grateful to all these individuals and institutions for their help, though on a daily basis it was the patience and understanding of my wife, Jacky Davis, who helped me press on to the end, and it is to her that this book is dedicated. As far as any errors or faulty interpretations, the blame for these is mine alone.

CALIFORNIA'S
Channel Islands

CHAPTER 1

California's Channel Islands: An Introduction

THESE ARE PLACES WHERE THE DEEP PAST SEEMS MORE STARKLY PRESENT.
LITTLE HERE IS OVERLAID, AS IT IS ELSEWHERE, WITH THE THICK MULCH
OF RECENT EVENTS. PHYSICAL REMAINS OF EARLIER AGES LIE
JUST BENEATH THE SURFACE, SCARCELY COVERED.
MODERNITY IS ALMOST ABSENT, CUT OFF BY THE [SEA].

Adam Nicolson
Sea Room: An Island Life in the Hebrides

Within the Southern California Bight, the rough arc of coastline between the cities of San Diego and Santa Barbara, the archipelago of the eight Channel Islands of California range in size from one square mile (Santa Barbara Island) to ninety-six square miles (Santa Cruz Island). The northern Channel Islands—San Miguel, Santa Rosa, Santa Cruz, and Anacapa—form an east–west chain off the coast of Santa Barbara County. The southern Channel Islands—Santa Catalina, San Clemente, San Nicolas, and Santa Barbara—are more widely dispersed, fringing the southern half of the bight roughly between the cities of Los Angeles and San Diego.

As one leaves the mainland, heading out to sea, each island swims into view, an undefined ridge floating in the haze. In the middle distance, they are usually gold and dark green. The gold is the dried brush and grasses dropping toward the cliffs. The dark green, mostly in the canyons, is the typical chaparral brush of California, sometimes interspersed with oak, fern, or pine. In spring, the brush is a luxuriant green with myriad yellow flowers, but that season is usually brief. Drawing nearer, as the distant Southern California mainland's solid layer of modernity becomes hazy and indistinct, the islands come into focus with their aura of existence before the measurement of time. Gradually they fill one's field of vision with a California before history. These are entryways to a wild California that has all but disappeared from the mainland, with the added appeal of plants and animals that flourish nowhere else on earth, profoundly shaped by the size of each island and its distance from the mainland—from the coastal proximity of Santa Catalina and Anacapa, to the remote wildness of San Miguel, San Nicolas, and San Clemente.

As one reaches five of the six islands where the public is welcome, cliffs often soar forbiddingly above, while at approach level waves crash into vertical rock bases, hissing and booming in sea caves. Shearwaters skim the surface and the cries of seals, sea lions, gulls, and other seabirds create a cacophony of sound far removed from the machine hum of daily life to which we are accustomed.[1] Here ruggedly dressed visitors shoulder their packs and step through a dramatic time portal. Signs of human habitation are perhaps reduced to a basic dock, with flights of iron stairs ascending a cliff above, or a sturdy wharf leading to a road that disappears around a bend into a valley hidden from view. Santa Catalina differs. Avalon, its main port, resembles a Mediterranean seaside village in France or Italy or perhaps a coastal California town from the 1940s or 1950s. With a tidy yacht basin, it is anchored at one end by a domed casino and at the other by well-kept, steeply climbing streets. Here thousands of visitors stream off the hourly ferries, wearing every type of outfit from flimsy resort wear to sturdy backcountry hiking gear.

In the interior of the islands, visitors discover a California seemingly frozen in time. Minimal human habitation intrudes. California as it appeared in pre-contact days is the visible reality, with distinctive flora and fauna. The work of scientists from Charles Darwin and his successors of the present day reminds us that islands such as these are "unique evolutionary laboratories." They are high-resolution demonstrations of the evolutionary forces that shaped the plants and animals that we find on them today.

The Southern California maritime boundary differs from a typical continental shelf in that it encompasses large depressions as deep as almost seven thousand feet below sea level and island peaks as high as almost twenty-five hundred feet above the sea. The geological evidence suggests that coastal and offshore Southern California changed from a more typical shelf-slope condition to one of basins and ridges in the cataclysms beginning twenty-five to thirty million years ago. Converging tectonic plates, shearing and tearing each other, were accompanied by fiery volcanoes in an age that lasted until about ten million years ago.

It was at this time that Southern California emerged as a distinctive part of the North American land mass. Today's California Channel Islands came to be formed in embryo, changing their sizes and shapes as this part of the planet went through ages of fire and ice. The islands probably became distinct from the continental land mass in the Pleistocene Ice Age, which began about 2.6 million years ago and was characterized by a complex mixture of plate tectonics, volcanism, and the raising and lowering of sea levels.

The Channel Islands are continental islands, outliers of the western shelf of the North American continent. It seems likely that at the end of the last great ice age—about twelve thousand years ago—the four northern islands, San Miguel, Santa Rosa, Santa Cruz, and Anacapa, were connected, forming one large island that geologists call Santarosae. It was cut off from the mainland by a narrow but steep marine canyon. Pleistocene mammals on this large island included mammoths, which are said to have swum the narrow channel and evolved into a dwarf form. Other evolutionary examples were giant deer mice and two species of flightless geese.

With the melting of glaciers, the sea level rose about 150 feet, dividing the large Santarosae into the four individual northern Channel Islands approximately nine thousand years ago. It is only in very recent geologic time—about four thousand years ago—that the islands reached their present size, although we can trace the combination of uplift and changing sea levels over the past two million years from the characteristic wave-cut marine terraces on some of the islands, most notably Santa Rosa, Santa Cruz, San Nicolas, and San Clemente. On San Clemente as many as nineteen terraces are exposed above sea level, with another two below.

The topography of the northern Channel Islands can be described as the exposed top of a single, dissected mountain range. The island ridge is lower at either end (San Miguel and Anacapa) and highest in the center (western Santa Cruz and eastern Santa Rosa). The straits between the islands are described as broad transverse valleys that were exposed when lower sea levels allowed the islands to all be connected. Higher seas resulting from melting ice during warm interglacial periods, combined with local uplifting of the earth's crust, may have alternately submerged and exposed the islands at various times, except for the highest parts of Santa Cruz. The stepped series of marine terraces suggest that the largest part of their land mass was covered by water from time to time.

The sea around the islands today, the waters of the Southern California Bight, show another complex pattern. The cool California Current heading down the coast is altered by the bight, and an eddy system is developed in which the water swings inward toward the coast in the area of San Diego, with a surface flow up the coast forming the California Countercurrent. This countercurrent creates a transitional zone in which surface water combines with deep water welling up from below three hundred feet. This flow is blocked by the northern Channel Islands and diverted westward to merge with the California Current west of San Miguel Island. This system provides an important source of cold water and nutrients that rise up from the deep ocean, creating a rich oceanic ecosystem. The mixing of temperatures and salinity levels brings together northern- and southern-ranging organisms, a diverse array of fish, plants, birds, and marine mammals, to form an area hugely rich in biodiversity. More so than for other island chains, there is a justifiable claim that the sea makes these islands what they are. It not only defines them, it moderates their climates and creates conditions favoring the survival of species of plant life not seen on the mainland in millennia.

This eight-island realm is in the intertidal or littoral zone, where the land and sea overlap. In a constant demonstration of the edge effect, it contains characteristics of both terrestrial and oceanic habitats, giving rise to the richest zone on earth in terms of organism diversity. This is most obvious in the luxuriant kelp beds and tidal zones where a large variety of mollusks, sea mammals, fish species, and seabirds are prevalent. In general, if it were not for the islands of California, where nesting birds can find refuge from terrestrial predators, seabirds would be largely absent from the California coast. The avian and marine life of the California coast is rich and varied, and the islands represent relatively unspoiled coastal havens crucial to the continuation of that biological diversity.

While they share many characteristics, the islands are also set apart by differences. The northern islands are less arid, closer to shore, and closer to each other than their southern counterparts. They are also generally larger and higher in elevation. There is a trend toward greater ecological diversity and increased numbers of species on these larger wetter islands. The absence of terrestrial mammals such as coyotes, bears, raccoons, rabbits, and gophers, makes it highly unlikely that the islands were part of the mainland after the emergence of these creatures there, though other life forms did make the journey across the channel, probably by flotation, rafting, flying, and intentional or accidental transport.

The flora of the northern islands is characterized by a high proportion of species found on the mainland north of Point Conception. They hark back to prehistoric ice ages when northern species invaded Southern California during glacial episodes and then retreated during warmer times. Their remnants continued to survive, largely due to the cooling influence of the California Current, and some of the survivors of the island adaptation competition have evolved into endemics, distinct plant or animal forms restricted in their distribution to a particular insular locality.

The key factor behind the large number of endemics on the islands is isolation. The populations of several islands, especially those in the northern group, appear to be more closely related to populations found on the mainland from Point Conception north than to those along the drier, adjacent coast of Southern California. Ratifying island biogeography theory, the southern Channel Islands—Santa Barbara, San Nicolas, Santa Catalina, and San Clemente—support proportionally more endemics than do the northern ones, life forms that have grown and interacted in isolation—immigrants that continue to evolve after their arrival, to survive on their new island home. The natural selection within the limited island gene pool enhances adaptations that are valuable for survival in an island environment. The housecat-sized Channel Islands fox, a dwarf form of the mainland gray fox, is found on all the Channel Islands except for the two smallest, Anacapa and Santa Barbara. Its coloring and body proportions are similar to the mainland fox, but its overall size is much slighter. Another mammal that has evolved to suit island life is the island spotted skunk, found on both Santa Cruz and Santa Rosa. These creatures have a larger head and body than those on the mainland, but a shorter tail and fewer white markings. Larger than its mainland relative, the island deer mouse is the only terrestrial mammal common to all eight islands, though each island has its own distinctive subspecies. Birds too have developed on the islands as species and subspecies. The most distinctive is the Santa Cruz Island jay, a third larger than its mainland counterpart and considerably brighter blue in color. In all, there are thirteen birds that have evolved into island endemics.

The islands' human prehistory, stretching back to the earliest human life on the continent, is a tapestry of intersecting currents and themes: climate change, invention and adaptation to that change, and commerce and alteration of the insular environments by the people who called these islands their home for thousands of years.[2] In the post-contact era, the last 450 years or so, the islands' recorded histories reflect in many ways the strong personalities and vision of the Europeans and European Americans who stepped forward and claimed all or part of them. Often with the best of intentions, they engaged in activities that over decades altered the island ecosystems even more dramatically than the actions of previous inhabitants over many millennia.

The post-contact era saw the decimation of the Native human population through disruption of local economies, introduced disease, and violence. This was related to the virtual elimination of the otter, the northern fur seal and the northern elephant seal early in the nineteenth century through overhunting. The removal of the Chumash Indians and their southern cousins to mainland missions opened the way on some of the islands for Mexican government land grants, and, later, U.S. government ownership of the others. With the rationale of nineteenth-century land husbandry and a focus on profitability, the agriculturalists who followed the Chumash people provided a series of examples of the magnified effect of species introduction into a circumscribed insular environment. Uncertain rainfall meant that populations of sheep and cattle swung between good years, when their numbers were allowed to soar, and drought years, when they starved or were killed for tallow, fleeces, and hides. A proportion of the goats, pigs, and sheep deposited on most of the islands soon reverted to a wild state and reproduced rapidly, often extirpating many plant species and certainly altering almost all plant communities. Before the modern era of "scientific range management," the numbers of introduced animals often exceeded the carrying capacity of the islands. A lack of predators meant that they were allowed to seriously damage fragile plant communities that had existed for thousands of years isolated from grazing pressure. It was not until the twentieth century on Santa Cruz Island and Santa Rosa Island in particular that conservative ranch management principles were put in place.

The prehistory of the Native peoples and the documented history of the last four centuries form two strands, and taken together they span at least thirteen thousand years, if not more. The habitation of the Channel Islands can be divided into four main phases. The first was the prehistoric phase, lasting perhaps thirteen millennia, overlapping with the era of Spanish exploration, which ended when the islands were largely depopulated, either by voluntary or involuntary removal of the Native populations to the mainland or by the ravages of diseases to which the Indians had no immunity. The last known Indigenous resident on any Channel Island was the so-called Lone Woman of San Nicolas, who was taken to Santa Barbara in 1853. Her story is taken up in chapter 8.

The first recorded contact between local Indigenous populations and Europeans was in the great age of Spanish exploration, in 1542, when two ships, *San Salvador* and *La Victoria*, traveled among the islands under the command of Juan Rodríguez Cabrillo. In the reports of the expedition, written years afterward, the northern islands of the group were referred to as the Islas San Lucas. At the end of the century, in 1595, Sebastián Rodríguez Cermeño visited some of the islands, although it is unclear which ones. It is thought that they were Santa Rosa, San Miguel, and Santa Catalina. Three years later the Manila galleon *San Pedro* was wrecked on Santa Catalina Island and the ship's company was stranded there for several months. In 1602 Sebastían Vizcaíno explored the west coast of North America, visiting several of the islands and later publishing extensive notes. This was the last recorded voyage in the initial burst of Spanish exploration. Thereafter, the imperial Spanish found themselves distracted by the complexities of administering and defending the richest and most complicated empire of the age.

It would be 167 years before the discovery routes of Cabrillo, Cermeño, and Vizcaíno were again followed. In 1769, with the Spanish monarchy now troubled by Russian and British threats to its empire's vulnerable Pacific coast, Gaspar de Portolà was dispatched to mount a land and sea expedition. The expedition's land-based contingent founded Mission San Diego de Alcala that year, and the maritime element of the expedition visited several of the Channel Islands, notably Santa Cruz and San Clemente. As if to validate Spain's fears, the maps that finalized the names of the eight islands off the Southern California coast resulted from the voyage of George Vancouver, flying the British flag in 1793.

The next historical phase was the era of Spanish occupation of California that followed the Portolà expedition. Spurred by the perceived threat of Russian and British explorers and settlers, the aim of the expedition was to take possession and title to all California lands in the name of the king of Spain under the Laws of the Indies. This phase lasted fifty-two years, ending with the nine-year Mexican revolt against the rule of the Spanish Empire and the independence of Mexico in 1821.

The following Mexican era lasted just twenty-seven years, until the Treaty of Guadalupe Hidalgo of 1848 that concluded the war between Mexico and the United States. During this period the islands of Santa Cruz, Santa Rosa, and Santa Catalina were granted to private individuals by governors acting for the Mexican government. After the treaty of Guadalupe Hidalgo, title to the other five islands passed to the U.S. government, marking the beginning of the latest era of the Channel Islands. As we approach the present day, this era can be divided into two periods. The first focused on husbandry, principally of livestock, which severely affected the islands' flora and fauna. The second, continuing today, focused on reclamation and recreation under the auspices of nonprofit conservation organizations and the federal government. The Nature Conservancy controls 76 percent of Santa Cruz Island, and the Santa Catalina Island Conservancy controls 86 percent of Santa Catalina. The National Park Service controls the remainder of Santa Cruz, along with all of Santa Rosa, San Miguel (by agreement with the U.S. Navy), Anacapa, and Santa Barbara. The federal government retains control of the remaining two islands, San Nicolas and San Clemente, which are used for military purposes, with access limited to accredited scientific researchers.

No small amount has been written about the engaging and colorful individuals who populated the Channel Island in the last two centuries, but it is with the first thirteen or so millennia of human activity, as the islands emerged from the last great ice age, that we should first concern ourselves before examining the story of each individual island.

CHAPTER 2

The First Inhabitants

In the dim predawn light on Limuw Island, it would be easy to miss the stationary figure poised on the rock at the edge of Swaxil Village (later Scorpion Anchorage) where the point juts out into deep water. The man knows that the kelp-bed fish come close to the shore at this time of day, in these still, calm conditions. If the omens are right, there might be a larger fish swimming close enough for a spear throw. He has set his fishing lines, baited with disguised bones that will lodge in the throat of the fish that swallows them. These take care of themselves, so it is on his stone-tipped spear that he concentrates, waiting for the right moment. As the sun rises higher, he can see other members of the small tribe working their way carefully over the mussel beds, gathering the basis of today's meals. The muffled sound of the pounding of acorns drifts across the small inlet to where the fisherman stands. The scene is as it has always been, for himself and for his ancestors as far back as collective memory reaches: the same fishing, shellfish collecting, and nut and seed grinding in this little cove where a small stream flows down from the hills of the island. This is a society marked only by the smallest of changes through the generations. The life the fisherman knows here in the cove and in the seasonal settlements where his little tribe collect acorns or birds' eggs is virtually unchanged from the time described by the storytellers when the tribe made its first tentative explorations millennia ago across the then-narrow channel.

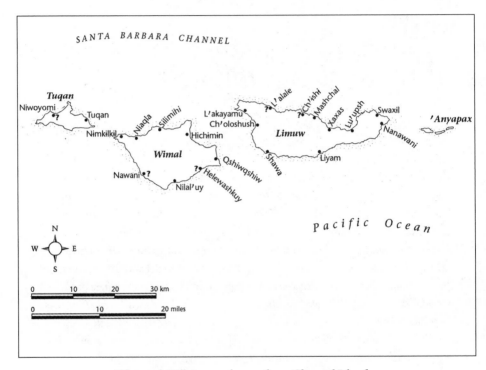

Chumash Villages on the northern Channel Islands.
Used by permission from Michael A. Glassow, Editor and Compiler,
Channel Islands National Park Archaeological Overview and Assessment.
National Park Service, Department of the Interior, 2010.

Facing a coastline so populated, celebrated, and defined by modern culture, the Channel Islands of Southern California contain starkly undisturbed evidence of a much older world compared to the relatively indistinct pre-history of the mainland. It is a world of deep time reaching back to the first incursions of humans into the Americas. As the last of the ice ages lowered sea levels by as much as four hundred feet in some places, a land bridge was revealed between Asia and the uninhabited Americas. The first explorers to cross found a continent fringed by a complex coastline of bays and islets, a resource-rich habitat that was home to sea mammal and shellfish food sources that sustained the maritime peoples as they migrated down the Pacific coast. The California islands of today hold the evidence to chart the lives of these early peoples over more than twelve millennia and trace their development, as some of the earliest documented human inhabitants of North America, into one of the most sophisticated forager cultures ever known.[1]

The island environments of these ancient peoples have particular advantages as subjects for interpretation and analysis by anthropologists and archaeologists. They are discrete geographic units on which resource diversity, abundance, and scarcity can be accurately measured, and because island ecosystems are by definition delimited, they are easier to understand. Analyses and discoveries over the last twenty-five years indicate that these islands were a destination of a seaborne coastal migration begun at least as early, if not before, the first terrestrial migrations down the center of the continent that have long claimed the attention of archaeologists. From San Clemente, Santa Rosa, and San Miguel Islands in particular has come evidence of settlements that required not only the capability for sea travel but also fishing technology for subsistence, and social and economic links to the mainland. These were people who had the maritime craft and skill to travel on open water. This sea-based culture began with some of the earliest settlements on the continent and ended thirteen millennia later with one of the first cultural collisions of the European Age of Exploration. Santa Rosa and San Miguel Islands have the highest concentration of prehistoric sites in all of North America, dating to nine thousand to thirteen thousand years ago or more and containing evidence of adaptation in response to climate change, technological development, and food availability.

Like similar societies in other parts of the world, the island Indians of California could rely on the sea for food. The food came to them—they did not have to move in search of it as did land-based foragers. They also had relatively easy access to bulbs and corms, as well as plants containing nuts and seeds, either by collecting these themselves or trading with their neighbors for them, removing the imperative to domesticate animals or cultivate particular crops. Other cross-cultural comparisons show similarities in the development of cooking and food storage vessels, like the soapstone ollas (jars with wide bodies narrowing at the neck) and woven baskets that groups on different islands excelled at making.

The coastal and island world encountered by the first human settlers in the Terminal Pleistocene and Early Holocene (thirteen thousand to seven thousand years ago) was barely post–Ice Age and significantly cooler than the one we know today. The recent arrivals adapted and developed their culture as the climate of the area became warmer and drier over the next two millennia. At the same time this climate change seems to have challenged the local population, which struggled to respond to changing conditions. The most dramatic of these, as the great ice sheets and glaciers melted about nine thousand years ago, caused the Ice Age mega-island that geologists call Santarosae to divide into the four northern Channel Islands. Sea levels rose, diminishing the insular land area by more than 75 percent to give the islands the outlines they have today. The pine forests were now in retreat, to be replaced by new flora, like chaparral and oaks, that were more suited to the warm, dry conditions. By about five thousand years ago, it appears that the Indigenous people were adapting to these changed circumstances with new tools. Archaeologists note the appearance of stone mortars and pestles, metates, and manos to grind pulpy plant parts, including nuts, acorns, and bulbs that had become an important food source. The plant resources supplemented the marine foods that the Indigenous peoples had now begun to hunt with stone-tipped spears. On the northern islands, shellfish such as clams and particularly mussels remained an important part of their protein-rich marine diet.

It was at about this time that two language groups became established in the region. The Chumash of the northern islands spoke a language related to the family of languages spoken by the peoples on the mainland coast across the strait. This differentiated them from the Tongva speakers, who are said to have emerged about two thousand years later, the so-called Gabrieleños of the southern islands. Theirs was a Takic language associated with tribes of the Great Basin and the Mojave Desert. All together the Indigenous peoples are often referred to as Canaliño Indians, people of the channel.

By five thousand years ago, all of the larger islands were permanently inhabited, in small settlements mostly near sources of water. We know from these habitations' refuse middens—essentially the accumulation of the debris of everyday living—that the island peoples' nutritional reliance on shellfish, including abalone, gradually expanded to include sea mammals and fish inhabiting the islands' luxuriant kelp beds. Seal and sea lion blubber, a critical dietary component where plant foods were unable to supply sufficient carbohydrates, became prominent, along with whale meat when they could get it. Experts are not in complete agreement about the reason for this shift, but it would appear that the causes were both rooted in the human impact of overfishing and longer-term climate change creating warmer sea and land temperatures. We do know that the development of fishing technologies—hooks, nets, and spears—kept pace with the changing climate and dietary needs. By about eight hundred years ago, fish was the most important component of the islanders' diet, caught using harpoons with a detachable foreshaft for spearing large fish, and curved, circular fishhooks made from abalone and mussel shells for catching smaller fish.

The most important innovation, the plank canoe called *tomol* or *tomolo* in the northern islands and *tiat* in the southern islands, dates from fifteen hundred to thirteen hundred years ago, with prototypical variants appearing perhaps as early as four thousand years ago. It was the linchpin of the Channel Island fishing and trading systems. The much prized and admired seagoing canoe was the Southern California variant of the sewn-plank craft tradition, akin to that of northwestern Europe and northern Asia. There are also examples of this type of construction predating the Iron Age from the South Pacific, thought to be particularly useful in areas of rough surf and where regular beaching of the craft was necessary—exactly the conditions in which the tomols operated.

Researchers are not agreed on dating the appearance of the craft in the area, but whatever the role and timing of the tomol in Chumash cultural history, Channel Islands evidence indicates that it was an elaboration of much earlier seafaring experience, reaching back to the time of the arrival of people on the coastal islands. The island Indians' tomols, at five meters or more in length and capable of carrying more than a ton of cargo, enabled them and their coastal mainland counterparts to venture into deep water, using their harpoons and spears to catch fish, particularly the larger species like sword-fish and sea mammals like dolphins, as well as seals, sea lions, and otters.

We owe many insights into the construction and function of the tomol to Fernando Librado (Kitsepawit). Born in 1839 at Mission San Buenaven-tura in present-day Ventura, California, he was the last known full-blood island Chumash. Librado had seen tomols being built when he was a boy in the 1850s. Two years before he died in 1915 he made one for anthropologist John P. Harrington.[2] Harrington's records are the most detailed indication of how they were built. Constructed from driftwood, the tomol was between eight and thirty feet long. A heavy one-piece deck had three or four rows of planks attached to build up the sides. The rows of planks were glued together with a melted mixture of pine pitch and hardened asphalt called *yop*. The asphalt was collected from the natural hardened oil seeps at the base of some of the Channel Island sea cliffs. After this adhesive dried, each plank was fastened to the one below by first drilling holes on each side of the seam and then tying the boards together with twine made from hemp. The holes and seams were filled with more hot yop. Finishing was done using sand-stone and sharkskin. Then the canoe was painted and decorated, sometimes with crushed mother-of-pearl from abalone shells, making it glitter in the sunlight. The typical tomol held a crew of three, though larger craft could carry as many as ten people. With seawater often seeping into the boats, one member of the crew would act as permanent bailer. The typical lifespan of the tomol is unknown but undoubtedly depended on the use and wear and tear.

The owners of tomols were persons of wealth and significance who con-trolled much of the means of production and distribution of money, food, and resources among the islands and between the islands and the mainland. Eyewitness accounts indicate that boat owners did not actually have to go fishing themselves but loaned out their craft and were rewarded with a share of the takings of the expedition. The tomol was critical in the transporta-tion of the islands' manufactured items, especially the heavy objects made on Santa Catalina and San Miguel Islands—the ollas and cookware such as *comals,* mortars, and pestles, which were manufactured for export to the mainland and, to a lesser extent, to other islands. They were also essential for the transportation of food, shell beads, and other trade goods that went from the mainland to the islands.

Xaxas (later Prisoners' Harbor) in the predawn light, around one thousand years ago. The village of grass-covered dome houses along the stream behind the beach is beginning to stir. The smoke of cooking fires rises straight up into the windless sky. On the far mainland, mountain peaks stand out sharply. The break along the shore barely rattles the beach pebbles. Wind and water conditions are perfect for fishing and traversing the channel to the mainland, and two tomols are getting ready for departure. The navigators have been studying the sea conditions for several days and feel confident that the calm conditions will continue for a few days more. The larger of the two boats, with a crew of eight, is being loaded with stone blades, digging stick weights, fish, and abalone. These, along with several dozen strings of shell beads and an otter pelt to be exchanged for acorn meal, are watched carefully as they are placed aboard by the caped chief, who is also the owner of the tomol. The smaller tomol with its crew of four is bound for the deeper parts of the channel to hunt for ocean fish—dolphin, tuna, or swordfish. The owner of that tomol is also present in the small crowd on the beach, watching as the crew members load their nets, lines, and harpoons. The light is brightening over the eastern hills of the island. The navigators confer quietly between themselves and the owners of the tomols. Then, with a minimum of fanfare, the boats are launched into the small wavelets of the harbor. The crews start up a repetitive chant as their paddles dig into the water. The larger boat heads directly for the mountain peak that marks the navigation point for the large town of Syuxtun (Santa Barbara). The other boat turns toward the rising sun, its decorations glittering in the light. It will follow the shore along the length of the island toward the fishing grounds. The crowd disperses into the village, now fully awake and preparing for the day.

These islanders formed part of a coastal mosaic of tribal groupings interconnected by trade and largely unhampered by religious and linguistic differences, with a role played by bilingual individuals who spoke both mainland and island Chumash. The island Chumash and Gabrieleño Indians traded heavily with their mainland neighbors to offset their resource limitations, bartering their island assets—food, furs, and soapstone vessels—for nuts, grains, and grasses that were more readily available on the mainland. The islanders' life expectancy was about thirty-five to forty years—roughly equivalent to European levels at the time—although exceptional individuals lived into their sixties and seventies.

There was even manufacturing specialization on some islands, in particular on Santa Cruz Island where certain villages became specialized in the manufacture of shell bead money, which was regularly used as a medium of exchange with villages on the coastal mainland and beyond. The shell bead money was manufactured principally from pieces of marine snail shells called Olivella (purple olive). Each shell section was placed on a stone slab and drilled by hand using a chert tool. The rough pieces were strung on a rod or thong and rolled on a shale slab to smooth out the edges to create beads of a uniform size. The value of a strand of beads was based on the rarity of the pieces of shell used and how many times it could wrap around a hand, essentially the amount of time invested in the making of it.

The discovery that they could barter their shell money for food to supplement their island resources was an economic breakthrough that allowed the island Indian populations to steadily increase and enhance their diet. Use of this money indicates the importance of trade between island and mainland communities. It was an important step whereby these specialized villages discovered that the manufacture of a medium of exchange was a superior occupation to hunting and gathering. This trading pattern was not necessarily a late development in the prehistoric period. Some of the island shell beads, approximately ten thousand years old, have been found more than 620 miles from the coast, evidence of wide-ranging regional exchanges and a clear indication of contacts between coastal and interior groups, reaching far back in time. In fact, significant numbers of shell beads have been found at a site in central Oregon estimated to be 8,600 years old.[3]

Vigorous inter-island trade is also evidenced in the artifacts found in mainland and island middens—spatulas, knife handles and projectile points, distinctively barbed fishhooks, and soapstone effigies from different island sources. Their control of the medium of exchange and having a reliable means of transport enabled the island Indians to enjoy the staple of the coastal diet, acorn meal. Using a pestle and mortar of sandstone or stone of volcanic origin, the dried, shelled acorns were ground to powder. After washing to remove the bitter tannins, water was mixed with the flour and this was cooked in a watertight basket by the addition of red-hot stones. These baskets were able to hold water because they were lined with the same asphalt mixture used to caulk the seams of the tomols. Stirring heated stones in with the acorn powder and water soon brought it to a boil, which eventually thickened it, making a soup that was eaten with every meal.

The population of the entire area including what is now San Luis Obispo, Santa Barbara, and Ventura Counties, and part of Los Angeles County, as well as the islands at the time of contact with the Spanish in the sixteenth century is estimated at about twenty thousand people. Of the northern Channel Islands it is estimated that Santa Cruz Island had ten villages, that Santa Rosa had eight, and that San Miguel had two. The total island population, extrapolated from baptismal and marriage records kept at Mission Santa Barbara was about three thousand at the end of the eighteenth century, many more than at any time since. Santa Catalina Island probably supported population densities similar to those of Santa Cruz and Santa Rosa, whereas the more remote San Nicolas and San Clemente appear to have had a Native population level similar to that of San Miguel. The Indians had an abundance of food, even in the winter months, and were able to support relatively dense populations without agriculture. They lived in large domed houses clustered closely together in settlements at every major drainage watercourse along the mainland coast, and along the shores of the islands.

Most southern island middens yield metates, which were probably used to grind acorns, cherry pits, and dried meat. The Indians had many types of bowls and ollas made of steatite (soapstone), all of which was apparently mined from outcroppings on Santa Catalina Island, where large partially carved bowls can still be seen embedded in the outcrop as though the islanders had just put down their tools in the expectation of returning soon. Catalina soapstone was prized on the islands and mainland for its relative malleability in the making of cooking utensils, bowls, pipes, club heads, ornaments, shamans' paraphernalia, gaming stones, and fishing-net weights. Because of its stability, soapstone can withstand exposure to heat, which it holds for a long time, making it highly useful in cooking. Serpentine, a stone with similar properties to steatite, was more commonly used on the northern islands.

Another type of stone, the chert found on the northern islands, was essential to some of the new technologies that the Chumash were developing in the period about one thousand years before the appearance of the Spanish.

Chert can be worked to produce a sharp cutting edge and is therefore useful in fashioning cutting and carving tools and arrow and spear points. The readily available abalone shells and sea mammal bones provided the raw materials for fishhooks and lures for kelp-bed fish that were now an essential part of the Chumash diet. The shells were drilled and filed to the desired shape, with both a point for penetration and a shank for keeping the fish attached to the hook. The islanders also made composite fishhooks, consisting of pieces of bone joined to make a V, or two pieces of wood bound together to form an acute angle capable of catching and holding a fish. The southern Channel Island Indians also used twisted cactus spines in their fishing. These devices gave the island Indians access to 125 species of kelp-bed and ocean fish, supplementing the abundant shellfish that was a staple of their diet. Chert spear heads and harpoons enabled the Indians to hunt seals and sea lions for their meat, bones, and pelts. Given the islands' position in relation to whale migration routes, these great sea mammals occasionally washed ashore to become a bounteous source of meat, bones, and oil.

One distinctive aspect of Chumash villages struck the chronicler of a 1767 Spanish expedition, the enthusiastic Fray Juan Crespi, who described "the inhabitants living in regular towns with very good sized grass houses, round like half oranges, some of which are so large within that they must be able to lodge without hindrance sixty persons and more."[4]

The houses, twelve to twenty feet in diameter, one to a family, which so impressed the Spanish were made by first creating a circle of willow poles fixed in the ground. Next a dome was formed by bending the poles in at the top. Smaller saplings were then tied crosswise to the poles and a covering of bulrushes or cattails was layered on, starting at the bottom, with each row overlapping the one below, creating a thatched, rainproof covering. The roof had a hole for air circulation and smoke ventilation when the inhabitants had a fire inside. This could be covered with a skin when it rained. Most cooking was done outside, but there was a fire pit in the center of each house in case of bad weather, providing warmth as well as a heat source for cooking. A chief's house could measure up to thirty-five feet across. Members of the Vizcaíno expedition in 1602–1603 talked of a village on San Miguel Island of two hundred of these houses, though this is likely to be a significant exaggeration.

The houses were laid out in relatively formal rows, but there was more to the villages. Other structures could include an enclosed ceremonial dance floor, menstrual huts, childbirth huts, male puberty huts, storage structures for grain, and smokehouses for curing meat and fish. It is likely that the most significant structure would have been the sweat lodge. Most settlements had at least one—half buried, semicircular, and earth-covered. The interior was tall enough that a man could stand in the center. The roof was supported by four substantial forked posts with cross beams and had a hole near the center for access and to let smoke out. A ladder was used to climb in and out. Sweat lodges were always located near water, either the sea or a stream, and it was said that their use was usually confined to the male members of the community.

Accounts from the time tell us that clothing was not a highly significant feature of everyday Chumash life. Women typically wore a knee-length skirt of fiber, deerskin, or sealskin. The men and boys usually wore nothing at all, or sometimes a belt or a small net at the waist for carrying tools. For warmth in cold weather, capes might be worn, and a chief often wore a cape as a sign of his status. For special occasions, the Indians wore body paint and jewelry. Dancers and singers at ceremonies had special costumes with feathered skirts and headdresses.

There was a basic division of labor in the villages, with the women and children collecting plants, seeds, and shellfish and the men hunting and fishing. Men dominated the woodworking and bead and arrowhead making, while the women did most of the basketry. The island population centers tended to be the densest along the coasts, notably on the islands that were better endowed with water and other resources, like the east end of Santa Cruz Island.

Chumash basketry was an intricate and much-admired art form whose objects were used for every imaginable daily and ceremonial task. Baskets were used in food gathering, preparation, serving, and storage. Some were made to be watertight, others for measuring foodstuffs for trade, others for gifts, gambling, and ceremonial uses. Usually made of straw, tan in color, they were easily recognizable by their border, about an inch wide below the rim. Decoration included subsidiary designs, vertical bars, horizontal bands, and other patterns, but excluded human or animal figures. Although some baskets were woven tightly enough to hold water without the addition of lining, some were augmented by asphalt coating made by pulverizing asphalt and then melting it inside a container by mixing it with hot stones.

Most settlements included "a community place for playing, consisting of a very smooth and level ground, like a bowling green, with low walls around it."[5] Chumash games included throwing a spear or shooting an arrow through a ring or hoop that was rolling along the ground. There was also a simple guessing game that did not require much space, in which opponents had to identify which hand held a black or white stick or bone. This could be played by individuals or teams and could go on for some time, until as many as fifteen tokens were correctly indicated. There was also a version of field hockey that would pit an entire village against another as part of an important ceremonial gathering. It usually involved large numbers of participants, and bets were often placed on the outcome. With the potential of more than one hundred players armed with sticks on a field, trying to put a small wooden ball through an opponent's goal, there was ample opportunity for rough conduct and fighting, but once the dust had settled, wounds tended, and all bets collected, there was the genteel custom of the victorious side giving half of its winnings to the hosts to help defray the costs of the gathering.

These assemblages were attended by many people from Chumash towns on the mainland, and one can suppose that the same or similar activities were found on the islands. The ceremonial gatherings also included ritual dances that honored creatures that were special in the Chumash world, like the blackbird, raven, fox, swordfish, and barracuda. The swordfish was one of the most important. The principal dancer might wear an actual swordfish skull decorated with shell inlay or a headdress to symbolize the sword of the fish. Chumash tradition held that swordfish were the marine equivalent of humans. They were offered beads and other gifts in recognition of their position as chiefs of all the sea animals. The Chumash believed that swordfish drove whales ashore to provide plentiful food for their land-based kin. Swordfish remains have appeared in archaeological finds dating to about two thousand years ago. This seems to generally coincide with the development of the tomol, which gave the Indians maneuverability on the sea and access to swordfish, and the barbed harpoon that could be used to kill the fish when it basked in calm waters. In addition to their appearance in middens on the islands, swordfish remains dating from two thousand years to nine hundred years ago, though relatively rare, are much more widespread on the mainland than one might expect.

The swordfish remnants shed light on changing environmental conditions that allowed fish to be hunted and caught in the seas off the mainland where they are unknown today. From this evidence it seems that between two thousand and nine hundred years ago, the sea temperatures were warmer in the channel, encouraging the swordfish to look for food in this area where they would be a target for coastal as well as insular Chumash.

With their well-organized villages, crafts, trade, ceremonies, and mastery of their environment, this was one of the most complex forager civilizations encountered by the Spanish. Fray Juan Crespi expressed his enthusiastic appreciation of their culture in 1769:

> This is entirely a very cultivated, quick, clever folk, skilled in everything, as is bespoken by the flint knives, very gorgeous, that they carry on their heads; the gorgeous and very elegant rushen baskets and bowls worthy of the admiration of any person of good taste; and the bowls made from wood and very shiny solid stone, so splendidly carven. I do not know whether anyone using tools for the purpose could do better. . . . To this add the canoes, so well made out of planking not two fingers thick, so smooth and so even—and they not possessing any [metal tools].[6]

This considered assessment is strikingly at odds with the impressions gathered by the first Spanish expedition to encounter the Chumash of the northern islands. Cabrillo's account of 1542 described the northern islands people: "The Indians of these islands are very poor. They are fishermen; they eat nothing but fish; they sleep on the ground; their sole business and employment is to fish. They say that in each house there are 50 souls. They live very swinishly and go about naked."[7]

While this description is in some respects accurate as to fishing and clothing, it is a harsh assessment that probably tells us as much about Spanish attitudes as it does about the inhabitants of the islands they visited. It also underlines the difference between the people of the islands, the Canaliño, and the mainland, which was largely one of access to resources. The mainland people had a more varied diet through their access to a greater variety of plants and animal life, and they lived in more impressive settlements.

Regardless of the views of Cabrillo, the overall image that emerges from the records of early Spanish travelers is an attractive picture of the ample Canaliño life, yet the traditional view of California's prehistoric peoples as the heirs of paradise should be carefully handled. For more than a hundred years, this rosy scenario painted by early researchers fit comfortably within a centuries-old European mythic tradition—Rousseau's noble savage—living in a benign climate and subsisting off bountiful seas and teeming wildlife. While it appears true that the story of California's prehistory was essentially about forager ingenuity that progressively tapped a larger and larger share of natural abundance, recent research argues that to view these societies as the best of all possible worlds "creates an unrealistic narrative about prehistoric culture change."[8] The reality is doubtless complex, and it must include the possibility of overexploitation based in human frailty and the role of other stressful factors, such as climate change. Looked at through this prism, the fishing intensification of the latter prehistoric period could be interpreted as a move compelled by depletion of alternative food resources, such as pinnipeds and shellfish, rather than an advanced stage of maritime cultural evolution.

Many people imagine that overexploitation of natural resources is a relatively recent problem in human history, associated primarily with modern industrial or agrarian societies. In contrast, forager societies are typically viewed as environmentally benign, restrained from overharvesting plants and animals by a deep reverence for nature, or so small in numbers and so technologically limited as to minimize their impact on the natural environment. Recent research concludes that it is highly probable that early cultures had an intense impact on the ecology of the islands through practices such as burning native vegetation to encourage food production. The early inhabitants of the islands also engaged in hunting and gathering restricted only by their available technologies, and they undertook the accidental and intentional transportation of plants and animals between the islands and the mainland. The natives exerted a significant impact on island vegetation through food-gathering activities, perhaps including cutting down certain trees or shrubs for shelter, fuel, or raw materials for baskets. A geographer points to one example. "The arrival of fire-using humans on windswept San Miguel must have opened up a new chapter in episodic landscape stripping."[9] Given that these activities took place within the circumscribed environments of the islands, "the full range of ecological effects [caused by Natives] . . . must have been profound."[10] At the same time, it must be noted that these impacts pale in comparison with the effects of Western agricultural practices in the nineteenth and twentieth centuries.

In the background of these pre-contact trends was significant climate change in the centuries before the appearance of the Spanish explorers. Beyond the earlier gradual warming trends that had affected the cultural and technological developments of the islanders, we also now know of even more drastic swings in temperature and moisture as the region experienced recurrent droughts of "epic" magnitude between about A.D. 800–1300. In what is referred to as the Medieval Climatic Anomaly (MCA), California's Indians, owing to their comparatively high population density and reliance on stored foods (acorns, for example), were probably as vulnerable to drought-driven crises as the Indigenous populations of the American Southwest. Scarcity of vital resources such as water and food appears to have been an important factor in bringing about significant patterns of culture change in coastal Southern California during these five hundred years not long before the arrival of the Spanish explorers.

As opposed to more gradual changes that allowed the Indigenous population to gradually modify their culture to suit the climate, these rapid changes were marked by intensified warfare, new trade alliances, and altered settlement patterns, as well as declining levels of health on some if not all of the islands. Recent skeleton studies suggest that around one thousand years ago the violence on this part of the coast reached a peak, then subsided dramatically. In the centuries before the appearance of the Spanish there was something of a Canaliño cultural flowering, based on a realization that all the Chumash were in the same situation and that their survival depended on enhanced interdependence. A more formal societal structure, control of trade, resolution of disputes, and distribution of food supplies led to a more peaceful and well-functioning society with a Chumash population density, on the islands in particular, higher than any other along the Pacific coast.

Despite the lack of formal agriculture, and despite a largely subsistence lifestyle based mainly on marine products—fish, shellfish, and sea mammals—and on wild plants such as acorns, this was a highly complex forager society. The inhabitants had a common medium of exchange in their shell money, and they controlled their environment through burning to increase desirable plants. They had created adaptive strategies to respond to environmental changes and climate variability over thousands of years by learning to store both food and water. For the Chumash, human and spiritual existence intersected in an unbroken continuum, interpreted through myth and story, which proved effective over millennia in taming, understanding, and defining the challenging environment in which they lived.

At the time of European contact, the islanders' culture, like that of their cross-channel neighbors, was well suited to the types of resources available to them. It was based on specialized crafts, cross-channel trade, and a modest degree of political and religious centralization, arguably the most complex societal and economic organization in western North America. As one archaeologist notes, this was a forager society without rigid stratification, a warrior class, or slaves, which managed to thrive until the arrival of exotic diseases and enforced missionization.[11]

———————◦•◦———————

With Spaniards arriving on the Southern California coast a mere twenty-three years after Cortez began his conquest of the Central American mainland, the Channel Islands were one of the first points of contact between the surge of sixteenth-century European explorers and the Indigenous societies of North and South America. Actual records are sketchy, though the effects of contact between the Spanish and the Native peoples of the Southern California coast are not in doubt. Because of the limited nature of islands, the effects on the Chumash are among the most measurable in terms identifying the lethal biological and cultural consequences of this collision.

During the hiatus between the voyage of Cabrillo in 1542 and Portolà's land and sea expedition of 1769 there is evidence of regular direct and indirect contact with Spanish sailors crossing the Pacific on yearly Manila galleons, and with the Spanish colonizers of the Southwest and Baja California. Documented visits from the likes of Vizcaíno in 1602 and other likely but unrecorded contacts in the following years resulted in goods being exchanged and deadly European pathogens being disseminated. As the Indians visited the Spanish ships and the Spanish sailors explored the Native *rancherías*, they were participating in a process that led to the poignant destruction and disappearance of these societies that had developed over many thousands of years, accelerating as it approached the end.

The devastating diseases that ravaged Native populations in all parts of North and South America played a central role in the decline. In the chillingly descriptive phrase "vectors of death," one archaeologist relates how diseases like measles and smallpox raced through Native populations many miles from the initial point of contact.[12] Doubtless the effects were magnified in the relatively enclosed societies of the Channel Islands. Anthropologists point to evidence of regional epidemics following the visits of European ships to the Southern California coast and islands. On Santa Cruz Island, for example, the Native population declined by two-thirds in less than a decade. Beyond disease, there were the highly disruptive effects of the sudden appearance of powerful strangers in these societies. Manufactured glass beads of European origin partially supplanted the local shell-bead money, and superior iron tools for hunting and fishing quickly dominated the native chert and shell, part of a constellation of highly destabilizing trends that disrupted trade and social relations along the coast.

In these circumstances it is not surprising the see the rise of a "crisis cult" in Southern California at the end of the eighteenth century, which spread to the southern Channel Islands. The Chingichngish movement was a counterpart of other North American Native movements like the Ghost Dance, which was inspired by a Paiute Indian shaman and spread across much of the West in the nineteenth century, professing to give its followers protection from the European weapons. The cult hallmarks shared by Chingichngish with other crisis cults were ceremonies conducted by religious societies from within the communities, with membership restricted to initiated adult males and with the heightened importance of the role of shamans. In Southern California, a shaman-like figure, Chingichngish, was said to have taught a body of beliefs that grew out of existing ideas and practices and became mixed with them.

What made the cult different from the system of principles that had gone before was a more explicit moral order that was enforced by a new class of spirits, "avengers" such as the rattlesnake, spider, tarantula, bear, stingray, and raven, whose role was to ensure observance of the shaman's laws and punish those who violated them. In this it was a combination of Christian and shamanistic practices—the messianic Chingichngish and elements of divine moral oversight that formed the amalgam between Native and imported religious elements. Earlier coastal and insular religious observances had previously been largely free of moral overtones, being mostly concerned with healing, divination, and the stages of life, from birth, to puberty, adulthood, and death. For centuries, Chumash shamans had held that disease resulted from problems with a person's spiritual state, so they concentrated on healing the spirit through songs and prayers, dietary restrictions, and special medicines.

The new religion included highly formalized ceremonies taking place in sacred open-air enclosures called *yuva'r*. These were marked out by elaborate poles decorated with banners and feathers and featured the sacrifice of raptors. Only senior tribesmen with great power could enter the enclosure. According to a nineteenth-century account, these sacrifices created a communication pathway between humans and the creator gods. Offerings of food and goods were presented to an image of Chingichngish as well as to representations of the owl, raven, crow, and eagle.

In the spirit of the times, European explorers with ideas formed by the militant Christianity of the Middle Ages found this appalling. An encapsulation of the predictable clash of cultures is contained in the diary of the friar who accompanied Sebastián Vizcaíno on his visit to Santa Catalina in 1602. He noted that the Spaniards had been effusively greeted by Indians, who made

> demonstrations of joy in proof of their happiness . . . [but the atmosphere was poisoned when the explorers] found on the way a level prairie where the Indians were assembled to worship an idol. There was a great circle surrounded with feathers . . . the Indian told the General not to go near it. . . . The General told the Indian that the idol was evil, and placed the sign of the Cross on it. When the soldiers arrived there were two huge crows inside the circle, larger than ordinary crows. One of the soldiers took aim with his harquebus and killed them both. At this the Indians began to lament and show great emotion.[12]

Here in a nutshell was the story of the contact between the two cultures— joyous welcome by the natives, which turned to terror at the desecration of their holy site. The natives were caught between fear of their gods' retribution and the physical fear of Spaniards' advanced weaponry. The practices of the Chingichnish cult, which it was said would protect the natives from the intrusions of the Spanish culture and Spanish diseases and weapons, continued on the more remote islands, like San Clemente, well into the colonial period.

In the final decades of the Indigenous societies, there was pressure from more than Spanish religion and weaponry. Word of the natural resources of the area spread northward to Alaska, where established traders in otter skins, supplying the elites of Chinese society, were ready to direct their activities toward the coast and islands of Southern California. The Russians brought Alaskan Aleut Indians to the Channel Islands, and Euro-Americans brought Native Hawaiian hunters. Both groups were heavily armed and more than a match for the Canaliños' spears and arrows. The result was tragedy and ruin.

Caught between the establishment of the mission system and the depredations of the sea otter hunters, it was the end of island culture. This was the local eighteenth-century version of globalization, and the Channel Island culture was not the first or the last to succumb to its rigors. In 1803, the master of the Boston-based otter-hunting brig *Leila Byrd* recorded an encounter with one of the last groups of Native holdouts on San Clemente Island:

> In this miserable [cave] resided eleven persons, men, women and children: and although the temperature was such as to make our woolen garments requisite, they were all in a state of perfect nudity. Their food was exclusively fish, and having no cooking utensils, their only resource was baking them in the earth.... I had been familiar with Indians inhabiting various parts of the western coast of America, but never saw any so miserable, so abject, so spiritless, so nearly allied to the brute.[13]

When a huge earthquake hit the area in 1812, most of the remaining Indians on the islands took it as a sign that they should submit to missionization. Mission records suggest that the last Indian inhabitants of Santa Cruz Island left around 1820. Those of San Clemente departed for the mainland in 1829, possibly the final fragments of a maritime forager culture reaching back to the end of the last ice age.

From this point, the account of the Channel Islands will feature the lives and stories of hardy agriculturalists who sought to apply the received land husbandry wisdom of the times to these circumscribed, often wind-besieged and wave-battered outliers of the continent. The role of the original inhabitants was relegated to history. Their civilization had disappeared so quickly that artifact collectors in the early nineteenth century who tried within the limits of their understanding to piece it together often found themselves witness to objects for which they had no reliable explanation. At least two of these collectors interviewed local Native peoples and recorded such information as they could recall, but it would be the scientists and researchers of the twentieth century who would build on this early work to develop an accurate picture of the disappeared world of the Chumash.

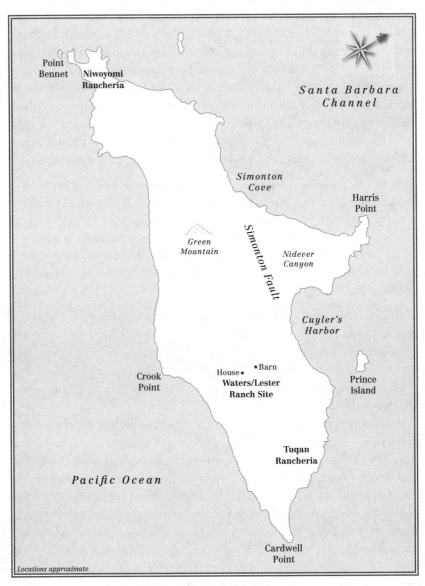

Point
Bennet

**Niwoyomi
Rancheria**

*Santa Barbara
Channel*

*Simonton
Cove*

Harris
Point

*Green
Mountain*

Simonton Fault

*Nidever
Canyon*

*Cuyler's
Harbor*

Crook
Point

House • • Barn
**Waters/Lester
Ranch Site**

Prince
Island

**Tuqan
Rancheria**

Pacific Ocean

Cardwell
Point

Locations approximate

San Miguel Island.
Map by Gerry Krieg.

CHAPTER 3

San Miguel Island

The westernmost of the Channel Islands is San Miguel, lying twenty-six miles south of Point Conception, where the elbow of the coast of California turns eastward. Visible from the mainland on a clear day leading the procession of northern Channel Islands, it is three miles west of its closest neighbor, Santa Rosa Island. San Miguel gets the full force of the Pacific winds out of the northwest. Combining with the wind is the sweep of the cool California Current, which flows south of Point Conception to meet the California Countercurrent. These factors led one geographer to describe San Miguel as "one of the windiest, foggiest, most maritime and wave pounded areas on the west coast of North America."[1] Others have noted its air of desolation and mystery: "Stripped bare in many places by persistent winds, the land reveals the skeletons of its past: ancient shells, trees, bones, and the remains of Native American and more recent habitations."[2] Out of the eight islands in the chain, at 9,325 acres it exceeds only Santa Barbara and Anacapa Islands in size.

Often enveloped in wind-whipped fog, it presents a much lower and more mysterious outline than most of the other islands with their high peaks and impressive valleys. It is also considered one of the most dangerous to approach by sea. With the prevailing northwesterlies tearing across its landscape, and a variety of submerged rocks and shoals, San Miguel has claimed enough shipwrecks to deserve the name Graveyard of the Pacific. Its sparse vegetation, only now making a comeback from a century of overgrazing by livestock, speaks for the dogged determination of hardworking ranchers to eke out a living in unusually harsh conditions. Yet at the same time much of San Miguel's significance lies in a story of human interaction, enterprise, and inventiveness that stretches back more than thirteen millennia. While artifacts and structures on some of the Channel Islands speak eloquently of the two hundred years of land exploitation and husbandry in the post-contact era, on San Miguel there are in addition remnants of a far older world, thought to include one of the oldest settlements in the region.[3]

The island's geological structure is a combination of Pleistocene terrace deposits toward the west (5.4–2.4 million years old) with older Miocene volcanic rocks (from 25 to 5.4 million years before the present) confined to the eastern end of the island. Green Mountain, at 831 feet, dominates the island's outline from its position slightly to the west of the center point. An impressive caliche forest, near Cuyler's Harbor (named for an early surveyor), with its fossilized remains of trees and other growth, serves as a reminder that San Miguel once supported a much more varied flora than it does today. Caliche, named from the Latin root for limestone, is a hardened deposit of calcium carbonate which cements together other materials including gravel, sand, clay, and silt. In the case of the San Miguel caliche forest, it has taken the form of the ancient remnants of the trees and shrubs that once covered the island before the effects of climate change and stock raising were felt.[4]

Much of our knowledge about indigenous life on California's Channel Islands relies on specific data taken from places like San Miguel's Daisy Cave, a rock shelter on the mainland-facing side of the island, dating back to the Holocene Age, 11,000 to 5,500 years before the present. It was here that researchers found startling evidence of the early development and technological advancement of the Indigenous island culture. Analysis of an ancient midden at this site, the oldest coastal shell midden in North America, suggests that the Indigenous inhabitants fished extensively around the islands, using boats and the earliest recognized examples of hook-and-line fishing on the Pacific coast. The analysis of the Daisy Cave midden further indicates that a large variety of fish provided more than half the early inhabitants' diet. We are able to see in the latter millennia of occupation how effectively these ancient people used their tomols and their expertise in the kelp beds and rocky shores to capture a diverse array of fish, exploiting the local marine habitats and resources, including marine mammals and seabirds. These were the first fishers of the Pacific Coast region with nets, spears, rods, lines, and hooks. Their technological foundations enabled the people of this island—who called their home Tuqan—to survive and flourish. At least two villages on San Miguel demonstrate the increasingly complex culture that thrived on the Channel Islands for thousands of years before contact with the Spanish.[5]

From San Miguel has also come evidence of the cooler air and water temperatures that once dominated the region before the warming trend that created the island outlines of the present epoch. This evidence has been gathered through paleontological investigations that have confirmed the existence of colonies of ancient puffins, which lived on the island in the late Pleistocene. In our era, puffins have rarely nested farther south than the Farallon Islands off San Francisco. Evidence from San Miguel shows that between sixty thousand and thirty thousand years ago, during one of the ice ages that shaped our continent, the waters around the islands were the equivalent temperatures of those found off the coasts of Washington and Oregon today and were home to colonies of puffins. Fossil evidence also indicates the existence on the island of the previously mentioned giant mouse and dwarf mammoth in the Pleistocene period.[6]

As on several of the other islands, the first contact between the Chumash and the Spanish explorers of the sixteenth century was with the Cabrillo expedition in 1542. On October 18 that year, the feast day of St. Luke, Juan Rodríguez Cabrillo happened on and predictably named the two northern-most islands in the chain the Islas de San Lucas. He seems to have recon-sidered afterward and renamed San Miguel, calling it Posesíon, after one of his ships. At the time there were two Chumash villages on the island with about one hundred inhabitants in total. After exploring a bit up the coast and being driven back by northwesterly winds around Point Conception, Cabrillo is said to have wintered on the island, beaching his frigate *San Miguel* for repairs, although some versions of the story have him wintering on Santa Catalina Island. This was to prove one of his last acts. Whether it happened on the one island or another, it is indisputable that he accidentally broke one of his limbs getting out of a boat, and the resulting infection in the days before antibiotics had the predictable outcome of gangrene; his death occurred on the third day of 1543.[7]

Enough experts had agreed on San Miguel as Cabrillo's final resting place to encourage the Cabrillo Civic Clubs, founded by Californians of Portu-guese ancestry, to erect a stone cross in his honor above Cuyler's Harbor in 1937. After his death, the name of the island was changed to Juan Rodriguez or La Capitana in his memory. But this faded with the passing of the years, and in the 1740s it appeared on a map as San Bernardo, though the name that stuck was the one from the charts of George Vancouver in 1793.

During this late-contact period the Chumash and their island home were the subject of the hostile attention of otter hunters and the better-intentioned aims of Franciscans, though the result of both was the depopulation of the island. The destruction of otter colonies at the hands of rapacious hunters, who also wrought havoc with the peaceful Chumash way of life, and the workings of exotic diseases like measles and chicken pox, introduced by the Europeans, spelled the end of Chumash occupation of the island. By the early nineteenth century, San Miguel—the Chumash Tuqan—was largely abandoned to its seabird, seals, and sea lions. Thus ended a thirteen-thousand-year chapter of Indigenous occupation of the island.

The island received sparse mention in travelers' accounts in the 1830s and 1840s. Where it came in for notice, it was called barren and dry—a place where Boston sailors came to salt down the hides they had bought from coastal Californio ranchos and not much more. As on Anacapa and Santa Barbara Islands, no territory on San Miguel was officially granted in the Mexican period. Title to the island passed in 1848 to the U.S. territory of California, which became a state two years later. The existence of reliable drinking water in modest amounts attracted the attention of squatters and seasonal fishermen in the mid-nineteenth century, and they were closely followed by those with a more permanent intent. Locally they were considered owners, though that status was more a legal convenience than fact. The federal government, with its attentions elsewhere, maintained a light-touch policy regarding its islands without relinquishing title to them.[8]

In June 1863, the Santa Barbara County sheriff held a sale of the property of one of the squatters, Samuel C. Bruce, to pay debts that amounted to $1,487 [$26,600 in 2011 equivalent].[9] Frontiersman and trapper Captain George Nidever, the first of a line of settlers and sailors whose stories figure in the histories of several of the Channel Islands, won the bidding for the lease of the island with an offer of $1,800 [$32,300] for "all the right, title [sic], interest and ownership . . . in and to all the sheep, cattle and horses upon the said Island of San Miguel, consisting of 6000 sheep . . . 125 head of cattle . . . and 25 horses. Also the right, title, interest claim and ownership . . . consisting of a possessory claim to an undivided one-half of the said island."[10]

How Bruce obtained his interest in the island in order to be able to sell it to Nidever is unknown, but it was the first link in a chain of ownership that saw the island change hands at frequent intervals throughout the remainder of the nineteenth century and into the twentieth.

Nidever, who had originally come to California with a party of trappers in 1833, built an adobe house in an arroyo about four hundred feet above Cuyler's Harbor, in what is now called Nidever Canyon, and he set about running the sheep ranching establishment with his two sons. But after six years the sons were tired of living on the island and pressed their father to sell at least half his interest. Their argument was all the more persuasive after the severe drought years of 1863 and 1864, when the Nidevers lost 85 percent of their sheep and most of their other animals. By 1869, George Nidever was convinced of the futility of the project and sold half the family interest to one Hiram Mills and his brother Warren for $5,000 [$82,500]. In 1870, the Mills brothers bought the other half of the Nidever interest, which included their livestock. Once they had complete control of San Miguel, the Mills brothers sold their property over the next two years to three men who eventually formed the Pacific Wool Growing Company, with an office in San Francisco and other sheep-raising holdings on Anacapa and San Nicolas Islands. Pacific Wool sold its interests in November 1887 to a David Fitzgibbon, who three days later flipped owner-ship back to the Pacific Wool president, Warren Mills. Mills, in turn, sold a half interest to Captain William Waters for $10,000 [$237,000].

While all these transactions were taking place, the sheep population of San Miguel was chewing its way through much of the ground cover. One visitor in the 1870s noted, "There are no young trees . . . as the omnipresent sheep crop every green thing within their reach to the ground."[11] Others called the island an extremely desolate barren lump of sand. As early as 1878 Nidever repeated a story that the island was "almost covered with sand," though there was a conflicting report in 1887 from a visiting botanist who wrote of good grazing land covering at least part of the island.[12]

The erstwhile ownership merry-go-round slowed for a while as Captain Waters, his wife, and their adopted daughter moved to the island, taking with them their maid and some ranch hands. The other half interest continued to change hands, but the colorful Waters retained his half for thirty years. Waters—whose title related to his service in the Fifteenth Massachusetts Regiment in the Civil War—had moved west to San Francisco in the 1870s.

Mills Ranch, 1869–87.
Photograph by Pete Reyes, ca. 1910s.
Courtesy of Channel Islands National Park.

It was there he met and married the widow Minnie Richardson Scott, a woman of comfortable means but poor health. In an attempt to alleviate her health problems exacerbated by San Francisco's fogs, they moved with her adopted daughter south to Santa Barbara. Unfortunately for Minnie, while in Santa Barbara Waters developed an interest in San Miguel Island, the coldest and foggiest of the Channel Islands.

Despite any misgivings she might have had, Minnie gave her husband $10,000 ($244,000 in 2011 funds) to buy the half interest in the island and they moved there in January 1888. The Waters family settled into a ranch, located above Cuyler's Harbor and east of the Nidever adobe that included a small board-and-batten house and barns that had been built by the Mills brothers. Here they worked hard to establish a productive farm, with a vegetable garden and their own dairy cows, poultry, and pigs.[13] The climate was far from ideal for Minnie, though she did her best to make a home for her husband and daughter in the face of the prevailing harsh circumstances,

William Waters's road to the ranch, excavated by hand, 1903.
Courtesy of Santa Cruz Island Foundation.

rendered more acute by her health problems. She kept a diary for the first half of 1888, declaring that on balance she liked the island life, though not surprisingly she missed the civilized touches of town, like plumbing and heating. The constant wind was also a factor for Minnie, and she noted that it had blown the roof off their house on one occasion. Doubtless the wind and fog were a big factor in island life, but by Minnie's own reckoning the weather was moderate to good on more than half of the days in her diary. It was a life dominated at least six days a week by hard toil, except for Minnie, whose ills kept her in bed much of the time. As well as their regular farm work, Waters and his hands built fences and a road up from the harbor to the top of the island, still evident as a hiking trail today. In February a schooner brought group of shearers and the luxuries of fruit for the adults and candy for Minnie's daughter Edith, age fifteen.

Minnie's diary describes meals with the farmhands and Ida, her "servant and woman of all work." After dinner, they played popular card games like whist, pedro, and euchre. They talked or she sang until about nine, when it was time for bed. Another feature of life was séances in which they communicated around a table with dead relatives who enlightened the living regarding questions about the past or the future. The Waters family observed Sundays with an outing—abalone hunting or riding mules to some point on the island. Minnie's description of two of these outings, one which included the shooting of an eagle for sport and another where they invaded Daisy Cave and came away with a human skull and bones—speak of a world far removed from today's sensibilities toward Indigenous remains and island flora and fauna.

The captain was much occupied with his planting grain, gathering abalone, and raising animals, and Minnie did her best to be a dutiful wife, but after six months it was too much for her. Waters agreed with the new owner of the other half interest in the island to hire a ranch manager, and a few days after the new manager arrived with his wife and six children in tow the Waters family departed for San Francisco. Unfortunately for Minnie this did not alleviate her maladies, and she died of tuberculosis in January 1890. The widower Waters returned to the island after Minnie's death, with the very unwilling Edith accompanying him. Now seventeen, she greatly resented having to exchange the art and poetry of genteel San Francisco for the hard work, outdated clothes, and rough surroundings of San Miguel Island. She stuck it out for four years, seeing herself as a virtual prisoner, living in "a roughly built house in which railroad ties form a part of the construction . . . where the wind blows a gale all the time."[14] When it all became too much, she convinced a guano gatherer camped on the island to sail her to the mainland and largely disappeared from the island story, surfacing decades later to successfully challenge her father's will in which he left her one dollar. Edith's lawsuit scandalized Santa Barbara and was featured prominently in the press.

In the early 1890s Waters was cultivating fields on the mesa above Cuyler's Harbor, and there were various employees and hunters in residence, though seemingly Waters did not reside there permanently. After a confusing number of transactions, the owner of the other half interest in the island, Warren Mills, sold it after five years to another investor, Elias Beckman, in 1892. But conflict was brewing after San Miguel was featured in the San Francisco and Los Angeles press. Fueled by reports from Waters, papers in those cities reported on a major landslide of the sandy bluffs above the Cuyler's Harbor boathouse into the southwest side of the harbor, which had reshaped the island's shoreline. The land movement, identified by modern geologists as a large rotational (slump) landslide, continued from April to June 1895 and caused authorities to resurvey Cuyler's Harbor that November, triggering conflict the following year between Waters and government surveyors.

The next year the federal government assembled a party of surveyors to officially map the island. Believing that it was not a U.S. possession, basing this on newspaper reports and local belief that San Miguel had not been specifically mentioned in the Treaty of Guadelupe Hidalgo, Waters announced that he would resist attempts to survey "his" island and that he was the king of a new nation. President Grover Cleveland was not amused. Under his orders, the surveyors arrived on the island armed with a collection of rifles and shotguns. Waters met them on the beach and made a formal protest of their "invasion" before agreeing to the survey in the face of far superior numbers and firepower.

In 1897 Waters and Jeremiah Conroy formed the San Miguel Island Company with assets of three thousand sheep, twenty-five head of cattle, eighteen horses and mules, several small boats, and various pieces of equipment for sowing and reaping grain. They issued capital stock of $49,500 [$1.33 million]. In the following years the now-portly Waters carried on his work, with extra hired help in the shearing season from the local population of Barbareños. As on Santa Cruz Island, the men were paid with brass tokens with a hole through the center, manufactured by Waters as a form of currency redeemable for cash. The rate was around five cents for shearing a ewe [eight dollars] and ten cents for a ram—to be cashed in before the shearers returned to town along with their employer. During most of the year Waters kept his enterprise going through the use of caretakers like the Rawlins family. Mrs. Rawlins wrote in 1903, "My husband's work was to milk the cows and keep the water holes clear of sand, as we had sand storms which blew and filled them. You could walk over them if you didn't know where they were to keep them open. [In] spring the sheep would have perished for [lack of] water."[15]

The drifting sand was becoming a real concern. It had buried the old Nideaver adobe in its arroyo and was on the point of covering Waters's old ranch house in the upper canyon in 1906. It was about that time that John Russell and his wife became resident managers for Waters. There are no records to show who built the new house on the mesa above Cuyler's Harbor in a location where the sand blew in the wind but did not settle. It seems likely that it was done by Russell under Waters's direction. The materials for the

Wreck of the *Kate and Anna*, Cuyler's Harbor, 1902.
Photograph by Pete Reyes. *Courtesy of Channel Islands National Park.*

house were salvaged from shipwrecks and the cargoes of lumber schooners that had ended up on the rocks of San Miguel Island.

In 1905 Russell hauled redwood lumber from the cargo of the *J. M. Colman*, wrecked the previous fall just inside Point Bennett at the west end of the island. The house was built double-walled to withstand the winds and sand that blew almost constantly, sometimes reaching one hundred miles per hour. The house grew in size as the materials became available, with an ultimate length of 125 feet and a width of 16 feet, divided into eleven rooms. These comprised a bathroom, master bedroom, dining room, four small bedrooms, a serving room attached to a kitchen, pantry, and closet, a storage room, and a laundry room with a meat cooler. Russell and a later leaseholder, Robert Brooks, built a fence at an angle to the wind to shield the house. The store of building materials was replenished at irregular intervals from shipwrecks, and the house and outbuildings were all kept in a reasonable state of repair. A Santa Barbara newspaper approvingly noted, "The building has running water in every room and compares favorably with any city dwelling in the number and quantity of its modern conveniences."[16]

Waters and Elias Beckman, the owner of the other half interest, fell out and took their differences into the courts in 1908. This attracted the attention of the federal government, which once again moved to exercise its title over the island. In 1909 President William Howard Taft issued an executive order reserving San Miguel Island for the purpose of erecting a lighthouse. Waters wrote to the president in 1911, explaining that he had bought the island in 1887 and asking if the light could be placed offshore on Richardson Rock, six miles to the northwest of the island rather than on the island itself. He claimed that a forced removal of his stock and buildings would constitute an undue hardship on himself as a Civil War veteran who had worked for many years to improve the island. Government attorneys found his legal claims to be completely without foundation but—perhaps swayed by Waters's veteran status—granted him a five-year lease for five dollars [$124] per year. This was a good result, but by signing the document Waters was acknowledging government title to the island. He complained to the local *Daily News and Independent*, "The fact that I lived on the island for twenty-five years without anyone questioning my right, that I built a home and other buildings there, would, I think, be accepted in Federal courts as proof of my title to the property."[17] In fact, Waters lived most of the year in Santa Barbara, where he enjoyed a very active social life as a founder of the Santa Barbara Club, member of the Knights Templar,

Masons, and Jonathan Club, and commander of the California and Nevada Department of the Grand Army of the Republic, the association of Civil War veterans. Waters's lease was renewed in 1916, and the following year, over the objections of the Lighthouse Bureau, Waters, then seventy-eight, took on two partners in his island enterprise, Robert Brooks and J. R. Moore.

Waters died the following year and in 1920 Brooks and Moore renewed the lease for another five years at $200 a year [$2,180], starting a relationship with the island that would last thirty years. It was not an unprofitable enterprise. Their business statement for their first year noted a net profit of approximately $3,650 [$44,500], a figure that would triple within five years.[18] Brooks and Moore continued the pattern set by Waters, with their main residences and other ranch holdings on the mainland, and the day-to-day running of the island in the hands of managers.

In spite of the building of a lighthouse on Richardson's Rock and a bell buoy off the southwest end of San Miguel, the shipwrecks continued to pile up. In addition to the wreck of the *J. M. Colman,* the source of much of the building materials of the distinctive in-line house in 1905, there were wrecks in 1908, 1911, and 1914, and two more in 1923. In February that year, the four-masted lumber schooner *Watson A. West* ran aground and almost immediately broke up on the west end of the island. In September another notable wreck occurred when the Pacific Mail luxury liner *Cuba,* heading north for San Francisco, lost her bearings in thick fog and grounded on a reef off Point Bennett. Her 115 passengers and 65 crew were taken off safely, along with $2.5 million in gold she was carrying in the ship's safe [$32 million]. The abandoned vessel provided a golden salvage opportunity for local entrepreneur and character Ira Eaton, who was running a resort with his wife at Pelican Bay on Santa Cruz Island. He sailed back to Santa Cruz with his boat *Sea Wolf* so laden that her "scuppers were awash."[19] Whether he used the *Cuba's* tables, linens, and silverware to upgrade his resort's furnishings is unrecorded, but it formed yet another lively episode in the checkered career of one of Santa Barbara's more colorful characters, detailed in chapter 5.

When the lease for San Miguel came up for renewal in 1925, Brooks acted alone, bidding $600 per year [$7,460] for five years. The lease was then periodically extended into the 1940s. Brooks derived perhaps half his annual income from San Miguel but more importantly it gave him bragging rights and a place to go, especially at shearing time, where he could act out a special role as one of a select group of island grandees. Most owners of these

Aerial shot of the Brooks' house with barn and
Cuyler's Harbor in the background.
Photograph by John A. Swede, 1938.
Courtesy of Channel Islands National Park.

island ranches reveled in their positions as kings of their own dominions. To get the full complement of skilled and unskilled workers he required, particularly at shearing time, Brooks cleared the county jail of "the bums of Santa Barbara" and claimed that the city administration respected and admired him for it.[20] His method of raising lambs on the predator-free island and then transferring them to his ranch in Camarillo worked well, and it was only in 1923 that San Miguel suffered a drought. With the permission of his partner, E. N. Vail, Brooks relocated all but five hundred sheep to San Nicolas Island for 1923 and 1924. As the 1920s wore on, Brooks found that his ranching operation was facing complications, with its very survival at stake. His attempt to restock after the drought with sheep purchased from

Herb Lester on board the *Dreamer*;
boat owner's father in background.
Courtesy of Channel Islands National Park.

Santa Cruz Island was a failure, as he lost half of them to local poisonous plants. Preserving a good water supply required new equipment and regular maintenance. The expenses began to cancel out his margin of profit.

By 1929 Brooks was in desperate need of some resident long-term management on the island. It so happened that his old army buddy, Herbert Lester, whom he had met in Walter Reed Hospital just after World War I, was looking for employment. Brooks thought that this arrangement could provide a solution to his management problem and that the low-stress island life would be good for his friend. Lester visited the island for a sheep-shearing session and was charmed by the idea. He wrote to Elizabeth (Elise) Sherman, the East Coast blue blood he had been courting, and she agreed to marry him and move to San Miguel. The life she was taking up could not have been more different from her upbringing as a part of a cosmopolitan family. The onetime New York debutante, who had been introduced to society at Delmonico's restaurant and entertained by Enrico Caruso, packed five hundred books, family photographs, clothing, and linens and boarded the Vail and Vickers Santa Rosa Island cattle boat *Vaquero* with her new husband. The couple took up residence in the house built by Captain Waters, and Lester, delighted with his new home, christened it Rancho Rambouillet after the town where he had been stationed in France and for the breed of sheep first imported by Justinian Caire of Santa Cruz Island and then sold to other islanders over the years.[21]

Home for Herb and Elise Lester was now the long narrow ranch complex that had been constructed twenty-five years before. They had elaborate plans to buy the lease from Bob Brooks, but no sooner had they settled in than the stock market crash of October 1929 heralded the onset of the Great Depression. Most of those who Lester had thought might provide financial backing for his scheme saw their wealth destroyed in the ensuing months and years as the financial contraction worsened. Yet though their plans for the assumption of the lease ownership were more or less permanently on hold, they threw themselves into island life despite the economic situation. The rough, simple house was gradually transformed into a comfortable home. Having been raised with a household staff of seven, Elise Lester found the challenges of homemaking novel and exciting, working alongside her husband to domesticate the living conditions. Herb built a brick-and-stone fireplace that turned the living room into a cozy library and added many other features to his wife's homey touches.

There was much more to be done all over the island. Like his predecessors, Lester continued the tradition of proclaiming himself King of San Miguel. He found that island life suited him perfectly, and he seldom went to the mainland, much preferring the solitary splendor of his kingdom. The same was true for the rest of his family, which grew to include two daughters, Betsy and Marianne, born in 1930 and 1933. They and their mother remained in Santa Barbara after their births only until they had reached the statutory ten pounds, then they were off to San Miguel.

Like the Caires on Santa Cruz Island, the family relied on kerosene lamps and candlelight for any activities after dark until Lester installed a generator in 1938. Their daily contact with the larger world came through the living room's battery-powered Silvertone cabinet radio. Betsy Lester remembered

Transporting wool sacks down to Cuyler's Harbor, 1939.
Courtesy of Channel Islands National Park.

listening to comedians like Bob Hope, weekly comedies like *Fibber McGee and Molly*, FDR's fireside chats, Walter Winchell, the New York Philharmonic, and the Metropolitan Opera. The children relished the freedom of island life in their sturdy house on the hill above Cuyler's Harbor. In 1935, there was even the excitement of the filming of parts of *Mutiny on the Bounty* around the island, which won that year's Best Picture Academy Award.

The romance of their situation, their tiny schoolhouse (a gift from the Vails of Santa Rosa Island), and the personalities of the Lesters drew nationwide attention. There was a feature article in *Life* magazine in which they were dubbed the Swiss Family Lester. Journalists found the Lesters' story irresistible. They were a couple from comfortable circumstances but showed pioneering spirit in adapting to the rough, self-reliant island life. The

Lester family, ca. 1941.
Left to right: Elise, Marianne, Herbert, and Betsy.
Courtesy of Santa Cruz Island Foundation.

incongruity of details, like the use of Elise's silver tea service, only added to the romance of their circumstances. By necessity an early proponent of homeschooling, Elise Lester obtained teaching materials from the Santa Barbara County schools department and presided over the girls' lessons and occasional proficiency exams administered on trips to the mainland.

An infrequent supply boat brought them provisions, and family friend George Hammond, an early aviator with an airfield on his Montecito estate, flew in mail, stores, and small packages of Santa Barbara delicacies when the weather was favorable. Carrying a mailbag marked "George F. Hammond, Bonnymede, Air Mail, Kingdom of San Miguel Island," he landed on "Hammond Field," a nine-hundred-foot stretch of grassland east of the ranch complex, complete with boundary markers and a wind sock.

Herbert Lester developed a collection of San Miguel memorabilia for his "Killer Whale Bar," flotsam and jetsam collected from the island beaches. The house's walls were graced with the skulls of a ram and a Steller sea lion, the dried head of a mako shark, framed covers and liquor ads from the *New Yorker* magazine, and even a lithograph of a nude woman. It was here that Lester held forth to the delight of scores of fascinated visitors. The house's enclosed yard was littered with lifeboats, ships' tackle, casks, a "school bell" contributed by the Southern Pacific Railroad, and even fossilized remains of Pleistocene pygmy mammoths discovered by Lester.

Lester took a proactive approach to island maintenance, installing a new windmill, water tank, generator, and radiotelephone. His relationship with Brooks was one of friendship rather than employer and employee, especially in the straitened financial circumstances of the time, and Lester was even instrumental in saving his friend's life after Brooks fell on the pier and impaled his thigh on a rusty spike. In the meantime, control of the island was transferred to the Department of the Navy, and in 1935 Brooks signed a lease with the navy for $600 per year [$9,530]. The new landlords, concerned about overgrazing, placed a limit on the number of sheep. In 1938, it was twelve hundred, a number that was reduced in later years. A study requested by the National Park Service noted, "Nature is now forcing man to pay the penalty for gross malpractice committed many years ago. For this reason, 1100 sheep are now destructive of the remnant of the island's resources, although originally such a number might have been pastured there indefinitely with little or no harm." In 1942, the National Park Service recommended removal of all livestock and cats, as well as a program of replanting, though grazing continued for another twenty-five years.[22]

With the outbreak of war at the end of 1941, and panic rampant along the California coast, the navy stationed three sailor lookouts on the island and warned the Lesters that they remained there at their own risk. The presence of the outsiders upset the careful balance of the island family. Not long after, Lester lost two fingers in an accident chopping wood and had to be hospitalized. Now approaching his mid-fifties and never the most stable of characters, Lester fell into a deep depression over the state of his health. On June 18, 1942, he committed suicide. The Lesters' island idyll was over. Two days later his daughters, aged nine and eleven, were sent to the mainland. The following month the Coast Guard picked up Elise Lester and the family's possessions and took her to Santa Barbara, where they would live for the next thirty-nine years. Herbert Lester was buried on the island at a place he chose, above Harris Point, within sight of the ranch where he spent the happiest days of his life with his family as the "King of San Miguel." After her death in 1981, Elise, who in life had never returned to the island, was buried next to him.[23]

Now Brooks needed a new tenant manager, and he found one in Ulmar Englund, an old Norwegian sailor who lived for some time on the island with his wife until they were replaced by another couple, Al and Rosie Baglin. In the meantime, there was a war on, and as part of the Coastal Lookout Organization the navy had built a two-room shack with glass windows and an observation tower equipped with a radio transmitter and receiver near the ranch house. A bulldozed road connected the lookout post with the ranch compound and then went west to Point Bennett. It was part of a network of nine island lookout stations, abolished with the end of war in 1945.

The war also brought another link in the chain of tragedies that seemed to dog the island following the accidental demise of Ralph Hoffman of the Santa Barbara Museum of Natural History, who fell to his death from a cliff while collecting plants in 1932, and the suicide of Herb Lester ten years later. On July 5, 1943, a B-24 crashed into Green Mountain, killing all twelve crew members. It had been dispatched to search for the ten crew members of a similar plane who had bailed out over water, resulting in the death of two of them. The wreck of the B-24 was not discovered on San Miguel until the following year, when the remains of the crew were found and removed. Hikers rediscovered the site a decade later, and, after a mix-up over military records, a Coast Guard vessel was dispatched to check on the report. Adding to the island's somewhat sinister reputation, the vessel collided with a sailboat that sank, drowning two of its passengers.

The war ended with the management and use of San Miguel much the same as it had been for more than a quarter-century. Then in 1948 came a bolt out of the blue. Brooks, who had held the lease on the island for twenty-three years, was given seventy-two hours to vacate. The navy had decided to reclaim the island for "military purposes of a confidential nature." In essence, though the navy had one bombing range off the California coast, San Clemente Island, its leaders felt the need to make San Miguel into a second target range for guided missiles and bombing. In a notice issued in December 1948, the Coast Guard declared that the San Miguel Island bombing range was a "danger area" for the public.

Intermittent bombing of the island continued through the 1950s, with the exception of a temporary halt in June and July 1950 to allow Brooks to visit the island and retrieve the livestock he had been forced to leave behind when the navy bundled him off two years before. The island was categorized as a strategically important asset of the Pacific Missile Range and the navy refused to give up control of San Miguel, while at the same time agreeing with the Department of the Interior to jointly protect the "natural values and historic and scientific objects" on the island.

Throughout the 1960s the navy and the Pacific Missile Range continued active operations on and around San Miguel. Guidance systems were tested and fleet exercises were conducted, and the island's use as a target for air and sea ordinance continued. Predictably, there were increasing conflicts with recreational sailors and protests from environmentalists, airplane owners, fishers, and scientists, though some progress was made in the protection of the environment with the final elimination of the island's sheep in 1966. The next year a naval aircraft dropped a flare to warn off unauthorized visitors who had landed on the airstrip during a military exercise. The flare caused a grass fire upwind of the old ranch. The ranch house, by this time abandoned and heavily vandalized, was leveled, the fire consuming the remnants of personal belongings left by various residents over the years. All that remains of the structure now are a few pipes, the remnants of a couple of chimneys, and two cisterns. These mark the former center of San Miguel ranching life.

Throughout the 1970s, changes in the needs of the navy meant that the National Park Service was allowed greater administrative powers and spending for study and management of San Miguel. The idea of including the island in the Channel Islands National Monument, created in the 1930s under FDR and comprising Santa Barbara and Anacapa Islands, had been discussed for decades, but the determination of the navy to hold on to San Miguel decreased only gradually during this decade, starting with the principle of cooperation with the NPS in the management and preservation of natural resources. The position of the NPS was strengthened in 1978 with the establishment of a tightly controlled visitor program overseen by a ranger resident in temporary park headquarters in Nidever Canyon. After the creation of the Channel Islands National Park in 1980, the Park Service expanded its management role although the navy retained ownership.[24]

Not much development took place in the 1980s, largely due to the heavy restrictions placed on visitors, the extreme conditions on the island, and the distance from the mainland. It was decided that a small campground should be constructed. The temporary ranger station was developed into a more substantial building in the canyon, and finally it was replaced by a modern building up on the mesa in 1997. Powered by solar energy, with water from a modern well in Nidever Canyon, it sits next to the airstrip. With relatively few visitors, the work of the park rangers is focused on preserving the 170 species of native plants, predominantly the Coastal Sage Scrub vegetation, though there are no plants that are San Miguel endemics. The native terrestrial mammals include the San Miguel Island fox and deer mouse. The island is also home to a variety of birds and marine mammals.

With the disappearance of most of the traces of historic ranching endeavors and a rapid resurgence of vegetation, San Miguel's importance, and most of its attraction for visitors, is in its ability to connect them with the California of the Chumash, its caliche forest and its pinniped rookeries. The modern history of each of the Channel Islands has been marked by strong personalities, none more so than San Miguel, but today the Nidever adobe of the 1850s is barely visible under a covering of sand and brush, and the wooden house of Captain Waters dating from 1870 has completely disappeared. The Lester house, built by Waters and Russell, is rubble, and the road painstakingly constructed up to the mesa by Captain Waters and his men from Cuyler's Harbor is now reduced to a mere trail. It is planned that most of these signs of land husbandry from relatively recent decades will weather, disintegrate, and disappear with the passage of time, leaving the natural habitat and the "deep time" of the Indigenous people to come to the fore.

For lucky visitors there is always the lure of the rare calm moment in the blustery character of this island, captured in an article by the botanist Blanche Trask for the *Los Angeles Times* in 1906: "Nowhere are there days more calm nor nights more lovely than on San Miguel Island in good weather. The shadows fall from the cliffs and lie upon the sands, and the seaweeds sway to and fro and the furrows which the winds have plowed look like the tracks of some forgotten monsters. Birds sing in the little arroyos and the streamlets trickle away . . . ever in your memory San Miguel arises 'phantom fair' with the gray mantle of fog falling off the bare shoulders of the cliff whose yellow hair is streaming with seaweed."[25]

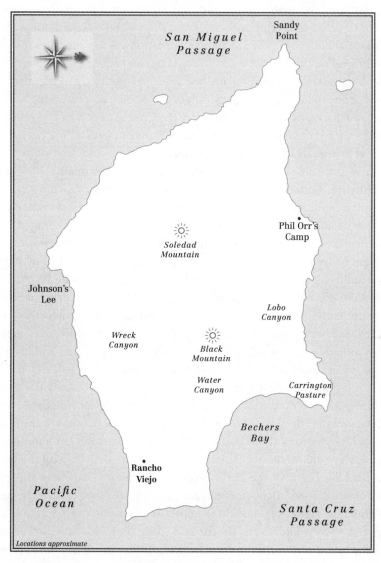

Santa Rosa Island.
Map by Gerry Krieg.

CHAPTER 4

Santa Rosa Island

Three miles to the east of San Miguel Island, Santa Rosa Island presents a more rounded outline to those driving on coastal Highway 101 about twenty-six miles to the north. The Island of the Cowboys, as it is sometimes called, is the second largest of the California Channel Islands, nestled between San Miguel and Santa Cruz Island. Its shape is roughly a parallelogram, ten miles by fifteen miles, whose corners approximate the cardinal points of the compass. Exposed to the prevailing northwesterly winds that cross its undulating contours and sculpt the trees around the island, particularly around the ranch buildings at Bechers Bay, it nonetheless has lived up to its description as a rancher's paradise, free of virtually all the major predators that menace fattening cattle on the mainland. Not even gopher holes mar the gently rolling hills that are its distinguishing characteristic.

Compared with the dramatic, rugged topography of its sister "spine islands" San Miguel, Santa Cruz, and Santa Catalina, Santa Rosa's eighty-four square miles have a smoother outline. The island's highest peak has never even been graced with a name. Santa Rosa's ground cover, which combines native and non-native grasses, and a terrain that holds significant ground water have enhanced its desirability for ranching for almost 150 years. The island has the capacity to grow, feed, and water livestock. These natural conditions provided the setting in the nineteenth century for one of California's finest sheep ranches and in the twentieth for one of its most admired cattle ranches. At different times, the island supported up to eighty thousand sheep and as many as eight thousand cattle.

With fewer rock strata of volcanic origin than any other Channel island, Santa Rosa, like its near island neighbors, is structurally part of the Santa Monica Mountains but with a comparatively gentler origin. It is said that if the water around the northern islands were lowered two hundred feet they would all be connected, as they once were, in the great ice ages of the Pleistocene, though they would still be separated from the coast by a narrow but deep strait about ten miles wide. Across this strait swam one of the more remarkable early inhabitants, the mammoth, which evolved on the island into a pygmy version standing roughly four to six feet high at the shoulder, only one-half to one-third the size of its mainland kin.

In the history of scientific exploration of the Channel Islands, it was this discovery, among others, that gave Santa Rosa Island attention. Throughout the latter half of the nineteenth century, starting with surveyors from the U.S. Coast Survey, visitors and residents of a scientific bent or otherwise regularly turned up Indian relics on the island. In the 1870s Reverend Stephen Bowers, sponsored by the Smithsonian Institution, gathered a ton of specimens, much of which he sold to collectors and museums, often, it is said, by the barrel-load. More scientific rigor was practiced in the twentieth century as would-be archaeologists excavated sites on the island, attempting to utilize the intellectual and cultural transformations that archaeology was undergoing in the teens and twenties.

The conclusions drawn from some of the Santa Rosa discoveries made later in the twentieth century remain controversial. Much of the evidence of early human habitation disappeared along with the shorelines that became inundated with rising sea levels at the end of the last ice age, but we can safely say that the first Native Americans arrived via a coastal route as the glaciers withdrew, approximately thirteen thousand years ago. As noted in chapter 2, the first of these migrants reached the California coast by sea from the far north and the Asian land bridge. DNA evidence from Santa Rosa and the other islands suggests a connection between the coastal Chumash language grouping and Indians now inhabiting the countries along the west coast of South America as well as Prince of Wales Island in Alaska.

On the Channel Islands, the abrupt meeting of land and sea meant a lack of wide drainages and few estuaries, giving rise to a subsistence pattern distinctive from that of contemporaneous mainland civilization. As they developed, the early Santa Rosa people appear to have been opportunistic foragers, exploiting shellfish and near-shore fish, depending on availability. There are still gaps in the record, and there continues to be speculation about when humans first reached Santa Rosa Island—some say it was as early as thirty thousand years before the present—but we do know that the island proved to be of sufficient size and contain adequate resources to support a Native population second only to that of Santa Cruz Island, with three villages identified by the first European explorers, though recent research has increased that number to eight.

These European voyagers were members of the expedition of Juan Rodríguez Cabrillo. After his death in January 1543, they carried on exploring the coast, and on the island the Chumash called Wima they found several hundred—perhaps more—Native people living in dome-shaped houses composed of whale ribs covered in sea-grass thatching, each with a hole in the roof to permit smoke to escape. Inside, the living space contained raised platforms of rush mats that served as beds. The Cabrillo expedition reported forty to fifty people living in each house in three *rancherías* or villages. Later chroniclers of the mission era, 250 years later, spoke of seven villages. One of these, at the site that would come to be called Rancho Viejo, near the southeast corner of the island, contained 120 people. The second largest village was located at Ranch House Creek, at the present-day ranch complex at Bechers Bay.

The Spanish noted the Natives' fishhooks and spears and their skill at hunting sea mammals. Their soapstone vessels and acorn-grinding implements were also evident, as were their much-admired tomols and their ability to manage these craft in rough conditions. The Cabrillo expedition found the Native people of the islands "very friendly," as would intermittent visitors in years to come. Four decades later the starving crew from Cermeño's Manila galleon, which had been wrecked at Drake's Bay in 1595, worked their way down the coast in an open boat and were given fish by Native people on Santa Rosa Island in exchange for some pieces of cloth. Seven years later, the ships of Sebastián Vizcaíno passed between Santa Rosa and San Miguel Island, which he referred to as San Ambrosio. Vizcaíno noted the friendliness of the islanders, with each Spaniard being offered "ten women to sleep with" if they would come ashore. What came of this oft-reported proposal is unrecorded. After this, almost two hundred years passed before George Vancouver affixed the name Santa Rosa on the Spanish charts he was using on his voyage in 1792.

In the first part of the nineteenth century, when Franciscan missionaries were attempting to entice the islanders to their missions at Santa Barbara and San Buenaventura, the island culture was in rapid decline from the deadly combination of disease and depredations by Aleut otter hunters. It is thought that along with the viruses and violence, to which they could offer little resistance, the earthquake of 1812, centered near the island, provided additional motivation, if any were needed, to move to one of the missions. The quake created a huge rift near Lobo Canyon on the island, one thousand feet long, one hundred feet wide, and fifty feet deep, and is still visible today. It is not clear when the largest removal of Indians took place, but the Santa Barbara mission records show a large number of baptisms in 1822, and the Santa Rosa Island Indians were largely a memory by the late 1820s.

The unceasing winds tore away the thatch from the whalebone framework of their houses. Rain poured in and grass grew in the earth tamped down by many generations of feet. The millennial age of the Chumash on Santa Rosa Island was over, and the age of the Europeans and Americans was about to begin, but first came an interregnum of almost twenty years with an absence of human activity broken only by sea otter hunters and other occasional visitors.

The link with the global market for sea otter and fur seal pelts, opened by the voyage of Captain James Cook in 1777, identified the source that would cater particularly to the Chinese luxury market. British, Russian, and American investors moved quickly to create a supply chain to feed that demand. The destruction of coastal and island cultures followed in short order. The Pacific coast fur trade was an exploitative industry that was expedited by force of arms. The Russian and British sea captains hired Aleut Indians who had the necessary and highly prized hunting skills. They used their small kayak-like boats to surround otters and then killed them with spears and later with guns supplied by their employers.

American investors, in contrast, hired Hawaiian hunters with similar abilities. Their practice was to shoot an otter from the shore and then swim out and retrieve it. It was a rough and violent industry, in which the Aleuts were the most avid practitioners. They were feared for their ability to land not only on the islands but also the mainland, where they killed livestock and occasionally inhabitants. They often clashed with other hunters, running them off and appropriating their furs and supplies. A firsthand description from 1837 by George Nidever details a series of armed skirmishes over several days on Santa Rosa Island that left several Aleuts dead or wounded. They had attempted to land from an unlicensed brig flying the British flag, and for the first time they met concerted armed resistance, a strategy previously decided upon by Nidever and his group. After three days the Aleuts and their English captain gave up and sailed off in search of easier pickings. Three years later, hired hunters killed the same captain, along with his half-Hawaiian wife off Santa Cruz Island. On this occasion the enterprising Aleuts mutinied, seizing the vessel and forcing the crew to sail them back to Alaska where they stole the cargo before releasing the ship.

Nidever initially hunted under a license granted by the Mexican government to William Dana, a naturalized citizen of Santa Barbara who hired hunters like Nidever and his Hawaiian helpers in exchange for half the pelts they acquired. The skin of an adult sea otter was substantial. It measured about five feet in length and two to three feet in width, and through the course of the nineteenth century, as the otter population was decimated, the price for these prized furs rose accordingly. In 1802, pelts sold for an average of $20 each in China [$420 in 2011 equivalent]. When Nidever began his operations, hunting on Santa Rosa, San Miguel, and Santa Cruz Islands in the early 1840s, he received $30 for each skin. By 1846, the pelts were retailing for $150 each [$4,400], and in the 1870s a good specimen brought $475 in London, but by that time the sea otter had all but vanished from Pacific waters.

Nidever, who later became widely known for his central role in the saga of "the Lone Woman of San Nicolas" in 1853, lived out a long life on Santa Barbara, hunting and following various agricultural pursuits on the islands, spawning a modest nautical dynasty in which his son and grandson piloted schooners and worked for island owners. As a young man, he had seen Santa Rosa Island in a virtually unspoiled, uninhabited state, though by the time he died in 1883 it was widely known as one of the biggest sheep ranches in the region.

It was concern about the use of the Channel Islands as a base for brigands that provided the impetus in 1838 for the Mexican government to order

Governor Alvarado "to prevent numerous foreign adventurers from appropriating important portions of [the islands] whereby they can do much injury to our fisheries, commerce and interests . . . [and to] proceed with promptness and prudence to grant and distribute lands in the said islands to citizens who desire them."[1]

The government recommended that the grant for Santa Rosa Island be given to brothers Jose Antonio and Carlos Barrelo Carillo. This recommendation became a casualty of the infighting that characterized California politics at the time, and it was not until Alvarado had been replaced as governor by Manuel Micheltorena, who was more amenable to the Carillos, that they could claim ownership.

The Carillo brothers were sons of a soldier who had arrived in California with the Portolà expedition in 1769. Jose Antonio, the elder of the two, had followed his father into the military and enjoyed a distinguished career in Monterey, Santa Barbara, and San Diego, notably protecting Santa Barbara 1818 from the depredations of the French-born Argentine freebooter, Hippolyte de Bouchard. Fresh from a triumphant capture of Monterey, capital of the province of Alta California, Bouchard was intent on subjugating Santa Barbara, but through a ruse that could have been borrowed from a comic opera, quick changes of uniform behind a screen of brush by Carillo and his men managed to convince Bouchard that the town was heavily defended and that he should negotiate. There was an exchange of prisoners and the brigands sailed off down the coast to the evident relief of the Barbareños.

Following his military exploits in the teens and 1820s, Jose Antonio Carillo developed a political career that spanned the unstable decade of the 1830s. He gained a reputation up and down the province as a lightning rod for trouble. In keeping with the spirit of the times, his politics included challenges to sitting governors, changes of alliance, political deals, and periods of exile. At one point he induced the Mexican government to appoint his brother Carlos as governor, but by 1843 he seemed to be more intent on valuable real estate transactions. One of these was the sale of Santa Rosa Island, one month after he had acquired it, to Carlos's two daughters. These two offspring of one of California's best families were married to two naturalized entrepreneurial Americans, Alpheus Basil Thompson and John Coffin Jones. Thompson and Jones enjoyed long careers in both legitimate and not-quite-legal activities along the coast in the 1830s and 1840s. There seems to be general agreement that it was the interest and influence of the husbands rather than that of the Carillo daughters that spurred the acquisition of the island from their uncle and father.

Before the end of 1843, the Carillo brothers made that sure formal possession was secured by transporting a party of local worthies to accompany a load of building materials for a house on the island. About a year later Jones shipped 270 head of cattle, 51 ewes, 2 rams, and 9 horses to Santa Rosa, the first documented livestock on the island. To carry out the terms of the grant, Thompson had his men build a house and corral between Skunk Point and East Point, south of Bechers Bay, a location that became known as Rancho Viejo. It was a simple structure, twenty-four by fifteen feet and nine feet high, with a shingle roof and one glass window. Four Hawaiian vaqueros were hired to look after the livestock.

With their grant secured, the interests of the two Americans diverged. Thompson took the lead in running the island operation, while Jones, dissatisfied with life in California and doubtful of his economic prospects with the rapid decline of the otter trade, sailed with his family to Boston the following year. He left Alfred Robinson, fellow Bostonian and representative of the firm Bryant, Sturgis, to represent his affairs in California.

The modest island operation required few people to keep it going. It ran like a traditional Californio ranch, in which livestock roamed free until they were rounded up to be slaughtered principally for their hides and tallow. The Hawaiian vaqueros were eventually replaced by a Barbareño and two Indians. The small number of sheep produced wool and meat for the local market. All this was transformed with the discovery of gold in Northern California in 1848. The subsequent Gold Rush, which lasted well into the 1850s, created a burgeoning market for beef, lamb, cheese, and butter in San Francisco and the goldfields. As it did for many purveyors to the hungry hordes of miners, the Gold Rush created fortunes for the owners of ranches in southern California who drove their cattle north up the coast or the central San Joaquin valley. One source tells us that by 1852 the Santa Rosa Island ranch was prospering, generating an income that year of $38,000 [$1.1 million] Others dispute this, but it is known that Thompson added brood mares, a stallion, hogs, and rabbits to enhance his holding around this time. After California achieved statehood in 1850 with a sharp increase in its population, the owners of the great ranches were called before the newly established Public Land Commission to prove the legal titles to their huge estates. Manuela Carillo de Jones and the heirs of her sister Francisca who had died in 1851 hired a San Francisco law firm in 1852 to represent their interests before the Public Land Commission and prove their ownership. In their petition they stated that they had established a large stock of sheep, cattle, and horses, houses and other improvements. They also filed documents showing the chain of ownership from the government of Mexico, represented by Governor Micheltorena, to their father and uncle and then to themselves. The commission initially rejected their claim on the grounds that it had not been proven that the Mexican government had authorization to grant ownership of islands, there was no map included in the petition, and other technicalities. In their appeal against this judgment, the value of taking witnesses on the first trip to the island to land building supplies became apparent, as these Santa Barbara worthies testified about the building of the house and the stocking of the island. Various other witnesses, among them vaqueros, the carpenter who built the house, and the captain who transported lumber and livestock, also supported the appeal. Under the influence of this testimony the district court confirmed clear title to Santa Rosa Island for Jones and Thompson in 1856.

Their title was now clear but trouble was brewing. In Boston, Jones was experiencing health problems and voicing concern about lack of returns on his California holdings. With the help of his Santa Barbara representative Alfred Robinson he sought to claim some income from the island operation he shared with Thompson. Even though his involvement had been negligible, Jones asked Robinson to investigate the business, as Thompson had never furnished him with any details of the operation. Robinson found that Thompson had been generating income through the sale of livestock, and Jones hired a local attorney to sue his erstwhile partner for an accounting of the business. With local feeling running high in favor of Thompson, Jones's lawyer petitioned for a change of venue to Monterey. Both sides lined up their witnesses. Jones let his fears about his former partner's intentions run riot, telling his attorney that Thompson had been plotting against him for years: "God forbid that his nefarious purposes be successful!"[2] Thompson, on the other hand, complained to his lawyer that he had paid out of his own pocket for stock, building materials, transportation, and employees' wages. He defended his sale of cattle as justified because of his expenses. As far as he was concerned, Jones and his wife had never spent "one dollar on the Island nor on anything thereon, neither have they given one hour's time in any way or manner."[3]

In spite of Thompson's protestations, in 1857 the court took the side of Jones, awarding him $7,370 [$190,000] from Thompson's assets and appointing a referee who reported to the court that Thompson had sold livestock to the value of $23,000 [$593,000], but that his management costs had been $40,000 [$1.03 million]. It was further noted that there were saleable assets on the island totaling $114,000 in cattle, sheep, and horses [$2.9 million]. The court ordered that enough of these be sold to satisfy a petition of the guardian of Thompson's children to pay off their debts, which had been prevented by Jones's legal actions. Two hundred head of livestock were put on the market and bought by Santa Barbara rancher T. Wallace More, the first of a series of transactions that would eventually see the transfer of the entire island to More and members of his family.

T. W. More and two of his brothers, Alexander and Henry, were forty-niners who had done well enough out of the mines for an initial investment in ranch land in Southern California. Seizing the opportunity to supply the voracious markets in the northern part of the state, they drove their cattle to the mines to sell at a substantial profit. This they invested in more ranch holdings, the history of which provides a window on the changing fortunes of the Californios, as they were forced to give way to U.S. legal rigor on boundary definition and Americans' determination to seize profitable opportunities as they arose. In Santa Barbara County, this trend gave rise to a complicated marital and legal history for the Mores and the Carillos. Alexander More was married to another of the Carillo daughters, but this did not prevent his brothers T. W. and Henry from using their financial muscle to foreclose on Rancho Lompoc, owned by Alexander's Carillo in-laws, in 1855, and then buy their Rancho Sespe near Ventura at a probate sale in 1862. A fourth More brother, John, bought a ranch at Goleta whose wharf would prove useful for the Santa Rosa Island operations, further enhancing the More family territorial ambitions.

The liquidation of the joint assets of Thompson and Jones continued through 1858. Court-appointed receiver Abel Stearns ordered an inventory and placed ads in California newspapers for the sale of eight thousand cattle, about a quarter of which were semi-wild, roughly sixteen hundred steers, six thousand to seven thousand sheep in a very wild state, and as many as three hundred horses. There had been no management of the stock for about three years and little management of the pasturage. Alfred Robinson, acting for the estranged partners, negotiated another sale of all the remaining cattle to T. W. More for $35,000 [$956,000].

The unwinding of the Jones-Thompson holdings proceeded, in spite of a welter of claims by Thompson's nephew, Dixey, and other former Thompson associates. By mid-1859 More had bought most of the island livestock, transporting them to his Rancho San Julian near Lompoc. Many of the animals died on the way or in the severe storm that hit the island and the mainland in December. By that time only two thousand cattle, fourteen hundred sheep, and nineteen horses were left on the island. The storm also destroyed the recently constructed pier at Bechers Bay. These setbacks seemingly did not deter More from his next objective, which was the purchase of the island itself. Thompson, who had given half his Santa Rosa holding to his children, had mortgaged his other quarter share of the island, and it eventually had to be sold at auction on the steps of the Santa Barbara County courthouse in October 1859.

The high bid of $3,000 [$81,000] was that of Thomas Wallace More. He talked it up with another prominent rancher, C. W. Hollister, who thought it sounded like a good investment. Hollister then floated the idea to an associate of buying the whole island to run as a sheep ranch, including buying a little steamer, and "set[ting] up a little Confederacy upon the Pacific of our own." He added that they could check with William Barron of Santa Cruz Island to see how he liked ranching offshore, "free from wild animals, already fenced, plenty of water, good climate . . . [and] Santa Rosa is said to be much better."[4] They did not act on the idea, and More continued with his acquisitions.

In 1861, John Jones died in Boston after a long illness, leaving his half interest in the island to his wife and children. After four years of negotiation, they sold their interest to Thomas More's younger brother, Alexander (A.P.), for $18,000 [$249,000]. Out on Santa Rosa Island, the Mores were now in possession of three-quarters of the interest. Given their previous experience with the Mores, the Thompson-Carillo offspring were understandably anxious to divest themselves of the property, and with the death of their father in 1869, on the basis that it was unlikely that they would find another buyer, they sold their shares to A. P. More for $6,000. After negotiations between the More brothers, by mid-1870 A.P. and Henry were joint owners of Santa Rosa Island, an arrangement that lasted for the next eleven years.

The drought-stricken years of the 1860s had created upheaval on the stock-raising ranches of Southern California, with the number of cattle in the state declining by almost half. Ranchers were forced to decimate their herds of cattle and sheep as pasturage dried up and disappeared, ringing down the curtain on a cattle industry that had dominated the region for much of the previous century. It is unclear how Santa Rosa Island fared in the great drought, but given the continuing negotiations between the Mores and the Thompson-Jones interests, it is unlikely that the livestock numbers increased significantly.

The Mores moved the headquarters for the ranching activities on the island from Rancho Viejo to its present location at Bechers Bay, and they began to act on their ambitious plans to create a large sheep ranch. By the early 1870s they had imported thousands of sheep to create one of the biggest holdings on the Pacific coast. An 1873 newspaper article noted that they were building a new house, a new wharf more than five hundred feet long, and a water pipeline from a spring two miles away from the ranch headquarters. The operation was centered on "a cozy ranch house, behind a group of high shouldered Monterey cypress, squeezed out of shape by the wind . . . [overlooking] a quiet little village composed of the vast storing barn and shearing room, stables, pens and sheds, and the dining and sleeping rooms."[5]

An *Overland Monthly* article from 1874 trumpeted the progress and prospects of the Mores. The writer, who had hitched a ride from Santa Barbara on the *Star of Freedom*, owned by the Santa Cruz Island Company, claimed that there were sixty thousand sheep on the island. He estimated that their three hundred thousand pounds of wool would produce an income of $100,000 [$2 million], of which $80,000 would be profit. One of the advantages of island ranches, said the writer, was their location near coastal shipping lanes, which enabled delivery of island products into the markets of San Francisco, Santa Barbara, or Los Angeles within thirty-six hours. He further noted that freight costs for shipping wool were less than from some of the interior ranches, making island wool more profitable. With the passage of time and the development of the California economy in the twentieth century, with its land-based transportation systems, this balance of advantage would change

Main Ranch, Bechers Bay.
Photograph by Mortimore (full name unknown), August 1965.
Courtesy of Channel Islands National Park.

significantly. The writer also speculated on the idea of introducing exotic game from all over the world to the island—buffalo, elk, deer, antelope, and others—creating a convenient hunting reserve that would provide a boost to regional tourism, as "few would pass over this coast without spending a day or two at Santa Rosa Island."[6]

At the Mores' operation on Santa Rosa Island, every six months there would be a *corrida* (roundup), and forty or more shearers were recruited locally to clip the sheep. It was said that a good shearer could clip one hundred sheep per day, which probably meant, between the corrida and the *trasquila* (shearing), that there was one to two month's work for these local transient laborers, who often went from island to island and ranch to ranch. Nationally, the 1860s and early 1870s were a boom time for sheep ranchers, with wartime needs and postwar economic expansion stoking the market for woolen cloth. The end came with the Panic of 1873 leading into the Long Depression of the latter 1870s, which eventually caught up with the wool industry. The enterprising Mores responded to the collapse of the market, reducing their herd by killing large numbers of sheep, skinning them, and boiling their carcasses in huge kettles. Between the sale of the sheep pelts and the tallow from the carcasses, a modest profit was attained and the island range stabilized.

In the late 1870s the Mores still did not possess their own vessel, choosing to rely principally on the Santa Cruz Island Company's *Star of Freedom*. But the availability of this schooner was reliant on the goodwill of the prickly superintendent of the company, J. B. Joyaux, and after some real or imagined slight he peremptorily informed Henry More that the schooner would no longer be available except on an emergency basis at $35 per trip [$800]. This encouraged the Mores to commission their own schooner. Built in Oregon, the sixty-one-foot *Santa Rosa*, with a carrying capacity of thirty tons, was delivered in 1879. She made regular runs between the island and the mainland, calling at Santa Barbara and the landing of the More holdings in Goleta, as well as making biannual trips to San Francisco for supplies.

In 1881 Henry More and his wife sold their half interest in the island to A.P., giving him sole ownership. A.P. hired his brother-in-law to act as superintendent, as he spent much of his time in San Francisco. Nonetheless, the life of the ranchero grandee would seem to have had strong appeal for A. P. More. A contemporary studio photograph shows him confidently staring into the camera, decked out in the traditional velvet suit of the Californio gentleman, his thumb hooked into his fringed cummerbund, with a carefully arranged bandana and sombrero completing the look.

Dressing the part of the grandee was one thing, but in 1884 More took his connection to the olden days, when the great ranchero's word was law, too far. After an argument and a scuffle on the island he shot and killed an employee who'd had the temerity to quit his job as ranch cook. At the ensuing trial in Santa Barbara, a deliberate fudging of jurisdiction—the shooting took place on the Bechers Bay pier, hence over water—allowed the powerful and well-connected More to walk from the courthouse a free man.

Nearing the end of the difficult decade of the 1880s, a San Francisco newspaper article declared that More was back on top, in 1887 shipping wool worth more than $210,000 [$5.2 million], for a profit of $80,000 [$2 million].

The writer noted that, aside from the times of the corridas, four men were capable of running the ranch. The island was said to be divided into four zones by fencing made of split redwood posts topped by two strands of barbed wire and with four horizontal boards placed low on the posts. Trained goats were used to move the sheep around the ranch and help round them up at shearing time. At the turn of the century, Santa Rosa was the most celebrated of the northern Channel Islands, featured in more than a few books and articles. The writers, many of whom spent time on the island, described the "village" of houses and barns at Bechers Bay, with its simple, New England–style house for the owners, sheltered by a group of wind-sculpted Monterey cypress, and other accommodations, including a developed cave that provided housing for temporary workers. There were detailed descriptions of the work in the shearing shed, which was laid out to aid the efficiency of the shearers, who could produce a fleece in around five minutes while keeping up a steady stream of songs and jokes. The fleeces were thrown onto a table for collection and the running numbers were called out and noted by the tallyman, though there is no mention of the exchange of a token to be cashed in later as was common practice on most of the other sheep-raising islands. The fleece went to the packer, who stomped it down in one of the huge burlap sacks hanging nearby. Once all the sheep were shorn and dipped in a noxious solution of heated caustic soda, sulfur, and lime, the trasquila shed was often carefully cleaned to provide the setting for a fiesta staged by the ranch hands, featuring dancing and song.

In an 1893 magazine feature, the "island kingdom" was said to be "one of the finest sheep ranches on the Pacific Coast" and was considered to have "perhaps one of the largest flocks of sheep now owned by one man in California."[7] For visitors there were long horseback rides to explore the island and excursions to Chumash burial grounds to collect artifacts. Personal memoirs of this time talk of a little white schoolhouse where some of the More children were taught by a teacher imported from Ohio. There was even an island hermit, who lived in the cave described by George Nidever in his recollection of the shootout with the Aleut otter hunters in the 1840s (*The Life and Adventures of George Nidever*).

A. P. More was no longer actively involved in the ranching by this time, having moved to the Midwest in the late 1880s. He leased the island to his brother Lawrence, who ran the ranch through a series of superintendents,

Santiago's Cave, also known as Nidever's Cave.
Photograph by Pete Reyes, ca. 1910.
Courtesy of Channel Islands National Park.

including Thomas More Storke, his grand-nephew. Storke, later a Santa Barbara grandee, newspaper owner, and politician, wrote that he "endured . . .
an interlude of managing a sheep ranch. . . . Life was rugged on Santa Rosa.
. . . At the time, it was one of the largest sheep ranches in California and,
under my uncle's ownership, had carried as many as 125,000 sheep at a time."[8]

This number is likely to be an exaggeration of a youthful memory, well in
excess of the carrying capacity of the island, but is an indication of the great
number of sheep involved. There was also increasing evidence in the late
1890s that all was not well, and the ranch was running down. The Depression that began with the Panic of 1893 made life difficult for many, and in
particular for agriculturalists. A. P. More died childless in Chicago that year,
leaving no direct heirs, though there was a clutch of offspring of his many siblings, creating a total of fifteen individuals with a partial claim on the island.
Over the next eight years, a series of claims and counter-claims, transfers
of ownership, and legal conflicts ensued. Responsibility for the estate of

A. P. More changed hands because of financial conflicts in an atmosphere of declining profitability. A.P.'s brother John, acting as executor, was found guilty of embezzling $80,000 from the estate, and in addition the schooner *Santa Rosa* was wrecked on the beach at Cuyler Harbor on San Miguel Island in 1899. The owners, who now included a San Francisco consortium, were reduced to using the services of a Chinese junk to conduct island business.

In April 1900 a state court authorized the sale of A. P. More's mainland real estate interests, which consisted of ranches near Goleta and Lompoc, but not the island. A probate report that year valued the island at $350,000 [$9.4 million], including about 8,000 head of sheep, 200 head of cattle, 170 horses, 25 hogs, 100 goats, and 200 bales of wool. Later in 1900 the court authorized the distribution of shares in the island to the twelve remaining heirs. Between June 1901 and October 1902, all of these except for one holdout sold their shares to two Los Angeles cattlemen, Walter Vail and John V. Vickers, for about $250,000 [$6.6 million], bringing the More era on Santa Rosa Island to an end.

The Mores, who had taken control of Santa Rosa from the descendants of one of Santa Barbara's first families, provided the transition to future agricultural development by creating the basic ranching infrastructure of roads and fences, but their cultivation of sheep had left the rangeland in a greatly altered state from the way how they had found it in the mid-nineteenth century. Santa Rosa was not as badly affected as San Nicolas, San Miguel, and San Clemente Islands, where the combination of sheep foraging and prevailing winds created large barren areas of creeping sand dunes that threatened to overwhelm the remaining vegetation, but the decades of sheep grazing had taken their toll. Over the years, the Mores produced a significant volume of wool and drew the attention of western writers to the island by following the template for stock-raising that dominated most of the Channel Islands in the nineteenth century.

At the same time Santa Rosa was exceptional as an agricultural entity, one of the last California ranching outposts of the era before fences. It was not only a successful sheep ranch that largely paid its way, it was also connected through the Mores and the Storkes to local Santa Barbara Californio royalty, playing a role in Santa Barbara's mythologizing of its Hispanic heritage.

One of the early ranch superintendents was the aforementioned Dixey W. Thompson, nephew not only of early owner Alpheus Thompson but also of T. W. More. A photograph from the 1890s shows him on one of the main streets of Santa Barbara, seated bolt upright on his horse, Van Dyke beard carefully trimmed, resplendent in ceremonial Californio decorated sombrero, jacket, and trousers. As Santa Barbara rushed to embrace its mystical Hispanic past he became one of its emblems, a local worthy and manager of the Arlington Hotel, greeter of the good and the great, including President Harrison on his travels in 1891. Another Santa Rosa ranch manager noted above, Thomas More Storke, was a son-in-law of T. W. More. He was viewed as the heir apparent of the Hispanic-Yankee tradition of Santa Barbara by being related to both the Castillo and Ortega families, whose roots went back to the founding of the Santa Barbara presidio in the days of Portolà. With the new century, Santa Rosa Island would maintain its exceptionalism but in a different way, under new management with a new philosophy.

The new owners of Santa Rosa represented something of a break with the past of the Mores and old Santa Barbara. The advent of Walter Vail and J. V. Vickers ushered in an era of ownership stability and cattle-raising that would dominate Santa Rosa Island in the twentieth century. With no particular connection to the real or imagined Hispanic heritage of Santa Barbara, these two represented a fresh chapter in the history of California and the West. They were part of the late-nineteenth-century wave of Pacific Coast immigrants, many of whom arrived having made one or more fortunes elsewhere, with an eye for western prospects in which to invest and the deep pockets to fund those investments. The decline of the great Californio ranching families and their holdings at the dawn of the new era had spelled opportunity for early Euro-American arrivals like Thompson, Jones, Stearns, and others, when Santa Barbara was easily as large and important as Los Angeles. But a generation later, with the swelling population of Los Angeles and Southern California linked to the rest of the United States by the steel rails of the Southern Pacific and the Santa Fe, the stage was set for a new group of entrepreneurs to complete the breakup of the huge old land holdings, to subdivide and develop and to help create the modern image and the reality of Southern California.

Like many young eastern men of his post–Civil War generation, Walter Vail headed west from New Jersey in 1875 seeking adventure and fortune. After working briefly as timekeeper of the California mine in Virginia City, Nevada, he lost his job when the devastating economic impact of the Panic of

1873 reached the mining towns of the West. Vail continued westward, arriving in San Francisco in the fall of 1875. After a bit of exploring in Northern California he headed south, where his arrival coincided with that of his wealthy ship-owning uncle Nathan, who had made his fortune transporting cargoes between Newfoundland and England. Nathan had plunged into the property market in Los Angeles and advised his young nephew to invest in land, suggesting cattle ranching in Arizona Territory as an affordable first step. Walter followed this advice and soon found a ranch near Tucson that suited his requirements. In order to fund its purchase, he returned to the Nevada mining towns that were starting to recover from the downturn of the economy, but it was soon apparent that it would take years to save enough money to buy the ranch. Walter Vail was a young man in a hurry, and he turned once again to his uncle, who effected an introduction to an Englishman with money to invest. By 1876 Vail and his new partner Herbert Hislop had bought a 160-acre ranch in southeastern Arizona Territory for a little more than $1,000 [$21,000]. Reflecting his optimism, they called it the Empire Ranch, which prophetically grew over the next two decades, with some early financial assistance from uncle Nathan and his wife Anna, into a huge holding of more than a million acres, one of the largest in Arizona. A commercial studio photograph from the time shows him as stereotypical western man of action—booted and spurred, with ten-gallon hat, neckerchief, and six-shooter. His gloved hand rests on the shoulder of his brother, Edward, who, by way of contrast, is dressed as a city dude, with bow tie and straw boater, though he makes the concession of leaning on a bale of straw.

Arizona ranching was not necessarily an easy road to wealth in those years. The local Indians, the fierce Chiricahua Apache, led by their quick-witted chief Geronimo, were a constant hazard to ranchers and livestock. Vail and his partner were working in rugged country where the line between success and failure was a fine one. It got to be too much for the English partner and he quit the scene, leaving young Vail to continue on his own. His land acquisitions, some made with his uncle as partner, expanded dramatically, particularly after the discovery and development of a highly profitable silver mine on one of his ranches. At its peak, the Total Wreck Mine was generating profits of $4,000 per day [$94,000], supporting a town with a post office, four saloons, three hotels, a bank, and a brewery. With a herd of ten thousand head of cattle and rail connections to both Los Angeles and Chicago, Walter and

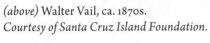

(above) Walter Vail, ca. 1870s.
Courtesy of Santa Cruz Island Foundation.

(right) John Vickers, ca. 1870s.
Courtesy of Santa Cruz Island Foundation.

his uncle incorporated the Empire Land and Cattle Company, and Walter rose to prominence as one of the leading cattlemen of the territory, even taking on the might of the Southern Pacific in 1890 when they peremptorily raised the cattle transport rates to exorbitant levels. He succeeded in driving nine hundred head of cattle from Arizona to Southern California, with his brother Ed acting as trail boss. When the other Arizona cattlemen showed solidarity behind the idea of making the trail permanent, the railroad backed down on their rate increase. The story of that drive, "Diary of a Desert Trail," told years later to the *Arizona Daily Star,* became Ed Vail's best known publication.

Walter Vail's family connections in Los Angeles led him to operate out of an office there with a successful real estate investor, Carroll W. Gates. Together they bought and leased ranches in California and Arizona, including a one-year lease on Santa Catalina Island in 1890 (during which they stocked the island with 2,500 head of cattle), and a half interest in an Arizona ranch owned by J. V. Vickers, who would eventually become Vail's partner in the purchase of Santa Rosa Island.

J. V. Vickers had come west at about the same time as Walter Vail but with access to greater resources, having sprung from more comfortable circumstances as the son of a wealthy Pennsylvania Quaker farmer. He arrived in substantial style at Tombstone, Arizona, as the representative of the New York Life Insurance Company, investing in a ranch east of town, adjacent to Vail's Empire Ranch in Sulphur Spring Valley. Vickers expanded his holdings to include more real estate and other ranches, investing in the Erie Cattle Company and cofounding the Chiricahua Cattle Company, where one of the principal investors would be Walter Vail. In 1890, he moved his family from the rough-and-tumble Tombstone to the more genteel environs of Los Angeles, building a substantial home on Seventh Street. Six years later, Vail would install his family in a house around the corner on Burlington Avenue, reflecting the changing balance of his investment portfolio, moving from the fading profits in Arizona ranching to the rising opportunities of Southern California.

With the cattle industry facing chronic problems of oversupply, Vail turned his attentions to investments in urban real estate, subdivision of the old ranchos of the Mexican era, and oil development. He and his Los Angeles partner, Gates, subdivided the Laguna Ranch into what would become the cities of Commerce and Montebello and purchased the Pauba Ranch in Riverside County. Vail and Vickers then partnered to found and develop the town of Huntington Beach, and in 1901 they made their first investments in shares of Santa Rosa Island. Throughout that year and the next they acquired an undivided seven-eighths interest from the estate of A. P. More, including the livestock and buildings on the island, giving them a free hand to manage and develop the ranch as they wished.

As experienced western ranchers and cattlemen Vail and Vickers were familiar with the hazards posed by cattle rustlers and transmitted diseases, and a ranch secured by at least twenty-five miles of open water would have been very attractive. Their experience also gave them a clear idea of the direction they wanted to take ranching on the island. In September 1901, before their acquisition was concluded, Walter sent his brother Ed to the island to make an inspection. Ed was accompanied by J. V. Vickers's brother and one of Walter's sons, Banning, to have a good look at what they had purchased. In a letter to his sister, Ed Vail commented favorably on the size and quality of the island horses, and the size of the cattle, "the fattest grass cattle I ever saw." The party rode over twenty miles a day, inspecting the "rich and abundant" grasslands. Ed commented on the "large barns, a large two-story ranch house, shearing sheds, and dipping vats for sheep etc., a wharf and boat-house with a lifeboat and a two story cottage furnished comfortably." He also noted the cool windiness of the climate, writing that "a fire was comfortable at night [in August], but there is not much frost in winter." The party amused themselves hunting foxes and digging for Indian relics. Banning went home with "a sack of bones, skulls, and some stone implements," which the family divided with a Professor Willard from Tombstone.[9]

With the views of the brothers of the two principals carefully noted, Walter Vail and J. V. Vickers set about gradually changing the More family's sheep ranch into a cattle stocker or fattening operation. Vail family lore has it that they rested the range for a couple of years while removing most of the sheep. Only then did they commence shipping in young steers from other Vail and Vickers holdings to fatten on island grass and be sold as "finished cattle" ready for slaughter. There was good logic to all this. More than half a century of sheep grazing had led to erosion and the spread of non-edible plants, which presented range management problems for ranchers continuing with sheep. Running the operation as a stocker ranch allowed flexibility to respond to island range conditions and changes in beef market demand, and it allowed the Santa Rosa Island ranch to be integrated into the overall Vail and Vickers ranching enterprise.

Wholesale change did not happen overnight. Reports in the California press in 1903 spoke of seven thousand to eight thousand head of cattle shipped in from Arizona, ultimately arriving via coastal steamers and the company's schooner, *Santa Rosa Island*. The sheep population gradually dropped to a few thousand, down from about ten thousand at the end of the More era. There appeared to be a school of thought that getting rid of all the sheep was not a wise decision, though there were regular shipments of the sheep to livestock dealers Sherman and Ealand in Santa Barbara. By 1904, the sheep population was reduced to about seven hundred, but it would be decades before the last remnants of the sheep herd were gathered for shipment to the mainland. In the meantime, the Vail family remained sporadically involved in sheep raising, with Ed running sheep and cattle on San Clemente Island and leasing San Nicolas Island from 1919 to 1934 for sheep-raising in partnership with Robert Brooks, whose story is detailed in chapter 8.

Throughout 1905 the move to making Santa Rosa a cattle ranch continued, and various members of the Vail family became more directly involved in its day-to-day running. The year 1906 began optimistically for the family, but, foreshadowing things to come, on April 18 a huge earthquake struck the San Francisco Bay Area. In the following days, the Los Angeles Chamber of Commerce organized a Citizens' Relief Committee, with Walter Vail as its executive director. Free train transportation from San Francisco to Los Angeles was made available to thousands of newly homeless people who flocked southward from the stricken city. Five refugee camps were located in various city parks, where ten thousand to fifteen thousand hot meals were served daily, organized Vail. By the end of the month, it was reported that Southern California had sent over a half a million dollars in cash and supplies for the relief of San Francisco [almost $13.5 million], all overseen by Vail, who had the entire Los Angeles Police Department at his disposal. On behalf of his army of volunteers, Vail accepted the thanks and recognition of his executive ability from Governor Pardee and the State of California.

In business terms, the development of the new ranch on Santa Rosa Island was going well, and with Thanksgiving Day approaching there seemed much to be thankful for. Walter, his wife, and their oldest son Nathan Russell were returning to Los Angeles from Redondo Beach on one of the city's street-cars, still a bit of a novelty after their introduction five years earlier. At the corner of Grand and Seventh, Walter alighted from the front platform and turned his back to Seventh Street to help his wife from the streetcar. At that moment another streetcar made the turn from Grand Avenue, and Walter, with the rumble and screeching of the wheels and rails unable to hear the warning shouted by his son, was crushed between the two cars. Suffering devastating injuries that were beyond the medical capabilities of the time, he lingered for four days, dying on December 2, 1906. To lose their figurehead at age fifty-four was a terrible blow to the family. Vail's obituaries in Los Angeles and Arizona hailed him as an "energetic worker, patriotic leader, and a devoted husband and father, a Cattle King." It was written that "ranchers from the mountains went to him for advice; business men appealed to his wisdom; friends found him sympathetic and sincere. . . . He was generous, open hearted and true."[10]

The family rallied. Twenty-three-year-old Nathan Russell (N.R.) Vail, who had been on the streetcar with his mother and father that fateful day, took over direct management of the Vail family holdings, including ranching operations on Santa Rosa Island. He stepped up to become the mainstay of the Vail family estate for thirty-five years. His younger brothers were brought in to manage other properties as they came of age. Mahlon Vail took on the Pauba and Santa Rosa Ranches around Temecula. A few years later, Banning took over management of the Empire Ranch.

In 1912 the Vail Trust was established as the entity that would carry on the family's business on the island in partnership with the Vickers family, who, in turn, were visited by tragedy the following year. J. V. Vickers died suddenly in 1913 from complications brought on by an abscessed tooth. The connection between cardiac and dental problems was little understood at the time, and his death came as a tremendous shock to both families, though the effect on the island was minimal, given his passive role in the Santa Rosa ranch holding. Vickers left an estate of almost a million dollars [$22.7 million], and his wife and daughters continued his business activities, placing their Santa Rosa Island interests into the Vickers Company in 1931, acting as silent partners in the functioning of the ranch, with Walter Vail's descendants actively operating it.

The story of Santa Rosa Island as a twentieth-century western cattle ranch is the story of the Vail family. Through four generations, with the assent of the Vickers interests, the Vails were the hands-on managers, and although some were more formal with their employees and others less so, they all knew how to direct ranch operations on the basis of personal experience and ability. Able to assess the state of the herd and the range, decide on the timing and shipping of cattle, and conduct business worth hundreds of thousands of dollars on the strength of a handshake or a phone call, they also knew the basics of riding, herding, and fencing. These were the skills that ensured the success and continuity of the Vail and Vickers experience on Santa Rosa. With operations directed from a mainland office, first in Los Angeles, and then, after 1961, Santa Barbara, there was heavy reliance on their superintendents for day-to-day operations. And these men responded by staying in the job for decades, adding a further layer of stability to the ranching business.

N. R. Vail had a formal approach to the job but was intimately acquainted with all aspects of the business, as an excerpt from a letter sent in the drought year 1918 to his uncle Ed (known by N.R.'s generation as Tio) demonstrates,

Am figuring on making a deal with people here or in the East to handle aged steers first. The cows will be next to be looked out for and with these out of the way I imagine the young steers and the heifers can get buy [sic] until things warm up a little in the northwest. I am anxious to play this so that at any time that we are moving, if we do get a rain we can keep as much stuff [cattle] on the island and impair our future receipts as little as possible.[11]

N.R. managed the island ranch from his father's death in 1906, through the prosperity of the teens and twenties, the hard times of the thirties, and the difficult early war years, then died unexpectedly of a heart attack in 1943. With the Vickers family's approval, N.R.'s brother Ed, ten years his junior, stepped into his shoes. Like the other Vails, Ed brought a wealth of ranch management experience to the job, having overseen family ranches in San Diego and Riverside Counties, as well as having leased San Nicolas Island as a sheep operation for some years. He had been living and ranching in northern Santa Barbara County for eleven years and was familiar with local conditions and the island operation.

With diverse interests like polo and sailing, Ed kept a certain distance from his cowboys, though he spoke Spanish and showed himself ready and willing to pitch in when needed for roundups, inventory, and shipping. Island cowboy Diego Cuevas, later foreman, characterized Ed: "He was always making trips just to see how the cattle [were] doing, how the feeding was, all of this thing. At round-up he come over to help separate the loads and weigh cows and all that stuff. . . . he like to tell you what to do and he like you to do it just exactly the way he told it . . . and if you make mistake you find out about it."[12]

With the death of Ed Vail in 1961, the mantle of management fell to his nephew Al Vail, who had been the boots on the ground for his uncle for more than twenty years, working as a cowboy on the island, which made the transition smooth. Having been born in Los Angeles, and raised both there and on the island, and with a degree in business from UCLA and courses in animal husbandry from UC Davis, Al had the management background to go with his cowboy skills. Cuevas said of him, "He was really nice, he was part of a team. He was in it with everybody. . . . he like [to] play around. He was not much about yes and no, sir, you know, these things. He was just a plain man. You have to do something, [and] he get on it and do it, he's a hard worker . . . everybody treat Al just like us."[13]

Another employee remembered Al Vail doing business over the phone, on the word of business partners, to deliver on deals that might reach a value of $200,000 [$1.4 million], sizing up cattle valuations quickly and accurately. These leadership and management qualities, passed on through the generations, inspired legendary loyalty among Santa Rosa Island employees. Foremost among these was Charles Wesley (Smitty) Smith. Hired by Walter Vail in 1890 to help him with a herd on Santa Catalina, Smith worked his way up the hierarchy of the Vail holdings, moving to the Empire Ranch where he was cowboy, then head cattle shipper, cattle boss, and division boss. In 1914 he moved to Santa Rosa Island. Planning to spend a year, he stayed a lifetime. He and his wife raised three children there, seeing them educated at the tiny island school until they outgrew it, continuing their education in Santa Barbara. In all, Smith worked for Vail and Vickers for fifty-five years, retiring to his house on Anacapa Street in Santa Barbara after World War II. He continued to be involved in the supervision of Santa Rosa cattle barges at Port Hueneme until his death in 1954.

Early in the Vail and Vickers era on the island, as mentioned above, the restocking of the grazing lands with cattle took place slowly to allow for the overgrazed vegetation to recover. This goal was reached in 1910 or thereabouts. Vail and Vickers raised their Hereford cattle on the island from calves, initially brought in from their holdings in Arizona, though later they bought calves from all over the West. The decision to focus on being a stocker operation fitted nicely with the need to find land that was less prone to drought than their mainland holdings. It also meshed with the public's taste for grass-fed beef that predated the taste for grain-fattened beef that developed some decades later. At the same time, developments in rail and road transportation gradually opened national markets for the Vail and Vickers product—cattle on the hoof.

In these first years of the Vail and Vickers operation, weaned calves for Santa Rosa Island usually arrived at the port of Los Angeles by train or truck, though in the early years it was not unknown for the Vails to ship them from Santa Barbara and after 1939 from Port Hueneme. Often the stock would be prepared for shipment to the island—branded, dehorned, vaccinated, and fed—at mainland ranches in Brawley, El Centro, Lancaster, Pomona, Santa Maria, or Ventura—while the owners waited for the best grass conditions on the island.

Vaquero at the dock, ca. 1925.
Santa Cruz Island in the background.
Courtesy of Santa Cruz Island Foundation.

On Santa Rosa there was also continuity in the physical division of the land by fence lines established in the middle of the nineteenth century, as the Vails capitalized on the infrastructure left by the Mores. The existing fences made sense of the landscape, and changing them would have been costly in time and materials. The sheep fences of the Mores—two or three one-by-six-inch boards fixed to posts, with wires strung above and below—were used as long as they held up, which in the case for many was into the 1940s.

The island was divided into eight pastures. The largest were the North and South Pastures, west of the ranch complex, separated by a twelve-mile-long fence, known as the Drift Fence. These held the cattle that were fattening for eventual shipment during the growing season. The next in size was Pocket Field, which held the young females (heifers). After new cattle had been held at the ranch complex when they first arrived, they would be sent to either Lobo Pasture to the north of the ranch or the Wire Field to the south for three weeks to accustom them to island life while the cowboys kept an eye on them before sending the new arrivals to the larger North or South pastures. Within these pastures the cattle tended to stay in relatively small herds, mainly because the features of the terrain hemmed in their natural tendency to roam. Carrington Pasture, which occupied the Carrington Point area, held cattle and horses that didn't have a destination elsewhere, functioning as another small holding area for new arrivals and the home for cattle that were not commercially viable because of accidents. They provided meat for the ranch kitchen, at the rate of approximately one per month.

The working horses were kept in the Horse Pasture in the low hills west of the ranch complex. Finally, the brood mares grazed in the Old Ranch Pasture to the south of the complex, site of the first ranch on the island. The grazing was managed by leaving the pastures under-stocked or not stocked at all during the dry months of summer and fall—all subject to adjustments to accommodate the weather. It was a system that required good judgment and constant fine-tuning, both on the part of the Vails and on the part of the cowboys who worked for them.

Of American icons, perhaps none is more recognizable or potent than the cowboy out on the range, doing his part in the roundup. Cowboy images, western music, and the accompanying rugged outdoor ethos permeate American culture in the modern era. Yet at the same time that cattle drives came to dominate the imagery of western fiction, movies, and advertising, they had all but disappeared from the reality of the West. The same was largely true of the cowboy out on the unfenced open range, though there were exceptions to be found in the most remote parts of the region. One of these was the ranch on Santa Rosa Island, where the idea and reality of the cowboy remained intact long after the lonesome horseman on a cattle drive had ridden into the sunset of the twentieth century.

Many of the cowboys who found their way to the island began their careers at Vail and Vickers ranches on the mainland. The island life, with its isolation, hard work, and enforced camaraderie was not for everyone, but for those who liked it, and there were enough of them, it was ideal, and they often stayed for many years, lending added stability to the operation. It was there that their independence, initiative, and intimate knowledge of the island, cattle, and horses were rewarded. Many had made their way north from Mexico. Spanish was often the predominant language of the bunkhouse. The cowboy way of life remained largely unchanged into the latter decades of the twentieth century, even as suburban sprawl covered the coast twenty-five miles away. The Vails made sure that their employees felt like part of a family, that they were well-fed and taken care of. The Vail family usually ate in the bunkhouse with the cowboys in a friendly atmosphere dominated by a long dining table. Al's sister, Margaret Vail Woolley, later recalled,

> There was always a cook there during when people were working [in the shipping season]. . . . It was a big strong husky meal . . . meat, tough meat from the cow and potatoes in some form or other and beans, beans, beans. . . . Lots of canned vegetables and oddly, bread instead of tortillas. . . . And breakfast . . . there'd be oatmeal, there'd be fried eggs, there'd be some kind of breakfast meat, there'd be coffee, tons of coffee. Just all you could put inside yourself. . . . And there were pies, pies, pies, lots of pies, lots of cakes, lots of dessert.[14]

As on the other islands, life during visits to Santa Rosa was a paradise for the Vail children, and a nice break for their parents too, who could generally leave them to their own devices, riding, exploring, and, as they got older, hunting wild pigs. They played with the other children on the ranch or brought friends from Los Angeles, as did their parents. Sometimes the parents did not come with them, leaving Uncle Ed and the foreman to keep an eye on them: "He was a wonderful uncle for kids. He taught us or helped teach us all to ride, made us clean our tack, brush our horses, be sure their feet were clean. If we didn't sit down to trot he let us know about it. If the horse's bridle wasn't straight we heard about that too. Just so much fun."[15] It was a far cry from the Southern California mainland experience of the Vail children's contemporaries, and they were very appreciative of it.

The focus on continuity meant taking care of the needs of the employees to encourage them to stay, and that included taking care of the education of their children. During the 1920s and 1930s eight to ten children attended the one-room schoolhouse at the ranch, overseen by teachers hired by N. R. Vail and his wife, Nita.

The children had assigned desks, built on the island. The school day mirrored that of mainland schools, beginning at eight and finishing around three. The children were taught all the usual subjects, even typing. Occasional field trips lightened the school year, with the group visiting the old ranch, or going out in the channel on the ranch schooner *Onward*. The school closed around

Dock at Bechers Bay. Loading cattle, ca. 1940.
Courtesy of Channel Islands National Park.

1932 when the pupils reached high school age, and most of them made the transition to high school in Santa Barbara. The school building was later remodeled into a small house for use by one of the married ranch couples.

All these relationships formed a background to the main ranching business of Vail and Vickers. The continuity of ranch supervision on Santa Rosa Island had the added benefit of continuity of range management based on the Vails' own study of the scientific literature and their island experience. Al Vail summed it up: "Our policy has always been to under-graze rather than overgraze; keep some old feed . . . our business is 'selling grass.' "[16] Neither he nor his sister Margaret recalled significant change in the nature or quality of the island grasses in sixty years, though they acknowledged that the thickets of cactus they remembered from their youth had died off and been replaced by sagebrush. Their speculation was that the cochineal insects imported by a Santa Cruz Island neighbor to control his cactus had played a part.

On Santa Rosa, prior to 1948, when several corrals were built to supplement the existing two, at Arlington and China Camp, roundups could take as long as three months. The cowboys were sent to gather the cattle that had drifted into the canyons, accumulating them until there was a large enough group to start separating those fully grown and ready for shipment from those that would be remaining on the island for another year. At Las Cruces, Sierra Pablo (a corrupted version of the original "El Cerro Pablo"), Rancho Viejo and Water Canyon on the east; Pedregosa, La Jolla, and Wreck Canyon on the south; Pocket and Lepe on the west; Lobo and Green Canyons on the north; and finally Black Mountain in the high center, the cattle to be shipped were kept in tight herds by seven or eight horsemen and the cattle that were staying on the island were driven back to their grazing pastures. Each roundup session lasted approximately three days, with the cattle for shipment moved across the island using the trails or roads that led to the Bechers Bay complex. As the military, who had been a presence since the early 1940s, moved out in the 1960s, building materials became available from their abandoned structures, and new corrals could be built cheaply, facilitating roundups and reducing manpower requirements at a time when that was becoming an increasing cost factor.

The roundup traps—centralized locations suitable for gathering five hundred to one thousand cattle—were each furnished with a shack to accommodate the cowboys while they were working in that locale. Largely a place to grab a quick meal and a bit of sleep, they were rough and ready and fit for purpose. Some were made of timbers that had come ashore from wrecks, some from materials scavenged from abandoned military buildings. In the late 1950s, Margaret Vail and her husband refurbished and expanded a cabin built at China Camp using lumber and materials salvaged from the abandoned army camp near Black Mountain. Ranch workers enhanced the corrals there in the 1960s using materials from the former air force base at nearby Johnsons Lee. The road to China Camp, running from the Burma Road, built by one of the oil exploration companies, northwest along the island's narrow spine, with sharp drops into the canyons on either side, took its place in island lore as Rita's Road, becoming a story told in the spring to any new men hired that year. According to Al Vail,

> It was kind of an old tale that they used to hang on these boys . . . before they would go to China Camp they would always talk about seeing Rita, which was obviously a fictitious gal. But sometimes you'd get these boys, they'd . . . put on a clean shirt and bathe and get all ready to go see Rita. So that kind of lived on for years. . . . There were a lot of people that never did really know for sure [whether she existed] . . . or always wondered.[17]

China Camp cabin and its corrals remain as they were and the National Park Service maintains Rita's Road today, though an encounter with Rita herself is never guaranteed.

Another piece of island lore has to do with the naming of Clapp Spring near the head of San Augustine Canyon on the south side of the island. Despite the association of its name with venereal disease, water quality tests in modern times have shown it to be the purest on the island. The name was given to the source by an island old-timer who suffered from a case of chronic venereal infection. He claimed that drinking the water helped his condition, and the name has been used ever since, with the second "p" in the name said to have been added in deference to modern sensibilities.

Arlington and Wreck Pastures, the latter named for a shipwreck in 1929, were used as traps to consolidate cattle for separation into those for shipment and those that would stay for another year. After the cowboys had spent several days gathering and herding cattle into the enclosed pasture from the Pocket Field and North and South Pastures, small groups would be moved into a corral and forced into a fenced alley where they could be assessed by the foreman or manager. At the end of the alley were two gates. One opened into a corral for the cattle to be shipped and the other for those that would stay on the island. The cattle destined for Bechers and shipment were moved to the smaller pastures close to the ranch complex. There was always a trail or road connection between the trap pastures for the roundups and the ranch. In other areas there were corrals to enable the division of the herd but not a holding pasture, and it took a great deal of skill on the part of cowboys to move a herd from the open range into the corral. The Arlington roundup was the final gathering point for the northwestern and western sides of the island. The Wreck roundup performed a similar function for the pastures to the south.

In the 1990s, Diego Cuevas recalled life and work on the island half a century earlier:

> When I started working at the island we used to get up pretty early, [three, three thirty, four] o'clock in the morning, get up, drink coffee, or whatever there was to eat at that time, and then you have to go and saddle up your horse and get your horses ready to go to work. Then we leave the ranch with everybody on their own horse and we take about 12, 13 horses, unsaddled horses.... When we get there, we change horses, turn ours loose and then catch a fresh one and we drive those other horses home.[18]

The cowboys given the job of separating the cattle for shipment and driving them to the ranch got them settled in a corral or the House Trap. Then they sat down to eat, changed horses after their meal, and put the cattle in pens for shipping.

The children of N. R. Vail—Al, Russ, and Margaret—had been allowed to participate in the roundups from the time they were young and they remembered them as special occasions. Margaret Vail recalled being actively engaged in authentic cowboy work when her childhood contemporaries could only imagine it from television and movie westerns: "We'd be way over there [far from the ranch] having to go to the bathroom, being hungry, wanting to talk to somebody and I think once or twice they forgot us and started home and had to go back . . . but we thought it was pretty dramatic and we could pretend we were helping somebody that cut out a steer."[19]

The half-dozen cowboys and their horses were central to the operation of the ranch, and the horse herd, including yearlings, mares, and working, retired, and resting horses numbered more than one hundred. Mainly quarter horses, they were bred and raised only for use on the ranch. They were trained by the cowboys, each of whom had the responsibility for five or six. Cuevas said years later,

> You gotta learn from the horses, teach 'em to lead so you can walk to [them] and touch and play with their feet and make them gentle. . . . You know, train the horses from beginning, from baby to three or four years old. So you can drive it and then you start teaching it how to respond to the reins. Once you do that you start teaching it how to work cows. And you try your best to make a good gentle horse at the same time. Working horse and gentle horse . . . you can play with them and they make good kid horses, because on the island you always have somebody that never ride a horse and then you can put him on the horse and you can trust him.[20]

Given their offshore location, oceangoing vessels were another key aspect of the Vail and Vickers operation. The Mores had used their schooner *Santa Rosa* to transport livestock (principally sheep), wool, tallow, and supplies between the mainland and the island, though her career ended as a wreck at Cuyler's Harbor on San Miguel Island in 1899. When the Vails took charge of the day-to-day operations, they commissioned a new schooner, the *Santa Rosa Island*, which was built in Wilmington, California, in 1903. She was

eighty-seven feet long, with a beam of twenty-six feet and a carrying capacity of about two hundred cattle, yet it seems she was not totally fit for the
challenging conditions that often prevailed in the channel. On one memorable occasion in 1910 the schooner was unable to overcome the elements,
and after battling all day in the face of a northwest gale and swell she had to
return to Santa Barbara and unload her cargo of two hundred head of cattle
until the storm abated.

In 1913 Vail and Vickers took delivery of the *Vaquero* from Wilmington
shipbuilder William Muller. At 130 feet in length, with a 29-foot beam and a
shallow draft, she was specifically designed to suit the needs of a cattle ranch
out at sea. She had six staterooms and early on carried a crew of four to six,
making the voyage up from Wilmington in about twelve hours, though in
adverse conditions it could take as long as twenty-three hours battling up the
channel against the northwest swell. Her cargo capacity was one hundred
tons, approximately 500 calves or 210 fully fattened animals.

The *Vaquero* was the linchpin of the cattle operation for decades between
the mainland, the island, and the feedlot destinations of fattened cattle. The
usual routine was to load on the mainland late in the day, travel overnight,
and unload early in the morning at Bechers Bay. If the cattle had not been
prepared on the mainland, the island cowboys would do the branding, dipping in creosote, and so on in a squeeze chute for that purpose at the ranch
complex. Then, as described previously, the new arrivals were moved to pens
at the ranch where they could be fed and observed before being distributed
to the nearer pastures—Wire Field or Lobo Pasture—for approximately
three weeks of acclimatization. After this period of adjustment they would
be put out to the large, more distant North or South Pastures. Weather was
the limiting factor, along with the general condition of the range, with flexibility in numbers to allow for dry years. The usual level was six thousand to
seven thousand head in the spring, with the largest number of cattle on the
island at one time, mostly calves, being about nine thousand.

This schedule of the *Vaquero* suited Vail family life as well. The involvement of N. R. Vail's children in the island started at a young age. In the
shipping season, after the end of the school week they would leave Wilmington on Friday evening and arrive at Bechers Bay on Saturday morning.
The weekend would be spent in ranch and family pursuits, with the return
trip overnight on Sunday night, the children arriving with the dawn on

Monday morning at the port of Los Angeles, theoretically refreshed and ready for school. When she was not required for cattle transport, the *Vaquero* remained moored in Wilmington. For transporting food and supplies and communicating with Santa Barbara in those days before wireless telephony, Vail and Vickers kept the *Onward*, a gasoline-powered 65-foot schooner bought in 1921, moored at Bechers.

The Vails tried to keep the *Vaquero* busy when they were not using her, and she was often chartered for livestock transportation for other islanders, hauling cattle and sheep to and from Santa Cruz, San Miguel, and San Nicolas Islands. One summer she was used as a fishing barge in Santa Monica Bay. At other times, the *Vaquero* was put to use by movie companies, and she was used in Laurel and Hardy's *Saps at Sea*. She hauled wild pigs from Santa Rosa to Santa Catalina to provide a remedy for their rattlesnake problem, deer to Santa Rosa for sport hunting, beans from Port Hueneme, and tuna from San Diego. On one memorable occasion, the *Vaquero* made a cattle delivery to Gaviota, up the coast from Santa Barbara, where in the absence of a usable dock the cattle were pushed over the side and herded by skiffs to ensure that they swam toward the beach rather than out to sea.

As with their ranch operation, the Vails were able to achieve continuity in their boat's personnel, with the same man functioning as chief engineer and later skipper for twenty years. Several of his five sons were employed on the *Vaquero* as well. N. R. Vail, who took a personal interest in the operation and maintenance of the vessel, also had his son N.R. Jr. (Russ) work as deckhand, standing watch over the cattle on the 115-mile overnight runs, while the temperamental engine pushed her along the channel at a stately ten knots. Russ later put his experience to good use by serving as a merchant marine officer in the Atlantic during World War II.

By the latter 1930s, the costs of basing the *Vaquero* in Wilmington began to outweigh the benefits of direct access to cattle transport in the Port of Los Angeles. The price of fuel was rising, the port was unionizing, and the unions began to demand that the *Vaquero* increase its crew from four men to ten, so the economics argued for a move. The Port of Hueneme had recently been established as a commercial port, and in 1939 the *Vaquero* was one of the first vessels to use its facilities. Hueneme was not unionized and was less than half the distance from the island, cutting fuel and personnel costs. But with the outbreak of the war less than two years later, the *Vaquero* was requisitioned by the navy and sent to the South Pacific, where her shallow draft was useful in small island harbors.

This worked well for the navy, but the Vails were forced to find another solution to their transportation problems for the duration of the war. The answer conceived by N. R. Vail was to use barges and old navy landing craft to transport the island cattle. A full barge was towed from the island by a tug to offload into trucks in Port Hueneme, or the cattle were landed on the beach northwest of Ventura and then driven across Highway 101 to pens at the Taylor Ranch for onward shipment. At the island end, at Old Ranch or Water Canyon Beaches, the barge was kept from capsizing in the surf with two cables—one attached to the shore and another fixed to the tug. At the height of the war, 1944, the Vails scrambled to locate any landing craft or barge along the coast not taken by the military, finally discovering a stone-transport barge owned by the Wrigley quarrying operation on Santa Catalina, an arrangement that Al Vail said gave him "a hell-of-a-lot more gray hairs in my head."[21] Other supplies were shipped to the island using leased fishing boats.

The unpredictability and inconvenience of these arrangements with barges and fishing boats paid by the hour got to be too much by the latter 1950s, and in 1958, using a cash award from the government for the use of the *Vaquero* in the war, Vail and Vickers ordered a new *Vaquero* from the Santa Barbara boat works of Sugar Lindwald. Approximately half the size of her predecessor and conceived on the simpler, more efficient, and utilitarian lines of the traditional Pacific lumber schooner, the *Vaquero II* was launched from the beach at Santa Barbara. She is said to have been the last wooden vessel of this type built on the West Coast. The *Vaquero II* was ideal for the scale and financial constraints of the operation. With a carrying capacity of about 210 calves or 100 fattened cattle, she could be operated by a crew of two and make the crossing from Santa Barbara in about three hours.

After the wreck of Carey Stanton's schooner *Santa Cruz* at Prisoners' Harbor on Santa Cruz Island in a storm in 1960, the *Vaquero II* became the Stanton operation's first choice for hauling cattle, an arrangement that persisted for twenty-six years until the last cattle shipment off the island after Stanton's death in 1987. On the eastern 10 percent of Santa Cruz, after the wreck of their boat *Hodge*, the Gherini family used the *Vaquero II* to transport their sheep. Following the sale of Santa Rosa Island to the federal

Vaquero II at Bechers Bay dock.
This craft served the Vail ranching operation on Santa Rosa Island
from 1958 to 1998. *Courtesy of Santa Cruz Island Foundation.*

government and the end of livestock operations, the 1999 sale of the *Vaquero II*, a specialized livestock-transport vessel, ended a unique chapter in California maritime history.

With cattle on the island, the plan was to give them two green seasons, with a one-season overlap between new calves and finished cattle ready for shipment. When the new calves arrived in the wetter part of the year, half the cattle on the island would have been there for a year already. The finished cattle would be shipped off in late spring and early summer—ending about the Fourth of July. The growing calves would have the range to themselves until the new arrivals the following winter. This system had flexibility, allowing the numbers on the range to fit the conditions. In eighteen months on the island the calves would put on about six hundred pounds and then be ready for the market on shipment, a strategy that continued into the 1940s, when industry conditions and the public taste changed from range-fattened and grass-fed beef to feedlot corn-fed beef.

On the island the herds of cattle were free to wander in the large pastures, though they tended to stay in the area to which they were accustomed. There was no need for any additional feed, though this was carefully judged year by year. The economics of island ranching dictated that if the range conditions deteriorated because of lack of rainfall, it was cheaper to ship the cattle off the island to better range conditions than to bring feed to them, with its transport and labor costs. The island cowboys kept an eye on the herds but didn't get actively involved unless necessary. There was little roping. The Vails had a policy of keeping the cattle gentle by not forcing any extreme movement in the herds. The reward was general recognition of their quality at the market.

Spring, generally May, when the grass was beginning to turn from green to gold, was roundup season. The island cowboys left their general maintenance duties and focused on bringing cattle to the pens at the Bechers Bay ranch complex, readying them for shipment, assisted by Vail family members. At the ranch, the cattle were weighed and put into specific pens, with the sale price based on the weight at shipment. There was an acknowledged weight loss in the transportation period across the channel, then by rail—later road—to feedlots in California and other western states as far east as the Rockies. After four or five months in the feedlot, they were sent to the slaughterhouse and on to market as prime beef.

Among the islands that were economically reliant on some form of agriculture, Santa Rosa demonstrates exceptionalism—in its continuity and in its flexibility to change with market and island grassland conditions. Elements instrumental to the Vail and Vickers success were the simplicity of the business plan, the concentration on one product, and the financial resources to manage through hard times without requiring the participation of outsiders. Financial stability and flexibility allowed Vail and Vickers to maintain traditional working methods without having to compromise with the modernity that was reshaping the rest of Southern California.

In spite of the arrival on the island of motorized vehicles in the war and postwar periods, horses remained the favorite means of transportation

around the island. They were the backbone of the workforce and gave a
sense of freedom to the Vail children who could roam the island on idyllic
visits with their friends and siblings, having island adventures and picnics
in their own special world. Taken aback by the arrival of motor vehicles in
the wake of the oil explorers of the 1930s and 1950s, and the military in the
1940s and 1950s, they much preferred their horses for transportation.

Of course, the Vail and Vickers Company was a business that looked
to exploit whatever economic opportunity came its way, and like several
of its island neighbors, it responded favorably to requests from major oil
companies for exploration rights. The Standard Oil Company obtained an
exploration lease in 1932. It built three bunkhouses at Bechers Bay and a
road to the drilling site west of Soledad Mountain, with another road to a
water source in a nearby canyon. Standard Oil drilled to a depth of almost
6,300 feet and came up with nothing. The children thought the paved road
was scandalous and disliked the drillers' trucks that plied up and down it
between the ranch and the drilling site. Although their parents would have
welcomed the oil income, the children were gratified that none was found.
The same fate awaited the Richfield Oil Company in 1938 and the Superior Oil Company in 1947. It seemed to some on the island that every week
brought new boatloads of geologists and oilfield technicians, threatening
both the ranching business and the archaeological investigations that were
gathering momentum in those years. Vail and Vickers themselves, the views
of their children notwithstanding, cosponsored some oil exploration in
1949–50 and found nothing. After a gap of almost twenty years, there was
another attempt but with the same result. In 1971 the Mobil Oil Company
negotiated a lease that created a storm of controversy, as it was less than two
years after the much-publicized oil spill from a platform in the channel that
had blanketed the Santa Barbara County shoreline with thick, tarry crude.
Mobil, under pressure from public opinion and the State of California set
out to prove that they could drill successfully in environmentally sensitive
areas. They drilled six unsuccessful wells, the last of which was plugged
and abandoned in 1975. In more than forty years of exploration no usable
quantities of oil had been found.

Oil seekers were not the only outsiders attracted to Santa Rosa. Archaeologists had been interested in the island since the nineteenth century,
and researchers from UC Berkeley, the Santa Barbara Museum of Natural

History, and the Los Angeles County Museum of Natural History worked on the island in 1901, the 1920s and early 1940s. From the early years of their tenure on the island Vail and Vickers had continued the More tradition of supporting scientific study, but it was always with the proviso that it remain unobtrusive and scheduled outside of the busy times of roundup and cattle shipment. In the late 1930s, the Los Angeles Museum sponsored a series of expeditions to all the islands by a team of scientists representing various disciplines. A nine-man team spent a week on Santa Rosa in 1939, using the former schoolhouse at the Bechers Bay ranch as its base. N. R. Vail provided them with food and horses, and team members were much encouraged by their findings. A second visit was arranged to take place in 1941. Another Los Angeles Museum party arrived at the end of November 1941, an expedition abruptly curtailed by the attack on Pearl Harbor on December 7. With their scheduled boat diverted to wartime duty, they were stranded on the island for a week until taken off by the schooner *Santa Cruz*.

It was not until Phil Orr of the Santa Barbara Museum of Natural History engaged with the Vails that Santa Rosa research got started in earnest. He too had been mapping out his research in late 1941, flying over the island with Bessie Owen, renowned local aviator and friend of Amelia Earhart, on December 7. On their return to the airport, they learned about Pearl Harbor. It would be six years before Orr could once again take up his work. In the late 1940s he began the most extensive archaeological research ever done on the island. Orr built his camp in an erosion gully overlooking the channel between Soledad Beach and Sandy Point on the northwest side of the island, low down and out of the prevailing winds, trusting in a typically dry summer. In his first two months he collected two dwarf mammoth skulls and a large number of mammoth bones. Further expeditions were assisted by oil prospectors, who helped with transport as time allowed, and by Ed Vail, who permitted wealthy Montecito aviator George Hammond to fly in supplies using his own plane. By the end of the second expedition Orr had enough bones to construct a five-foot-high mammoth skeleton for display in the museum. His rough camp in the gully now had drainage to prevent a washout, though his luck held, as this was the time of the driest years of the century recorded on the island. Orr's small team scavenged building materials abandoned by the army and constructed sleeping quarters, a work area and kitchen, and garage shop.

Orr recorded 180 sites all over the island, and after thirteen years of effort, at a place called Arlington Springs, he made the discovery that would crown his career. Orr found a human female femur, preserved in a block of earth, carbon-dated to approximately thirteen thousand years before the present, the oldest documented human remains of the Pacific Coast. It was with his "Report from Santa Rosa Island" that Orr began, with the use of carbon dating, to develop his theories of island habitation by early Indigenous peoples. Throughout the 1950s and 1960s he continued his research and publishing, culminating with his "Prehistory of Santa Rosa Island" in 1968, in which he put forward his headline-catching theories of prehistoric geology and cultural and climatic change, particularly his dating of the human bone fragment found in at Arlington Springs to among the earliest such finds on the continent and coexisting with dwarf mammoths.

While these theories caused a certain amount of controversy among his colleagues, Orr's professional dedication was never in doubt. Known as "the bone man" to the island cowboys, Orr was something of an island institution during his long sojourns. One of the cowboys remembered that Orr dedicated very little of his budget to food and said that he was known to often turn up at the ranch just before dinnertime, always welcome both there and at the air force base because of his engaging personality.

After Orr's retirement almost ten years passed before further archaeological work was begun on Santa Rosa. In 1976 researchers unearthed a fire pit with mammoth bones that seemed to confirm a link between early hunters and pygmy mammoths, though this conclusion faced some skepticism. Through the 1980s and 1990s archaeological investigations continued, particularly after the federal government purchased the island for the Channel Islands National Park. Leading archaeologists conclude that Santa Rosa prehistoric resources are still relatively untapped and that the application of new technologies will undoubtedly produce new discoveries and insights into the island's complex prehistory.[22]

Oil workers and archaeologists notwithstanding, ranch life continued the traditions of earlier decades, but there was no evading the incursions from the outside world. One of these was the Japanese attack on Hawaii's Pearl Harbor on December 7, 1941. The torpedoing of a freighter off Los Angeles and the shelling of the Ellwood Oil Field up the coast from Santa Barbara by a Japanese submarine shortly thereafter heightened the anxieties

Army camp, island interior, that was also used as an oil exploration facility.
It is now called Scott's Camp. Photograph by Rufus W. Snyder, 1944.
Courtesy of Channel Islands National Park.

of the population. People called for coastal lookouts and ultimately for an early-warning system that could predict enemy attacks. Months before the outbreak of war, the government had contacted N. R. Vail about the installation of a radar post on the island. Plans called for a modest site located at the top of Soledad Mountain and a right of way for a road from Bechers Bay for a rental of $100 [$1,500] per year. Vail responded with a detailed list of requirements—road construction, cattle grids, fencing, limits on personnel movements on the island, and so forth.

With the outbreak of war, military plans expanded to include an army facility of almost 46 acres on the island and an open-ended lease that would expire with the termination of the national emergency. Construction took place between January and August 1943, with a small barracks and other facilities at Bechers Bay connected by road to a camp area near the center of the island, with sixteen wood-frame buildings, including barracks, mess hall, and other facilities for about seventy-five men. In Al Vail's view, the isolated and windy site seemed to be used more for punishment duty than defense. Certainly by the time it was completed in 1943, the Japanese threat to the U.S. mainland had receded markedly.

At the war's end, the army abandoned the camp and radar site, and Vail and Vickers accepted $3,000 [$33,500] in lieu of site restoration. It would have cost the government more to tear down and transport the buildings. The arrangement suited both sides, and over the next few years the Vails made good use of the lumber from the buildings and other abandoned equipment.

The military's interest in Santa Rosa Island was reawakened with the dawn of the Cold War, as postwar tensions with Russia and China over the Pacific Rim grew in the 1940s and 1950s. Both the air force and navy looked to the island as a base for early-warning radar and missile-tracking technologies. In 1950 the air force chose Santa Rosa as one of the sites in its network of detection stations that would be linked to air-defense installations capable of responding to any airborne threat. For an annual rent of $20,000 [$181,000] it took over four parcels of land totaling almost 337 acres, more than half of it covering the highest elevations on the island, for its operations center, and the remainder in and around Johnsons Lee, for housing and other facilities. The air force also committed to building a road to link the two installations.

In spite of the often-challenging weather conditions on that side of the island, the facilities were ready in early 1952, and the air force began work tracking and identifying every inbound and outbound aircraft on the Southern California coast. Staffing averaged two hundred servicemen and civilians at any one time, provisioned by PT boats three times a week. Upon a boat's arrival, a steel cage was lowered from a dockside crane to the rolling deck of the vessel, it was loaded, and then it was raised and swung over the dock. Staff worked an eighteen-month tour of duty, with three days leave a month, diverting themselves during off-duty time with music, pool, and table tennis, but the Vails forbade hiking or hunting as threats to their cattle. Morale was "surprisingly good." One of the airmen described it as being like "on a South Pacific island, except for the monthly visit to the mainland."[23]

The ranchers got on well with the air force contingent, and there was regular interaction, with a bar at the Johnsons Lee base becoming popular with both the Vails and their cowboys. There was even a formal dress occasion when the Vails took the *Vaquero II* around the island to call on their military neighbors. There were points of contention from time to time, when enlisted men trespassed or cows chewed telephone cables, but there was prevailing goodwill on both sides. The ranchers provided meat for barbecues and the air force invited the cowboys over for movies and beer.

In 1952 the navy built a communications station to track its missiles fired from Point Mugu on the mainland and San Nicolas Island, a smaller version of the installation it built on Santa Cruz Island. It leased 4.5 acres on what became known as Navy Hill. It was one of the many communications links of the Pacific Missile Test Center, based at Point Mugu, with other facilities on Santa Cruz, Anacapa, and San Nicolas islands. Although all traces of it are now gone, there was an unstaffed tracking station on Black Mountain as late as 1993.

By the early 1960s, the air force was reviewing the operations of its early-warning systems and noted that it could maintain the same radar coverage on Point Conception with considerable cost savings over its existing Santa Rosa site. The headquarters of the squadron aimed to conclude its deactivation procedure by early 1963, canceling its lease a few months later. Once again it became apparent that it would be more expensive to tear down and transport the forty buildings and structures spread across the site than to give all the buildings and equipment to Vail and Vickers. The air force buildings became a source of construction materials for all parts of the island, providing a new foreman's residence and a replacement bunkhouse, guardrails used for corrals, and water, heating, and steam system. The air force left behind useful articles such as cots, mattresses, and lamps, as well as the equipment from a fully functioning motor pool. In the 1990s, after three decades of deterioration and scavenging by cowboys and trespassing fishers, several of the buildings were refurbished and used in the first decade of National Park Service ownership. The site is now returned to its natural appearance except for one building that serves as a remote study and storage base.

While the air force and navy were winding up their operations, the structure of the ownership of the island was also undergoing changes. Since the first years of the twentieth century, the island and its livestock had been owned jointly by the venture called Vail and Vickers, with the Vickers family involved only on a financial level. Separately the Vail Trust owned two large ranches in Riverside County. With more and more descendant stockholders, in 1964 the Vails decided to liquidate the Vail Company. Ultimately, those who wanted to retain an interest in Santa Rosa Island were siblings Al Vail,

Margaret Vail Woolley, and Russ Vail, and their cousin Sandy Wilkinson. The latter three retained an ownership interest in the land, and Al had ownership of the livestock. The Riverside ranches were sold in 1965 to a consortium that included Kaiser Industries for a reported $20 million [$145 million]. With its mainland ranching interests ended, Vail and Vickers moved its offices to Santa Barbara.

The new simplified ownership structure was now ready to move forward with its cattle-ranching business, but larger changes were afoot. The same forces that had inspired the sale and breakup of the huge Vail and Vickers holdings in Riverside County—the booming economy, population growth, and the call for more recreational opportunities and environmental awareness—would also affect the company's tenure on Santa Rosa Island. After the increase in environmental awareness of the 1960s and 1970s and the insatiable demand for unspoiled recreation space, the long-debated Channel Islands National Park was finally authorized by President Jimmy Carter in 1980. It changed the islands of Anacapa and Santa Barbara from national monument status and added the other three northern islands. The Vail family made clear its objections to being included in the park, traveling to Washington twice to argue against inclusion, eventually winning a compromise whereby the Vails could continue their ranching and commercial hunting operations for twenty-five years once the park was established and the island purchased. The hunting operation was based on herds of elk and deer that had been imported to the island by the Vails earlier in the century.

Although the purchase of their island was designated in the act as taking first priority, it was almost seven years before the federal government bought Santa Rosa Island for just short of $30 million. Thus began a period of transition from commercial cattle ranch to environmentally focused recreational enclave. A five-year special permit was signed at the end of 1987, allowing the Vail and Vickers Company to continue operating more or less as it had before. But with the buildup of the park staff—and increased scientific study, monitoring and inventory of ecosystems, and documentation of rare plants and water quality issues—there was inevitable divergence of views about how the land should be managed.

In 1993 the National Park Service approved a range management plan. Although a second five-year ranching permit was signed, and most of the scientific community within the federal agencies agreed that the Vail and

Vickers Company was an excellent steward of the land, ultimately the NPS came to the conclusion that livestock production was not compatible with environmental protection. Around this time other government agencies entered the picture and were critical of the practices agreed upon between Vail and Vickers and the NPS. In spite of a new plan that would phase out grazing and hunting, pressure on the NPS and the Vail family mounted. At the end of 1996 the NPS felt compelled to reevaluate the responsibilities between it and Vail and Vickers.[24] Suits and countersuits were threatened. Faced with lengthy litigation and potential loss, Vail and Vickers consented to a settlement agreement that would phase out hunting and end the historic ranching operation. By 1998, just one steer remained on the island, in a corral at Bechers Bay.

The new millennium had scarcely begun when Al Vail, Santa Rosa Island patriarch, died at the age of seventy-eight. His life had spanned much of the twentieth century, and he had spent much of it on the island, as a child, as a cowboy, and as manager of island operations for almost forty years. He had been stung by the criticism emanating from the scientific community but bowed to the inevitable science-based management and restoration of the natural habitat of this land that no longer belonged to his family. With the death in 2005 of Al's twin brother Russ, the mantle passed to the next generation of Vails to continue the closure of their remaining island interests. Their twenty-five-year use and occupancy agreement of seven acres of the Bechers Bay ranch ended on December 31, 2011, and the family has now vacated the island. With the island fully in the hands of the National Park Service, the emphasis is now on restoration and preservation. One of the key features of the latter is to keep alive the memory of the ranching tradition and the historic ranching landscape that the Vails fostered and influenced.

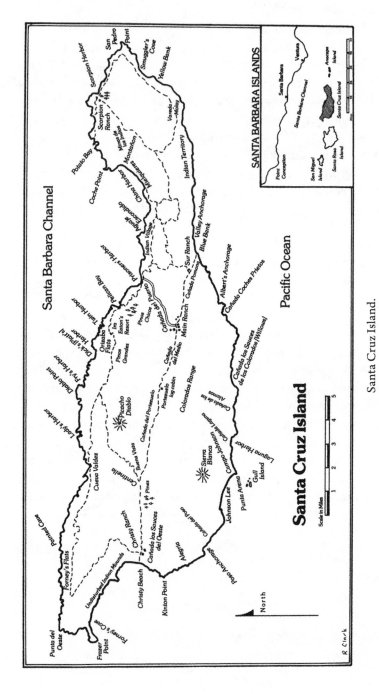

Santa Cruz Island.

Reproduced by permission from Helen Caire, Santa Cruz Island (Spokane, Wash.: Arthur H. Clark, 1993), frontispiece.

CHAPTER 5

Santa Cruz Island

The largest of the eight California Channel Islands, Santa Cruz Island's 96 square miles of rugged peaks and sea cliffs had been observed by Western explorers since the voyage of the ships of Juan Rodríguez Cabrillo in 1542. What he and the various seafarers who followed him in the sixteenth, seventeenth, and eighteenth centuries discovered was the complex and sophisticated aboriginal society of the Chumash, which dated back at least ten thousand years. At the inception of the California mission period (1769–1834) it is estimated that two thousand to three thousand Chumash lived on the northern three Channel Islands. There were some eleven villages on Santa Cruz Island alone. Because of their reliance on the sea for sustenance and trade, these villages were located in the coves and inlets of its coastline.

Santa Cruz Island purportedly got its name during the land and sea exploration led by Captain Gaspar de Portolà in 1769 that claimed California, including its islands, for Spain. After a visit to the island by the seagoing contingent of the expedition aboard the *San Antonio*, and an exchange of gifts with the Chumash at the village Xaxas (later Prisoners' Harbor), it was discovered that a staff topped with an iron cross had been left behind. Although iron was highly prized by the Chumash, the next day some of them paddled out to one of the expedition's ships in tomols to return the staff.[1] Thenceforth the island was called La Isla de la Santa Cruz, and it was recorded with this name on a map of the exploration in 1770. The name also appeared as Santa Cruz, along with Santa Rosa and San Miguel, on the maps of the expedition of George Vancouver in 1793.[2]

In the early years of the Spanish rule, the Chumash continued to live in their island communities as they had from time immemorial, but their days were numbered as diseases previously unknown took their toll. In 1803 there were still sufficient numbers of Indians on the island for the establishment of a mission to be strongly considered there, but by 1807 the decline in the island population, particularly from the spread of measles, had been so precipitous that the idea was abandoned. By 1822 the last of the island Chumash are said to have left voluntarily for the Missions San Buenaventura and Santa Barbara.[3] Their population had dwindled, their commerce in locally produced trading beads was destroyed, and they were subject to the depredations of Aleut sea otter hunters. They had neither the numbers nor the resources to resist.

It was the end of an era that had lasted at least ten millennia, and the beginning of a new time in the history of Santa Cruz Island. In 1821 Mexico finalized its independence from Spain, and under the leadership of Agustín de Iturbide (Agustín I) it laid claim to all the former Spanish possessions in Mexico, including Baja and Alta California. The impact of these events was felt on Santa Cruz Island only in 1830 when the Mexican government attempted to enforce an edict deporting convicted criminals to California presidios. In March that year the *Maria Ester* sailed into Santa Barbara with about eighty prisoners on board. Having previously been turned away from San Diego, the captain was not surprised to meet with strong resistance from the citizens of Santa Barbara. There are various stories about what ensued but one of the most widely accepted relates that after about a month of stalemate, the decision was made to deport thirty-one of the convicts, those deemed most incorrigible, to Santa Cruz Island to be left there with enough supplies to survive while they contemplated their crimes. Not long after they were put ashore a fire destroyed their provisions and the prisoners showed enough ingenuity to build rafts and sail back to the mainland where some were absorbed into the local population. Others, after a stint in the local guardhouse, were sent to the provincial capital in Monterey. They disappeared from the pages of history, but the memory of their brief sojourn on the island remains in the designation of the main harbor on its northern coastline as Prisoners' Harbor.[4]

The Spanish plan for colonization of its Alta California territories had relied on the tried-and-true combination of religion and armed force.[5] These were evident in a chain of four missions and their accompanying presidios.[6] Eventually this was supplemented by the concept of land grants to local settlers that could be made through the governor. In practice, little land if any was granted in the Spanish period, but in the era of Mexican rule the issuing of land grants accelerated, and private ownership of land expanded greatly, especially after the secularization of the mission system in 1834.

The 1830s and 1840s in Alta California reflected the tumultuous conditions prevailing in Mexico at the time. The machinations of the despotic general and president Antonio Lopez de Santa Anna resulted in a group of prominent Californios declaring independence under the governorship of Juan Bautista Alvarado. But the Californios splintered into several factions, with a peace of sorts in 1838, brokered through the efforts of Andres Castillero, a native Mexican and captain in the Mexican army. As reward, Castillero was given a land grant that permitted him to choose one of the Channel Islands. After a period of wavering, also considering Santa Catalina, he chose Santa Cruz Island, and Governor Alvarado granted this request in 1839, acting on behalf of the government of Mexico. Castillero thus became the first private owner of the island.[7]

Little development took place in the era of Castillero ownership. He was largely absent and distracted by his more lucrative discovery of the New Almaden mercury mine near San Jose, which intertwined his business affairs with a Tepic businessman, Alexander Forbes. Forbes and Eustace Barron (1790–1859) operated Barron, Forbes and Company with interests in various silver mines in Mexico. Barron and Forbes eventually acquired complete ownership of the New Almaden mine and also got involved in Castillero's Santa Cruz Island.

The conclusion of the 1846–48 war between Mexico and the United States made Californians U.S. citizens, and the 1848 Treaty of Guadalupe Hidalgo attempted to safeguard property rights of the former Mexican citizens living in the new territories of the United States. With the discovery of gold, the arrival of thousands of new immigrants, and statehood there was intense pressure to define the land titles of the huge Californio holdings from the earlier era. Congress attempted to resolve the problem by establishing a land commission that would examine the validity of all Californio land claims.

Castillero duly filed a petition to confirm his title to Santa Cruz Island, and in spite of the maneuverings of several local citizens this was confirmed in 1857 and upheld by the U.S. Supreme Court in 1860. After confirmation of the title, a survey was made, and a patent was issued, signed by President Andrew Johnson, which stated that the island had as its boundaries "the water's edge," and a plot of one hundred acres was reserved for the use of the government to erect a lighthouse.

A few primitive ranch facilities were constructed in the early 1850s and a Santa Barbara resident, Dr. James Barron Shaw, was hired to manage the operation. It was at this time that the first permanent ranch structure was built in the central valley of the island, and evidence suggests that this was the point at which pigs were first introduced. Virtually from the start, according to testimony in a court case at the time, the pigs were "unmanageable and had withdrawn to the mountains where they ranged in a wild state, not being worth the catching."[8]

In 1857, the same year that Castillero's legal title to the island was confirmed, he transferred the title to his agent William Eustace Barron, and in 1858 the island was advertised for sale.[9] The initial attempts to find a buyer failed and Barron, perhaps thinking that a going concern would attract more interest, instructed Dr. Shaw to establish a sheep ranch.[10]

Shaw, born in London and trained as a physician in England and Scotland, set about building a ranching operation. He is said to have bought one thousand head of sheep in Los Angeles and herded them to Santa Barbara for shipment to the island.[11] Within a couple of years, it is thought, the number of livestock had grown substantially and there were two hundred acres of animal feed under cultivation.

By the end of the 1860s, Shaw had established a well-recognized sheep ranch on Santa Cruz Island, with a herd of more than twenty-four thousand. Photographs from the time show several adobe buildings in the central valley, along with wooden corrals, shearing sheds, and a substantial wharf at Prisoners' Harbor. From here Shaw shipped animals to Santa Barbara and to cities along the coast, as far north as San Francisco. An effusive article in the New York Times from the early 1870s sang the praises of the island as a "splendid property," citing annual revenues of $76,000 [$1.48 million in 2011 equivalent], principally from the herd of forty thousand to forty-five thousand sheep, and annual profits of $48,000.[12] But during a drought two years later, a U.S. Geological Survey report underscored the perils of sheep ranching in this part of California, noting the thin pasture, and scrawny sheep,

Main Ranch, 1869.
Original superintendant's house.
Caire Family Archive.

saying, "It is impossible to conceive a more dreary waste than was here produced by over-pasturage."[13] It was said by Robert Glass Cleland in *The Cattle
on a Thousand Hills* that in the winter of 1876–77 seventy thousand sheep
were killed for their pelts and tallow on Santa Cruz Island. This figure seems
exaggerated, but the drought was certainly a disaster for the sheep-raising
industry on the Southern California mainland. There financial problems
and population pressures led to the breakup of the huge ranchos of earlier
days and a shift to more mixed crops and animal husbandry on smaller land
units. But although its herd was decimated, the island's unique geography
meant that it did not feel the same pressures, and the ranch remained intact,
largely dedicated to traditional open-range sheep-raising.[14]

In early 1869 the era of William Barron's ownership came to a close when
he sold Santa Cruz Island to a group of ten San Francisco investors headed by
Gustave Mahé, who became president of the newly incorporated Santa Cruz

Looking west down the central valley from the Main Ranch
in the year when the French Savings Bank bought
the island, 1869. *Caire Family Archive.*

Island Company.[15] Mahé was also the president of the French Savings Bank
of San Francisco, whose board of directors included Justinian Caire, who
had immigrated to the United States in 1851.[16] Caire, the successful founder
of Justinian Caire Company, sellers of chemicals, gold-mining supplies, and
winery supplies, was forced to significantly retrench after Mahé committed
suicide and was discovered to have embezzled bank funds. After about a
decade of hard work Caire emerged as the sole owner of the island: by 1886
he owned all the stock in the Santa Cruz Island Company.[17] Six years earlier,
notwithstanding his partial ownership, Caire's interest in the development of
the island began with a vision of creating a self-sustaining, diversified sheep
and cattle ranch and vineyard operation. This was the job that would occupy
the seventeen remaining years of his life. Born of the need to generate income
from this once passive investment in a distant island ranch, it became an elaborate and sustained construction and development program to domesticate
and cultivate the complex natural attributes of the island, realizing a return

Justinian Caire portrait, 1850s.
Caire Family Archive.

from its agricultural potential. His drive and energy succeeded in creating
the ultimate family retreat for this hardworking and private individual.

Justinian Caire's vision for Santa Cruz Island dovetailed perfectly with
the economic and cultural spirit of the times. Examples of huge ranch holdings, virtually feudal in nature, like the Rancho Tejón at the southern end
of California's Central Valley, were celebrated in best-sellers like Charles
Nordhoff's *California for Health, Wealth and Residence* (1882). Two years later,
Helen Hunt Jackson established the central myth of Southern California in
Ramona. This historical romance, unfolding within the gracious confines of
a self-sufficient hacienda, was mirrored on Santa Cruz Island—albeit with
a French accent—right down to the setting of the chapel in the vineyard.
In addition, it was the end of the cattle era, which had dominated Southern
California economic life for more than half a century, and the beginning of
the era of sheep and diversified agriculture.[18]

Fate had decreed that Santa Cruz Island become central to Caire's significant success as part of the Gold Rush generation of immigrants. As the
years passed, he came to cherish this unique California real estate asset. In
the waning days of his life Caire would make clear to his two adult sons that
it was his wish that Santa Cruz Island remain the central part of his legacy,
the mainstay of his family's holdings for generations to come.

Limuw, the island of the Chumash from time immemorial, now the Island of the Holy Cross—Santa Cruz—with its intermittent livestock operation, had changed little. Now, in the early 1880s, and for more than a century, it would bear the imprint of Caire's plan for commercial land husbandry across its hills, valleys and coastline. Over seventeen years his plan took shape, integrating sheep, cattle, and viticulture. Existing buildings were expanded and developed. Two kilns were constructed, one for the manufacture of bricks and the other for making limestone mortar. From these came the materials to build barns, warehouses, winery buildings, and, in 1890, a small chapel. Island stone was quarried and a resident blacksmith forged railings, balconies, fittings, and hinges. A comfortable two-story family home was built at the Main Ranch. Full-time and part-time employees included "ranch hands, team drivers, dairymen, vintners, grape pickers, sheep shearers, a wagon maker, butcher, carpenters, painters, cobbler and captain and crew of the schooner *Santa Cruz*."[19] Many of these men, particularly those associated with the rounding up and shearing of the sheep, were drawn from the local Santa Barbara population.

Justinian Caire threw himself into land husbandry. This domineering relationship to the land, prevalent in the nineteenth century, is nowadays often eclipsed by the passion for conservation of the natural world. But land husbandry, with its roots in the early pastoral vision of colonial America, was based on an older fervor for subduing nature and creating a controlled, fruitful environment in the face of an untamed howling wilderness. For religious Americans, it had the resonance of a new Garden of Eden, where nature would be dominated, nurtured, and improved. What better place to try to achieve this dream than a relatively untouched island? Caire was completely beguiled by this opportunity and resolved to make its development his life's work and to pass it on to his family so that generations to come might benefit from the fruits of his labor.

Blueprints were drawn up for enlarging and remodeling the houses at the Main Ranch and at Prisoners' Harbor (also referred to as La Playa) in a French Mediterranean style that Caire found congenial and a good architectural fit with the environment. By the mid-1880s the Main Ranch

Prisoners' Harbor with adobe house, warehouses, and wharf.
Glass plate negative by Helene Caire, ca. 1897.
Caire Family Archive.

buildings included the two-story family residence, the superintendent's house (enlarged to two stories), a bunkhouse, and a dining room for the hands. The number of workers swelled to several dozen to keep the development projects going, a number that increased during the roundup period, the grape harvest, and the winemaking season. The upgraded residences, ranch buildings for the workers, and associated corrals, barns, and other outbuildings now formed the northern and southern sides of a semi-enclosed great barnyard, approximately the size of a football field, bisected by the road that traversed the island for most of its length. The Main Ranch was the center of a world unto itself.[20] A visitor in the 1890s described it as "a gem in the very heart of the island, surrounded by high mountains, invisible and unsuspected from the not far distant sea."[21]

To organize the development of the business, Caire divided the island into ten separate ranches or centers of activity that worked together to form an integrated operation. In addition to the Main Ranch and Prisoners' Harbor, Caire oversaw the founding or development of Christy Ranch, Scorpion Ranch, Smugglers Ranch, Forney's Cove/Rancho Nuevo, Poso Ranch, Buena Vista Portezuela, and Sur Ranch.

The principal outer ranch to exploit the agricultural potential of the eastern end of the island was at Scorpion Harbor, with a subsidiary ranch at Smugglers Cove to control ranching operations in that vicinity. The men at Scorpion Ranch spent months hauling stones out of the fields and piling them in stacks at scattered locations where they remain today. By the end of 1885 the ranch had evolved into a busy and well-equipped colony. A road led from the harbor, went past a cave used for storing dairy products, and continued to the residential and shop area of the ranch. The old residence from the Barron and Forbes era remained, with its garden and chicken yards. Across the road a long line of small buildings had been constructed, more or less one long building with ten rooms in a row, including a carpenter shop, blacksmith shop, bake oven, toolshed, bakery, granary, provision room, general store, *matanza* (slaughterhouse), and butcher shop.

At nearby Smugglers Ranch, a house and outbuildings were constructed around 1885, but not until a masonry structure was built in 1889–90 did the ranch appear to be a permanent settlement, and even then the place did not remain settled full-time for long. In these development years, south-facing Smugglers Cove had orchards and grape vines. Caire noted the temperate climate and was encouraged to experiment with various vines and trees. At the height of its development, Smugglers Ranch had three residences, a bakery, a barn of fair size, a blacksmith shop, a water system, a vineyard, a vegetable garden, and orchards of walnuts, olives, and fruit. A good road led to the ranch from Scorpion Valley, yet at some time around the turn of the century the ranch was deemed a failure. Most likely, the olive orchard had not been large enough to make a profit, and likewise the fruits and nuts had not been profitable. The vineyard was not enlarged. Some have suggested that the ranch was built as an experiment and did not pass the test.[22]

The other outer ranches were situated to the west of the Main Ranch. A map from 1890 shows a small ranch complex fronting the beach at Forney's Cove, the westernmost extent of the island (Punta West). It had a ranch house, foreman's quarters and storeroom, sheep corrals, hog pen, pump reservoir, stable, and two hay barns or *zacaterias*.

Visitors and family members in front of the newly completed winery, 1890s.
Courtesy of Channel Islands National Park.

The Christy Ranch at the west end of the island was enlarged early on to take advantage of the miles of pasturage on the wide *potreros* (pastures) that end in bluffs facing the Santa Rosa Channel. At first called the West Ranch, it eventually took the name Christy in the early years of development. Caire had the fields expanded wherever possible and zacaterias built to protect the cut clover, alfalfa, and other forage crops from the weather. At this ranch Caire found at least one house and some corrals. He had the complex developed into the second major out-ranch of the company. The old house, built in 1864 or perhaps earlier, and known later as the Casa Vieja or Casa de la Cruz, acted as the centerpiece of the ranch, although a larger residence was built south of the creek before 1890. At the fullest extent of development, it boasted a second residence and a storehouse across the creek, blacksmith shop, carpenter shop, stables, saddle and harness room,

Scorpion Ranch, 1923.
Caire Family Archive.

storage shed, hay barns, a well, a windmill with storage tank, and a complement of sheep corrals, hog pens, and horse corrals. In the early years of the
twentieth century, the Caires occasionally travelled to Christy to stay the
night in the two-story house. As late as the 1920s there was a permanent
crew of occupying the old house, including a cook.

Other developments were simpler. Near the top of the pass, or Centinela,
leading from the central valley to the western ranches was Buena Vista.
There, and at Portezuela, the high valley midway between the Main Ranch
and Christy, simple ranch buildings were constructed or planned, with
vegetable gardens and a small vineyard. At the Main Ranch, the adobe-and-
rubble main house resembled those at Scorpion, Smugglers, and Christy
Ranches and was built at about the same time. The long *comedor* building,
partially built into the hillside, acted not only as dining room and kitchen
but also as carpenter shop. Its walls combined adobe and stone.

East of the Main Ranch about two miles was Rancho Sur. This small out-
ranch comprised a wood-frame dormitory constructed for the Main Ranch
in 1891 and later moved. It housed a kitchen, dining room, storeroom, stable,
and lavatories. The exact use of Rancho Sur is unknown, but in the early part
of the twentieth century the Caire family enjoyed riding horses out to the Sur,
where a barbecue had been built and a trail provided access to the beach.[23]

For the construction of many of the ranch buildings around the island,
in the time-honored tradition, adobe bricks were used. Made of island clay,
they were set out in forms to bake in the sun. But Caire also had more permanent, taller structures in mind, and for these he required kiln-fired bricks
and lime mortar. Two kilns—one at the Main Ranch for supplying bricks
and the other at Prisoners' Harbor for making lime for mortar—operated
through the 1880s and 1890s to provide building materials for the stables, the
chapel, and the winery buildings at the Main Ranch, and for the warehouses
at Prisoners' Harbor. The number of bricks made in 1887 alone was 185,000.

Sheep were already well established on the island, but Caire improved the
stock, adding purebred Rambouillet merinos from France and other breeds
from England to the Spanish merinos that had been introduced earlier. It is
thought that the Barron, Forbes Company had brought in Mexican cattle,
but Caire had them eradicated and replaced by imported Durham cattle. In
years of good or average rainfall, pasturage for the livestock could be found
in all parts of the island, particularly in the lush Cañada de los Sauces del

Oeste near the Christy Ranch, along the rolling Potrero Norte stretching eastward from Prisoners' Harbor and on the flats westward between the foothills that made up the northern range and its natural edge on the channel coast. There were also great fields flanking the road to the Sur Ranch at the east end of the central valley, which later became acres of vineyard. It was said that the salt-laden winds from the surrounding sea seasoned the forage so that the meat from the sheep and cattle had a particular flavor similar to that of French livestock that fed in the salty meadows of Brittany and the coasts of the Bay of Biscay. Over the years it was noted that the livestock had no interest in salt licks, having salt naturally available from the grasses and, where it was accessible, from rocks that lined the shore.[24]

In these early days, Scorpion and Smugglers Ranches also played their part as sources of forage and experiments in growing olives, vines, and other Mediterranean crops. Because of the difficulties of travel by land between the east end and the Main Ranch, which were separated by the transverse range called the Montañon, much of the animal feed and wheat was transported by sea to Prisoners' Harbor and then moved by wagon to where it was needed.

Horses were central to the island enterprise. Heavy draft horses were used for plowing and to pull the wagons needed for moving materials around the island. Saddle horses were essential for roundups, as well as for maintaining contact with various parts of the island. In 1915, even though tractors and trucks had begun to appear, an inventory showed 129 horses on the island.

Communication across such geographically complicated terrain was a perennial problem. The ride from the Main Ranch to Scorpion or Christy could take half a day, but the newly invented telephone technology promised a solution. Beginning in 1885, Caire had men at work stringing wires for what was said to be the largest private telephone communication system at the time in the United States, with hand-cranked telephones powered by 1.5-volt batteries. There was a line run from the Main Ranch three miles north to the caretaker's house at Prisoners' Harbor. Another ran approximately ten miles west to the office at Christy Ranch, and a third went about the same distance east, following the old trail over the Montañon to Scorpion Ranch. The lines were light, rust-resistant galvanized wire manufactured in England. They were magnetically charged, primed by a crank operated at the transmitting end, which provided a medium in which to send voice signals through the solid wire. "Each ranch was assigned a number of rings to identify it," remembered one of Caire's granddaughters, "so if [their] number sounded the foreman at that place would pick up."[25] Although of variable voice quality and dependent on the vagaries of weather and maintenance, it provided a workable solution for almost a century, lasting well into the Stanton era that began in the late 1930s.

As important as the telephone system may have been, most communication on the island was via the network of roads and trails. Given the need to import anything that could not be manufactured on the island and to export island products from the only harbor with a significant wharf, the most heavily traveled road was the one that ran up the Cañada del Puerto from Prisoners' Harbor to the Main Ranch. About three miles long, it had been laid out in the early ranching era under Barron and Forbes, and like the other roads on the island it was improved in the early Caire period. The Cañada del Puerto road ended at a T-junction facing the family residence at the Main Ranch. From this junction, the main road stretched east and west toward the two ends of the island. Beyond the western end of the expanse of the barnyard, the Camino del Carro followed the ridgeline of the Colorados to Christy Ranch, eleven miles as the crow flies, adding several miles more for the necessary curves demanded by the rugged topography.

Where erosion in the canyons caused regular washouts of the road, dry-stone walls were built at Caire's direction. Demonstrating building skills learned in Europe, these nicely fitted walls have stood for more than 130 years. Eastward from the T-junction of the Main Ranch, the Camino del Este ran about two miles to the Sur Ranch at the waist of the island and then turned into a horse trail leading to Scorpion and Smugglers Ranches.

Communication with the mainland was by boat. In recognition of the scale of the Santa Cruz Island operation, a post office was established at Prisoners' Harbor in 1895, with Arthur Caire, the elder of Justinian's two sons, as postmaster. Mail franked with the designation "La Playa" was received and dispatched from this post office for eight years until it was discontinued in 1903.

Throughout the American West of the nineteenth century, water was the great determinant of development. As the best watered of the Channel Islands, with five streams that flowed throughout the year in the central valley, Santa Cruz showed great potential. The Barron and Forbes regime had lacked a system to deliver this water to the places where it was needed,

Smugglers Ranch, 1890s.
Caire Family Archive.

but, with his customary energy and ingenuity, Caire set about remedying this, tapping into springs near the Main Ranch and storing this water in a 26,000-gallon concrete reservoir covered by a pitched wooden roof. The main supply was from a spring in the canyon to the west of the Main Ranch called El Pato, the Duck, which flowed into the central valley from the northern range. There were collecting tanks and rock dams at three other springs, the Gallina (Hen), the Dindos (Turkeys), and the Peacock, from which water flowed by gravity through pipes to the Main Ranch, or later to the winery and some of the fields. At the eastern end of the island, and in other places where the water supply was less predictable, wells were sunk. At Scorpion Ranch the well was hand-dug and lined with rock to a depth of around thirty-five feet, its water raised by windmill to a concrete reservoir.

In 1884, four years into his initial development plan, Caire began diversifying from a strict ranching operation with the planting of the first of the Santa Cruz Island vineyards. The president, as he was referred to by his

Workers in the vineyards east of the Main Ranch, ca. 1910.
Caire Family Archive.

superintendents, having judged that the climate and soil of the central valley and parts of Scorpion Ranch were favorable for the cultivation of wine
grapes, saw the original four thousand vine cuttings set out in December
1884.[26] Caire was not put off by the trials and tribulations of disease, boom
and bust plaguing his colleagues in the vine-growing regions of Napa and
Los Angeles Counties. By the time he planted his vineyards, a disease-
resistant American rootstock, *Vitis rupestris*, had been identified. European
varietals could be grafted onto this stock to reliably achieve the high-quality
product Caire wanted. In addition, the planting he was doing in 1884 and
1885 would not come to full production until the beginning of the following
decade, by which time it was expected that the market would have recovered.
By 1895, there were more than 86,000 gallons of wine maturing at the Caire
winery. As luck would have it, the phylloxera infestation did not cross the
Santa Barbara Channel, so the Santa Cruz Island vineyard, which would
grow to almost two hundred acres, was spared.

Though the new island vineyards escaped phylloxera, other pests attacked them, notably wild hogs. When it came to fencing, Caire, for reasons best known to himself, resisted the nearly universal western fashion for barbed wire and opted for smooth wire instead. For a 250-pound boar, this was an open invitation to charge between the wires into the vineyards. Guards were posted at night, particularly at the time of the fall harvest, and roamed between the vines with a gun or a long lance and a dog following the scent, but with so many acres the damage was sometimes prodigious.

Company records list vine stocks selected from France—the reds included Cabernet Sauvignon, Pinot Noir, Petite Sirah, Malbec, Cantal Mataro, and Hock. The whites were Muscat Frontignan, Chablis (Chardonnay), and Riesling.[27] The whites were sold with their varietal names, but the reds were often sold as generic "Burgundy" following the custom of the time for nonspecific varietals. Some of the cuttings were said to have come from Charles Lefranc, an old acquaintance of Caire who owned a vineyard in Saratoga, California for which he imported vine cuttings from France. Caire also reportedly purchased some of the original vines planted on the island from Charles Krug, first winemaker in the Napa Valley.[28] The island white wines probably kept their varietal names because of their high quality. Referring to the island whites, one expert asserts, "Few people in California at the time were growing anything better than Caire's Burger and Riesling."[29]

For more than twenty years Caire's wine was sold in bulk to distributors in Santa Barbara, San Francisco, and Los Angeles. Labels designed by Arthur Caire in anticipation of the time when they would sell directly into the lucrative bottled-wine market, pictorially told the story of the Santa Cruz Island Company. A circle of vines surmounted by a rustic cross enclosed a view of the schooner in Prisoners' Harbor, with a ewe, a lamb, and a sack of wool in the foreground. A banner below proclaimed Santa Cruz Island and Santa Barbara County, California. Based on company records, the yearly production averaged 42,000 gallons, though there was more in the better years, such as 1910 when 95,000 gallons were produced. An inventory of the wine cellar on the island by the San Francisco distributor in 1912 calculated almost 160,000 gallons on hand, about 90 percent of it red wine. The varietals mentioned in the report were Zinfandel, Mataro, Grenache, Burgundy, Carignan, Trousseau, Muscat, Riesling, Bordele, Burger, and Sauvignon, giving a snapshot of a changing pattern of the vineyards on the island.[30]

Pelican Bay Camp, 1928.
Run by Ira and Margaret Eaton from 1913 to 1937.
Caire Family Archive.

As for the superior quality of the Santa Cruz Island wines, the general conditions for viticulture were good to excellent, the vine stock was of the finest, the winemakers and cellar men were the best that could be found. For example, the Zinfandel was noted for being a full-bodied wine, fermented to dryness, with a higher alcohol content—qualities sought in many of today's top Zinfandels. From family lore, as well as company records, we can assume that the market enthusiastically accepted Santa Cruz Island wines. A local direct customer was the Raffour House hotel that stood on City Hall Plaza in Santa Barbara for many years. Raffour purchases in the first decade of the twentieth century averaged 275 gallons a year, and they also bought island turkeys at Christmastime. Distributors in Los Angeles and San Francisco ordered deliveries in thousands of gallons, and these were made in eighty-four-gallon puncheons, while smaller deliveries were made in barrels of 31.5

Santa Cruz Island wine label, designed in the 1880s by Arthur Caire.
Caire Family Archive.

gallons. Correspondence with these companies and customers was carried on in the native language of the proprietors—French, English, or Italian.

A distinctive feature of the early days of the island's vineyards was the positioning and building of a small chapel in a part of the vineyard on the north side of the central valley opposite the main family residence. The Chapel of the Holy Cross had been a project that Caire had nurtured for several years, and his daughter Delphine was convinced that he wanted to create it as a memento of the chapels that dotted the slopes of his native French Alps. This was truly an island project, lovingly composed of local materials by immigrant craftsmen. Their constructions are a testimony to the scores of immigrant workers who called the island home for some period in their lives. As had been the case with the warehouses at Prisoners' Harbor and the stables at the Main Ranch, the red bricks were made from island clay fired nearby and an expert French mason prepared the lime for the mortar. The island stone used for the entrance archway, arched window frames, and carved stone quoins for the corners was worked by a highly able Italian stonemason. The wrought iron railing in the interior that separates the nave from the sanctuary was the product of a master Sicilian ironworker.

At twenty-seven feet by eighteen feet, with sidewalls thirteen feet high and end walls rising to twenty-three feet, this was a triumph of rustic ecclesiastical architecture in miniature. Caire had the initials DOM, dedicating the chapel to God ("Deo optimo maximo"), carved above the door, as they are on many Italian churches. Above the initials a cross was carved in the stone, the same symbol that was chiseled on every alternate quoin. A little belfry, with its bell and cross above, completed the structure. The white, plastered internal walls rose to a gently vaulted ceiling, painted blue and studded with the stars that decorate so many Italian chapels. A plain raised wooden altar with a tabernacle surmounted by a simple dark wooden cross faced the congregation. This was a family chapel, with a capacity of no more than thirty people, but a large open area just outside the double doors allowed for expansion of the chapel's congregation if needed. A glass-plate photograph from 1891 commemorates the first services in the chapel. In it, the presiding priest, Father Genna, a Jesuit from San Francisco, stands in the decorated doorway of the chapel flanked by thirty-nine ranch hands in dark "city" clothes, gazing somberly at the camera from under broad-brimmed hats. The sun shines down on the little chapel set among rows of six-year-old, head-pruned vines, about three feet high, that march away toward the horizon under a cloudless sky.

In common with all Caire's investments in the agriculture and infrastructure of the island, the wine venture was for the long run, and Caire was confident that he and his descendants would succeed despite economic upturns and downturns. In these years, the labor force expanded to a size never seen before or since. In September 1889 there were 110 workers on the island. Seventy worked at the Main Ranch, ten at Smugglers Ranch, fourteen at Scorpion Ranch, eight at West Ranch, and eight at Portezuela. With this size workforce there was a substantial turnover. In all, approximately thirteen hundred workers spent time on the island between 1884 and 1906. Predictably the highest turnover was among general laborers, many of them immigrants, who applied at the San Francisco office and were sent down to Santa Barbara without ever having seen a ranch or the island and with no idea of what they were getting into. The company's payroll book for 1884–89 reveals that, with a few exceptions, the ranch workers' names were Italian.

In contrast, the names of all seasonal vaqueros and shearers are of Spanish/ Californio derivation.

Over this period there were thirty-four job titles listed in the company records, ranging from superintendent and majordomo to driver and laborer. Perhaps underscoring the exceptional nature of the island and the expanse of Caire's ambitions, there were masons, cellar men, farriers, dairymen, charcutiers, stonecutters, warehousemen, and sailors. Not only were there numerous jobs on the island to be filled, there was also an elaborate system of noting on what grounds employment was terminated. Employees were "thanked," "left voluntarily and honorably," and were "dismissed" or "discharged." All had different implications about whether they would ever be considered for employment again. Superintendents were expected to report on workers' conduct to the head office in San Francisco. Discharge or dismissal meant that the person in question should never be taken back.[31] Discipline was strict and the overall setup paternalistic, but on the whole it was not much different from ranches of similar size and complexity at the time, considering the isolated nature of the setting. It was a world that would suit a certain type of worker, and those who found it congenial stayed for years or returned seasonally year after year, even passing jobs from father to son. All in all, in its complexity of topography, work, output, and ambition, the development of Santa Cruz Island stands in marked contrast to Santa Rosa Island, where a much simpler regime held sway from the time of the purchase of the island in 1900 by Vail and Vickers.

On Santa Cruz, Caire initiated a tree-planting program. Seedlings were nurtured in the large lath house at the Main Ranch overseen by daughter Delphine. Groves of blue gum eucalyptus were planted as windbreaks to the west and east of the Main Ranch, and at the other ranches, growing quickly in the favorable island climate. Monterey pines and cypresses were planted in the central valley and around out-ranches. A nut grove of almost five hundred walnut and almond trees was laid out as part of the Main Ranch, along with a fruit orchard of peach, apricot, pear, apple, fig, orange, and lemon trees. As already noted, an olive grove and vineyard were planted at Smugglers Ranch. Around the family compound were oleanders, pepper trees, acacias, locusts, and Italian stone pines. The first of these pines was planted at the edge of the compound, having grown from a seed brought from Italy by Justinian Caire's wife, Albina. It eventually grew to a tremendous height

Family group with visitors by the chapel, 1890s.
Courtesy of Channel Islands National Park.

and a bench built around its trunk had to be periodically enlarged over the years. It served as a focus for outdoor socializing and singing, particularly after dinner on fine summer evenings. Often the concluding song at the time and at family gatherings for decades afterward was "Bon Soir, Mes Amis."

The expanded scale of the operation now required a larger, faster vessel that could reliably carry a quantity of livestock or other island produce such as wool and wine, one with auxiliary power to deal with adverse wind conditions. The *Star of Freedom*, which had been part of the purchase of the island, could take all day to cross the channel if the wind was against her. Caire turned to master West Coast shipwright Matthew Turner, commissioning him to build the schooner *Santa Cruz*. Launched in May 1893 at Turner's Benicia yards, she was 64 feet long and 18.6 feet in the beam. With her gasoline-powered engine, she could be relied upon to cross the channel

Caire family group under the Italian stone pine next to the family house, ca. 1915.
Back row, at right in dark dress: Albina; back row, with neckwear: Fred Caire and Lilian Caire. Caire Family Archive.

in less than four hours, the captain setting his course due south toward the island from Santa Barbara, aiming at the V-shaped dip in the ridgeline of the northern range behind Prisoners' Harbor. Fully loaded, the *Santa Cruz* could carry 200–250 head of sheep, enough to fill a rail car, or 15–20 head of cattle, which was sufficient for the local market. Following Caire's injunction to Turner, "Build her strong," she was easily capable of managing the channel in all weather and making the run down the coast with island wine or other produce for Los Angeles.

The outline of Caire's development plan was now in place. The Santa Cruz Island Company was a going concern, with income streams from sheep, cattle, wool, and wine. For 1880, an estimate of the gross income from the wool clip was $40,000 [$837,000].[32] Even in 1881, a dry year in which adverse weather conditions had forced a reduction in the sheep herd, the island shipped 14,500 sheep and showed a profit of $6,567 [$137,000] on revenues of $21,000 [$439,000].[33] In 1882, twelve thousand sheep were shipped to meatpackers in San Francisco. Between 1885 and 1896, the average yearly clip yielded approximately eight hundred sacks of wool. In spring 1894, livestock shipments brought income of $1,641 [$42,000] At Christmastime that year there were shipments of ducks, geese, turkeys, and chickens.[34] Caire's investment was paying off. His daughter Delphine speaks of the family's relief in May 1886 when he informed them that with the help of the island income he had cleared all his lingering debts from the French Savings Bank debacle of the previous decade.

Not long before Caire's death, he and his sons began to insist that the superintendent keep a diary and send copies to the San Francisco office every week. Many of these entries demonstrate the pattern of the spring and fall corridas, or sheep roundups, as they proceeded in a circuit around the island, starting at the central isthmus—Potrero del Norte and Potrero Sur near Prisoner's Harbor and the Main Ranch, to Pinos Chicos in the range to the west of Prisoner's Harbor.[35] From there the vaqueros moved on to Pinos Grandes in the northern range, then further west to Punta del Diablo. Working their way westward, the vaqueros moved on to Punta West and Christy Ranch, and then they headed south of Christy to Cañada Posa. Then they turned east through the Colorados, eventually sweeping up the potreros of the isthmus to catch any sheep that might have evaded them the first time. Lastly came the corrida at the east end. Statistics kept by the superintendents indicate that the corridas at the east end's Potrero Llano and Potrero Nord on the isthmus rounded up the most sheep.[36]

The vaqueros driving the sheep were for the most part local itinerant workers from the Santa Barbara area, many of them returning regularly to work on Santa Cruz and the other islands and ranches that had sheep operations—Santa Rosa, San Miguel, San Clemente, and San Nicolas. They also worked with cattle on the mainland as well, notably the Rancho San Julian near Lompoc. Though the majority were itinerants, more than a few stayed on after the roundups to help with general maintenance and ranching duties such as repairing the many miles of fencing. Known for their skill on horseback, able to roll a cigarette at a canter, they would arrive at the island with their homely baggage of canvas valises and bundles, clean-shaven except for soup-strainer moustaches, but within weeks their faces would be largely hidden by whiskers and thick shocks of coarse hair.

The pattern of the corridas was set before the ownership of the Caires and continued relatively unchanged well into the twentieth century. As a general rule, the days of the corrida started at the Main Ranch before first light, with the hands circling around the *mayordomo* to hear their assignment, be it the northwestern coast, at Pinos Chicos or Pinos Grandes, on the rolling hills of Potrero Norte, the long roundup that began at Christy Ranch, or any of a dozen other places. When the last man reached his appointed position at the farthest outpost of the territory being covered, the roundup began.

It started with a shout and a crack of the short braided leather quirt, the *chirrion*, and the vaqueros in the near vicinity closed in gradually. The canyons and hills resounded with whoops, shouts, and snapping of chirrions. Under the watchful eye of the mayordomo the men pursued the sheep, following their every move. The tough island horses could follow the sheep almost anywhere, responding to their breaking movements. Here and there a temporary wing fence helped guide the sheep in the right direction.

The drive went on through the day. The band of sheep increased, as did the semicircle of vaqueros behind them, closing them in and urging them forward. By midday, having been in the saddle for as long as eight hours, there was a break for a chuck-wagon lunch, with lamb barbecued on long sharpened sticks. After a short siesta, the drive toward the Main Ranch, Scorpion Ranch, or Christy resumed. Two or three men rode ahead to open gates, while others were closed behind the last riders.

Schooner *Santa Cruz* in Prisoners' Harbor, 1920s.
Caire Family Archive.

If the destination was the Main Ranch, the corridas would arrive at the great barnyard trailing clouds of dust, with a pandemonium of bleating, shouting, barking, and whistling. As the final sheep were driven across the yard, the riders appeared behind them, urging the laggards on. The last of the gates closed on the herd in their pens and the dust began to settle. The men unsaddled their horses, washed up, and got ready for dinner. After the evening meal the skilled shearers among them prepared their equipment for the shearing that would begin the following morning.

Just as the days of the corridas, the shearing (trasquila) days began early. The sheep could not remain too long in their pens or they would begin to suffer. If the shearing was at the Main Ranch, the normally silent large shed on the north side of the great barnyard hummed with activity. From the corrida the sheep had been driven into the large roofed corral directly in front of the shearing shed. From here they were herded into a long runway along the length of the shearing area. When it was filled to the end, heavy gates on

Vaqueros' carne asada lunch during a corrida, 1920s.
Caire Family Archive.

rollers were closed, separating the runway into small pens. A narrow gate from each pen opened into the shearing area. Now the cacophony included the snipping of the shears, the tapping of sheep's trotters as they were pulled out of a pen, the thuds as sheep landed on their backs, the shuffling of feet as the shearers brought each fleece to the mayordomo to get their token or *ficha* for each pelt. Snatches of song and whistling and joking punctuated the continuous bleating of the sheep in the pens. During the shearing the mayordomo sat on a high seat built in the narrow space joining the two sections of the shearing shed. Across his knees sat a wooden shelf with slots in its surface. Into these he put the small metal token, each about the size of a penny and stamped with a cross mounted on a hill, signifying the island ranch, with the company's initials, "SCICo," curving above. When each shearer had finished with a sheep, he wrapped the fleece into a bundle, tossed it onto one of the broad shelves flanking the mayordomo, and took a token. After re-sharpening his shears on whetting stones, he would choose another sheep and pull it from its pen by a hind leg, bending once more to his task.

The other section of the shearing shed was the packing area, where wool was stuffed into ten-foot sacks, weighed, marked, and stored until it was taken down to the warehouse at Prisoners' Harbor to wait for shipment to the mainland. At the top of a ten-foot-high scaffold was a metal hoop that held open a large burlap sack. The packer, dressed in bib overalls and wearing a green eyeshade, sat on the planks surrounding the hoop, dropping in fleeces tossed up by his work partner. When there were enough fleeces in the sack to start packing them down, he lowered himself into the sack using a rope hanging down from above. Once the sack was completely full, it was loosened from the hoop and eased down to lie lengthwise. With a large curved needle and heavy thread, the sack was sewn up, leaving ears at each corner for handling. The packer and his partner then rolled the sack to the scale and weighed it. The sack, usually weighing between three hundred and four hundred pounds, was recorded then and rolled over to join the others previously filled. It was then stenciled with the company initials and was now ready for transfer by wagon to Prisoners' Harbor. As each day of shearing drew to a close, the shearers would form a queue at the superintendent's office, where they handed over their fichas to be recorded and added to their daily pay.

After the shearing, the flock was divided into those animals to be shipped to market, those to be castrated, and those to be released back onto the range, the numbers dependent on the state of the market, the available feed, and the condition of the terrain able to sustain their numbers. These protocols of the corrida and trasquila changed little over the ensuing decades, despite changes that were taking place on mainland ranches. As one observer noted:

> The Santa Cruz Island Company operated its sheep ranch quite differently from most mainland ranches: no herding occurred, instead the sheep roamed freely in the vast mountainous pastures of the island. . . . On Santa Cruz Island, the large flocks roamed miles into the hardly accessible canyons and mountainsides, with hundreds becoming wild and rarely seen. This posed a problem to those rounding them up, forcing the continued use of the traditions dating from early California, where no fences held the livestock and hardy men and horses scoured the rugged mountains and valleys in lively *corridas* or roundups.[37]

In this sense, Santa Cruz Island was a ranch much more in the model of the great ranches of the Mexican period, a fact commented on by many visitors who found this central to its charm. This quaint view overlooked the efforts of Justinian Caire and his sons to control the herds of sheep through fencing to minimize erosion and build up pastures with good feed, restricting grazing when the range became poor. Overstocking combined with drought had been demonstrating adverse effects when Caire took over ownership of the island, and much investment was made to reverse these trends, though the wildness of much of the terrain meant that it was sometimes literally an uphill battle.

Santa Cruz Island Company financial returns continued to show that Caire's investment was worth the effort. The diary notes the business totals for the second quarter of 1896: almost five thousand sheep and more than seventeen thousand gallons of wine shipped from the island. At an estimated price of two dollars per head for the sheep and twenty-five cents a gallon, this would have represented a quarterly gross income of $14,250 [$363,000].

The superintendent's diary also has more than a few entries relating to fishing, an endeavor lightly regulated by the Caires early in the century. Beginning in 1906, Margaret Eaton spent months at a time on the island as the wife of the Santa Barbara fisherman Ira Eaton. She describes a life so removed from the doings at the Main Ranch that it might well have been on a different planet. These were halcyon days for harvesting the rich and abundant marine life, and fishers paid little if anything for the privilege. It was their contention that the land was public domain up to fifty feet above high tide, and they claimed it their right to squat on the shore. Under the original terms of the patent that confirmed Castillero's land grant, the boundaries of the island ranch ran to the water's edge, increasing and decreasing with the tides. Nonetheless, in these largely unpoliced days, fishermen formed a small rough-and-tumble community of temporary fishing camps on the island. They helped each other in times of trouble but were not averse to raiding each other's traps or lines if the opportunity arose. It was in 1906 that Santa Cruz Island Company managers, after years of feeling their generosity abused by the fishers, attempted to begin profiting from their activities, signing an exclusive contract with Ira Eaton on the understanding that he would warn off other fishermen, for which he would receive ten dollars a month.

In the spring of 1896, having fallen ill, Justinian Caire left his beloved island for the last time, but his presence was not necessary for the continued operation of the island enterprise. Filling his place, as he had been gradually doing for almost two decades, was eldest son Arthur, riding the trails to the out-ranches, taking the schooner down to Scorpion, inspecting the various ranches and their activities, and keeping a watchful eye on the superintendent and foremen.

Justinian Caire died at home in Oakland on December 10, 1897, at the age of seventy. His death was given front-page coverage in Bay Area and Santa Barbara papers, where he was extolled as a business pioneer and entrepreneur, "one of the best known merchants of San Francisco."[38] The man who had devoted the last quarter of his life and a considerable amount of his fortune to the building of the Santa Cruz Island enterprise was gone. Christmas that year must have been a somber affair at the island, at the Caire home in Oakland, and at the offices in San Francisco, though business continued as usual after a respectful pause for funeral arrangements. This is what he wanted. Caire's intention for the line of succession in the running of his enterprises was made clear in his will dated 1892. Indeed, his sons had been actively involved in management for almost two decades. Nevertheless it must have been a time of uncertainty. Justinian Caire had put the island on its course, but the end of the year 1897 signaled the end of an era in ways that his family could not foresee. His vision of land husbandry and an integrated, self-sufficient agricultural enterprise would be carried on by his sons, but the development phase was largely complete.

For the time being, in the absence of the founder, all was as before. The business of the Justinian Caire Company and Santa Cruz Island Company carried on as usual. There were the typical ups and downs of business and good and bad years for agriculture, and superficially things seemed fine. Slowly, however, pressures and resentments were starting to grow within familial relations. Caire's sons-in-law, Pietro Carlo Rossi, who had married Amelie Caire, and Goffredo Capuccio, who married Aglaë Caire several years after Justinian's death, came to regard the legacy of Justinian Caire as something that should involve them more fully and enable them to share more completely in its management—and its potential liquidation. This was an attitude that would be strenuously resisted by family members determined to follow Caire's wishes that his legacy remain intact. In a curious conjunction, the rupture of tectonic plates that would before long occur in the San Francisco Bay region would set off a clash of temperaments and a fundamental disagreement about land husbandry and the management of Caire family finances.

Caire had fulfilled a young French immigrant's wildest dreams, creating a domain in microcosm. It seems only common sense that his first wish was that his most highly prized accomplishments, the Justinian Caire Company and Santa Cruz Island Company, carry on intact after his death. The year before he died, Caire called Arthur into his San Francisco office on Market Street and asked him to produce all the stock certificates of both companies. He then carefully endorsed each one to his wife Albina, remarking to Arthur, "If anything happens to me, your mother will have no annoyance."[39] Mrs. Caire was now the sole owner of all the stock in both corporations.

Although the codicil to his 1889 will gave his six children—in the event that Albina died first—equal shares in his estate, he specifically stated two things. First, his sons were to be the executors of his will and act as "guardians of their sisters."[40] Second, his businesses were to be carried on by his two sons "with as little change and alteration as possible."[41] Today guardianship refers to representation of a minor or a mentally incompetent adult, but in the world of the 1880s it is much more likely that Justinian Caire, as a man of his times, meant the guardianship literally. His daughters were to receive an equal share of the profits, but they and their husbands would not take any part in the management of the business interests. These were to be directed by his sons for the benefit of the entire family, including their sisters.

By today's standards, this designation of the sons for an active role and the daughters for a passive one might seem manifestly unfair, and whether this was due to a perceived lack of business acumen we can only speculate. But we are looking at the world of 1889, and three of Caire's four daughters were still living at home in Oakland, aged twenty-two, twenty-five, and thirty-four, enjoying the genteel life befitting the comfortable economic circumstances created by their father. The one married daughter at the time, Amelie, was burdened with the first six of her fourteen children and profoundly reliant on her mother and siblings for material and emotional support. For her this was a deeply stressful time as childhood diseases took their toll (three of her children died in the Caire home), and her husband focused on the development of his career, working in his pharmacy in San Francisco all week and eventually at the Italian Swiss Colony winery in Asti every weekend. In addition, she had a mercurial temperament, marked by significant mood swings, which was generally acknowledged within the family.[42]

To Amelie's increasingly successful husband, P. C. Rossi, the notion of guardianship by his brothers-in-law, Arthur and Frederic, as stipulated in Justinian Caire's will, must have seemed like a rank insult to both his wife and himself. Having received significant help from his father-in-law in establishing himself, Rossi was by now the president of the Italian Swiss Colony Wine Company and vice-president of the Italian-American Bank in San Francisco. He undoubtedly saw himself as an accomplished businessman whose advice and views should be respected. On the other hand, a year before his death, Caire, whose business ventures with his son-in-law had often been less than satisfactory, confided to his sons that he had become uneasy about Rossi trading on the Caire name.[43]

For Rossi's part, by the early twentieth century, having built a career and a holiday home centered on the Italian Swiss Colony vineyards at Asti in Sonoma, his attitude and that of his wife toward the island was bound to be cooler and more calculating than that of her siblings. The island income now represented a small percentage of Rossi's annual earnings and held no special importance for him and his family. Its only real value was what might be achieved from its sale. Rossi's attitude about selling the island, verbalized after the death of his father-in-law, was presumably shared with his new brother-in-law Goffredo Capuccio and his son-in-law Ambrose Gherini.[44] Capuccio had married Caire's daughter Aglaë in 1903, and Gherini married Rossi's eldest daughter Maria in 1906. Rossi's views on the island put him on a collision course with Justinian Caire's two sons, who had been designated to maintain his legacy. In this, they were being urged by their mother to honor their filial and familial duty. She and her husband had taught their children the value of family solidarity. This was the time-honored way by which immigrant families prospered in a land that owed them nothing. For their sons it was unthinkable that the family would divide his legacy.

For a time after Justinian Caire's death everyone in the family got along reasonably well. Superficial tremors may have been felt early in the first decade of the twentieth century, but the bedrock of family harmony and unity seemed as solid as the building that housed four stories of Caire offices and a showroom on Market Street. That all changed on the morning of April 18, 1906, when the realignment of the Pacific and North American tectonic plates caused an earthquake and subsequent fire that destroyed much of San Francisco, including the Caire family's building.

It was now a struggle to acquire essential supplies for the island and to maximize income from it, but another problem troubled Arthur and Fred in the spring and summer of 1906, and that entailed their mother's will. Albina Caire was overseas when the earthquake struck, having traveled with her daughter Hélène in May 1905 to visit her family in Genoa and also her daughter Aglaë, now married and living in nearby La Spezia. Arthur and Fred's concern was that Albina's will had been destroyed along with all the other papers and stock certificates in the company safe on Market Street. The will had detailed the disposition of her estate, essentially all of the holdings of the Justinian Caire Company and the Santa Cruz Island Company left to her by her husband.[45] In those days, intercontinental travel was considered significantly more hazardous than it is today, and if something were to befall her and she died intestate, the family would have to apply to the courts for an executor rather than having one who had knowledge of the family background and the intentions of Justinian and Albina. The oft-voiced contentions of the two sons-in-law—particularly after the earthquake—was that the best course of action would be to liquidate the Caire family assets, including Santa Cruz Island, and share out the cash. This was a situation that Arthur and Fred knew that Albina wished to avoid at all costs. After correspondence with their mother, they determined that a new will should be drawn up and sent to Italy for her signature. This was duly accomplished and sent on June 24 by registered express mail in care of the office of Goffredo Capuccio at the shipyard in La Spezia. The expectation was that it would arrive in the usual eighteen to thirty days.

For reasons never satisfactorily explained at the time or afterward, the envelope addressed to Albina was opened at the shipyard and its contents read by Capuccio, who was enraged to find that his wife and her sister Amelie were to receive their one-sixth share of their mother's holdings as a life estate, with their brothers as trustees. This would thwart his and P. C. Rossi's financial ambitions to realize the cash associated with their wives' share of their father's legacy.

The exact details of what followed are ambiguous, but one thing is certain. Albina never saw the envelope containing the will, although she did not depart from Italy for San Francisco, via Paris and Le Havre, until August 2, almost six weeks after it was mailed. What is also beyond dispute is that Capuccio made copies of the will and sent the original chasing after Albina in her European route homeward. At the same time, one of the copies was quietly sent to P. C. Rossi, who had been advocating the sale of the island for years. Just after the earthquake he had advised putting the island on the market as a remedy for recent economic problems of the Justinian Caire Company. When he saw the will, Rossi was infuriated that he and his wife, Amelie, would have their share of her mother's estate administered by her brothers. Rossi wrote back to Capuccio immediately, "I cannot do without remarking the insult that such a document hurls at Amelie as well as me, just as against Aglaë and you. . . . For the time being I would advise you not to even mention it to Aglaë, because it would cause her too much sorrow . . . but *when the opportune moment comes we will see what we will have to do.*"[46]

The repercussions of the theft, inspection, and copying of Albina's will by her two sons-in-law would influence their attitudes and ambitions in ways that no one could predict, but now that Rossi and Capuccio knew about the trust limitations on their spouses' inheritance, their interest in Santa Cruz Island as a going concern ended. Their aims would only be served through a forced breakup of the company and a sale of its assets. The stage was set for resentment on all sides, particularly after the return from Italy of Aglaë and her husband in 1910. The situation was exacerbated by intemperate remarks made by Capuccio as he worked in the position that had been found for him in the Caire enterprises and while his family was ensconced in Albina's home in Oakland. After their return to California, Capuccio talked about how they had come hoping to influence Albina into giving Aglaë's share of her estate to them immediately. He and his wife also complained about the low income they were getting from their nominal 7 percent share of the Santa Cruz Island Company. It later emerged that Capuccio had confided to friends in Italy that he anticipated an early return to his native country with a fortune of $400,000 [almost $5 million].[47] Capuccio's brothers-in-law also overheard him provocatively speculating about their mother's longevity. The friction increased around the rebuilt offices of the Justinian Caire Company, where Fred and Arthur were regularly subjected to Capuccio's unsolicited opinions.[48] The powder keg was ready to explode, but there was as yet no spark to set it off.

By late November 1906 on the island, the fall corridas were concluded with a total of twenty-four thousand sheep rounded up. The 1906 wool clip was sacked and weighed. An agreement was concluded with Thomas Denigan Sons, wool merchants of San Francisco, to buy it for 16.5 cents a pound—totaling just under $20,000 [$455,000]. In spite of the setbacks of the months since the earthquake and fire, 1906 was turning out to be a reasonably good year, at least in terms of income, with $30,000 from sheep, wool, and wine. The Santa Cruz Island Company Secretary's Report for 1906 noted "failed" corridas, the sufferings of cattle, and a smaller than usual grape crop. But wine sales were booming, "to such an extent that we may be obliged to refuse orders from anybody except our Santa Barbara customers, [and as a result of favorable weather conditions] we will be able to produce all the hay necessary for the Main Ranch without being obliged to carry it from Scorpion as is done at present." Showing marked contrast to the smooth managerial transitions on neighboring Santa Rosa Island, the report notes the struggle to find management stability, with three different superintendents employed over the course of the year. These were the Revel brothers. The first, Ulrico, quit because of ill health; the second, Ottavio, was fired after four months for incompetence; and the third, Ugo, was judged to be satisfactory and would maintained his position for nine years. Even with all these trials and tribulations, the gross earnings for the year were more than $25,000 [$595,000], not including the almost $20,000 for the wool clip, which had been sold but not yet delivered. Expenses totaled $27,494, the majority of which were salaries and taxes.[49] The year ended with a relatively modest loss of $4,538 [$112,000], which, given the tumultuous events, was better than expected.

The Santa Cruz Island Company seems to have been recovering strongly. The 1907 company report showed that revenue had doubled to more than $50,000 [$1.1 million] but expenses had risen to almost $35,000. The blame for this was placed on rising taxes, the bill for the repairs to the schooner, and a labor shortage in the area that had led to an increase in costs. This was said to be "due to the passing away of the competent old-time *vaqueros* ... the younger element is composed of careless and lazy men who have no love for their work.... If we could manage to retain a few Europeans on the island for a few years, we would be free in a certain measure from the tyranny of the dishonest *Barbarenos.*"[50]

In the following year more than 84 percent of the island income was based on the combined wool sales of 1907 and 1908, and total revenue was down from the previous year to just under $44,000. It was ominously noted that "sales of wine have been somewhat affected by the prohibition movement in southern California and were smaller than during 1907." This harbinger of what was to become a nationwide trend illuminates the changing character of the Southern California population as it was influenced by waves of immigration from the conservative and abstemious Midwest. Additionally, although overall rainfall figures for the year were above average, "the water fell so irregularly and in such great quantities at one time that our crops did not receive any benefit from the downpour. The result was that our fields did not receive any moisture towards the end of the season and our hay crops were not satisfactory—in fact we can say that a good deal of our work went for nothing." But in spite of these gloomy notes and the overall reduction in revenue, expenses were still well below this figure, though a paper loss was shown because of the disbursement of $25,000 [$581,000] in dividends to Albina and all her children, based on their putative shareholdings that she held in trust for them.[51]

In 1909, net revenues increased to a healthy $16,000, based on wool and livestock sales with a small contribution from the winery. On the expense side Arthur noted a bill for $3,150 [$75,000] for the repair of the schooner. He further notes, "Our stock needs an infusion of new blood, that means care must be taken to get rid of all the *coludos* [wild males] and scrub sheep that roam over the island and greater attention paid to the preparation of stock for the market." Perhaps following the lead shown by Vail and Vickers on Santa Rosa, a heavy sum was credited to the cattle account for that year—from the sale of 299 head. This was "the first large sale of these animals we have ever made," Arthur wrote. "We are confident that we are in the right path so far as the development of the cattle industry is concerned." He also noted the need for new residences at Scorpion Ranch and the Main Ranch.

The year 1910 showed a paper loss of approximately $3,000 [$71,000], with revenues of almost $50,000 [$1.17 million] and expenses of almost $53,000. Arthur noted in his report to the shareholders, "Either because of low prices or severe competition we sold practically no wine during the year and the trouble we had in effecting a settlement with the Santa Barbara butchers delayed the sale of cattle until too late in the season." Included in the expenses were several extraordinary ones, notably a small dividend for each family member, a refit for the schooner, new tanks for the winery, and the building of the new family house at the Main Ranch. The approximately three-thousand-square-foot residence, with ten rooms and several bathrooms as well as a five-hundred-square-foot living room, cost $6,290 [$147,000] and was enthusiastically described in the local press as one of the finest summer homes on the coast.

Commenting, as he had in 1907, on the general problems with the local labor force, Arthur informed the shareholders:

> We find that the difficulty in obtaining capable *vaqueros* for the gathering of the sheep during the shearing season will oblige us to have recourse to some measures that will enable us to overcome the trouble due to the incapacity and the ill will of the *Barbarenos* who are now employed at the *corridas*. For this reason during the past year we have laid out lines of fences that will separate the various districts and enable us to gather the sheep and cattle a little more easily. Several of these fences have already been built and we expect that it will soon be possible for us to keep certain districts entirely free for a time and thus allow the pasture to be renewed . . . thus creating a reserve for the feeding of our animals.[52]

This is evidence of a general trend in which both rising prosperity and increasing competition for their skills had made the traditional Santa Barbara casual labor force more reluctant to accept the terms and conditions laid down by the Caires. Where their fathers had been happy for the work, their sons were not so enthusiastic about the enforced solitude and discipline inherent in the Caire management and island life.

Sheep shearing at Christy Ranch, 1929.
Caire Family Archive.

All in all, the years up to 1911 on the island were not untypical. The sheep herd remained at or above their twenty-five-thousand-head average for this period, with the herd in 1911 rising to the highest level it would achieve in the twentieth century, a little over thirty-five thousand.[53] The 1910 and 1911 corridas were especially successful, with between twenty-two thousand and twenty-four thousand sheep shorn.[54] With a good price for wool in San Francisco, this would have represented a substantial income for the company, in excess of $20,000 [$468,000]. The cattle herd had grown steadily, from 841 head in 1906 to 1,409 head in 1911. So in spite of the downturn in demand for wine, 1911 was one in which a small profit was eked out, approximating the annual average of $50,000 [$1.2 million] for both revenue and expenses. With the winters of 1909, 1910, and 1911 averaging a substantial twenty-eight inches of rain, feed for the large herd was plentiful.[55] The vineyard was producing well. Because of the lowered demand for its output, in 1911 the winery had almost 230,000 gallons of saleable wine on hand and about another 20,000 gallons maturing.[56] This would have represented more than $25,000 in potential income for the Santa Cruz Island Company, as the island maintained its place as the jewel in the crown of the Caire family's holdings.

The financial records painted a rosy picture, but far from the island in 1910 and 1911 three somber occurrences took place that would have dramatic impact on Justinian Caire's legacy and lasting repercussions for all his heirs.

At Christmastime in 1910 Albina Caire made a gift to her children of shares in the Santa Cruz Island Company. The children received full possession of the seven shares left to each by Justinian Caire that he had endorsed back to his wife. For each child, including the two married daughters, it represented a 7 percent ownership interest. Albina was almost eighty years old and had been a widow for thirteen years. She knew that the shares and their dividends were causing tensions in the family, and possibly she hoped that giving actual ownership to her two married daughters would keep the peace.

Despite Albina's hopes, the gifts only seemed to inflame Amelie's resentment. Perhaps because she was troubled by Amelie's attitude, Albina distributed five additional shares in the company in June 1911 to Arthur, Fred, and Delphine, giving the sons a total of fourteen shares each and Delphine twelve shares. The original distribution to the children was spelled out in her intercepted will of 1906, where she left equal shares of her personal estate to each child, but the two one-sixth shares for Amelie and Aglaë would be in the form of a life trust, with their brothers as trustees.[57] As we have seen, by following the example spelled out by her husband, Albina's decision enraged her sons-in-law.

The year 1911 was marked by two other significant events, one dramatic and shocking and the other unnoticed. The first of these was the sudden death of Amelie's husband, P. C. Rossi, in Asti. Thrown from the carriage in which he was riding, he died from head injuries. The family rallied around Amelie as her husband received a well-publicized funeral at Saints Peter and Paul Church and interment at San Francisco's fashionable Holy Cross Cemetery.

The second event of 1911 remains a central mystery in the dissolution of Justinian Caire's legacy. In the same month as Rossi's death, the annual notification for the payment of the State Corporation License Tax was received at the office of the Santa Cruz Island Company at 573 Market Street, where the company had rebuilt in the same location after the 1906 earthquake. As usual, the form required the signature of Arthur Caire and a payment of five dollars by November 30. It was placed on the desk of the company's cashier and secretary, son-in-law Goffredo Capuccio, the man who had played a central role in the surreptitious copying and distribution of Albina's will and whose position in the company had been engineered by P. C. Rossi the year before.[58] From there it disappeared, along with a second reminder, and their absence went unnoticed by the Caire brothers until two days after Christmas, when they were notified that they had failed to pay the tax and had consequently forfeited the corporate charter of the Santa Cruz Island Company. The corporation was technically in liquidation and required the unanimous agreement and consent of all stockholders to reinstate its charter. Amelie's son-in-law, the attorney Ambrose Gherini, who had married her oldest daughter Maria Rossi in 1906, was said to have exclaimed, "[This is] the first ray of light that we have been waiting for."[59] The majority stockholder trustees—Albina, Fred, Arthur, Delphine, and Hélène, with 86 percent of the stock—were now suddenly and fatally exposed to the whims of the two married daughters with their 14 percent.

On January 2, 1912, the first business day of the new year, Fred and Arthur began their efforts to reorganize the company. All the shareholders signaled their agreement, with the exception of the newly widowed Amelie. Thus began the war of words that grew into an intra-family lawsuit, resulting in the breakup of the Santa Cruz Island Company and ultimately precipitating the sale of the island.

Within a month, the Caires had gone from an ostensibly close-knit family sharing a valuable but not easily saleable piece of real estate, to a family threatened by litigation and the forced sale of property that had been accumulated and husbanded for more than half a century.

The legal sparring began. In June 1912, Arthur was served with a "Summons and Complaint" in the suit of Amelie's son Edmund Rossi against the trustees of the Santa Cruz Island Company. Suffering from the ill health that had plagued most of her adult life, Amelie had transferred her seven shares to Edmund, who now assumed the role of lead plaintiff. The same papers were served in the following days on Amelie's brother Fred, her sisters Delphine and Hélène, and her mother. Albina received her summons on June 13, 1912. It was her eighty-first birthday.

It was almost a year later that Judge George A. Sturtevant of the San Francisco Superior Court ruled in favor of the plaintiff, Edmund Rossi, acting on behalf of his mother.[60] Albina, Delphine, Arthur, and Fred, as controlling trustees, were directed to wind up the affairs of the corporation since it had forfeited its charter. The court's opinion stated that all shareholders were entitled to an accounting of the corporation's assets, which should be distributed according to their respective shares as of 1911 when the charter was forfeited. This was a major blow to the Caires attempting to keep Justinian Caire's legacy intact. They announced that they would appeal the decision. Four days after the adverse ruling, a disconsolate Albina signed a codicil to her will revoking the gift of Santa Cruz Island Company shares to the two daughters who had dragged her into court. She transferred those shares to her other four children and excluded her married daughters from other parts of her estate. The lawsuit rumbled on in the background as most of the Caires attempted to keep the Santa Cruz Island Company and the Justinian Caire Company operational and profitable.

Unfortunately, the weather added to their troubles. The winters of 1911–12 and 1912–13 were two of the driest and coldest on the island in the early years of the twentieth century. Adding to the family's woes, almost the entire 1912 rainfall came in March, and most of the rain in 1913 fell in February, with subsequent damage and loss to crops and island infrastructure. Unable to flexibly manage their range and livestock population like their Santa Rosa neighbors, and with sheep and cattle dying from exposure and the threat of more litigation hanging over them, the Caires hurried their livestock to market. The forced sale in 1912 meant accepting rock-bottom prices, 25–50 percent under what they might have expected in normal years. The books for the year 1912 made dismal reading, showing a loss of $24,000 [$550,000]. The Caires were forced to sell their entire livestock herd in 1913. It would take seven years for the sheep population to recover, and the Santa Cruz Island Company never regained its former levels of meat or wool sales.[61]

Over the next two years, the prices for saleable cattle responded to wartime demand by almost doubling, but the company had reduced its livestock to such low numbers that there was no basis left for growth of the herds and therefore nothing to sell. The lawsuit was beginning to dominate company strategy. In 1917, Arthur noted with bitter prescience that his sisters and in-laws "are people who absolutely refused to help to conserve their own interests, who absolutely did their level best to jeopardize said interests and who forced these interests into a position where a loss was bound to be sustained, clamoring for the condemnation, under a charge of mismanagement, of those who were trying to obtain good results!"[62]

Negotiations and legal appeals followed through the years 1913–16, with the fortunes of both sides waxing and waning, but the legal principle of the Rossi and Gherini "vested interest" that resulted from the technical death of the corporation continued to stand. In 1916 the California Supreme Court handed down its ruling, which seemed to offer a ray of hope to the other Caires.[63] In its decision, the court reversed Judge Sturtevant's ruling that the trustees must sell all the corporate property and distribute all the cash. If the corporation had sufficient money to pay off the corporate debts, trustees could distribute the assets to the shareholders, including land in kind, rather than force a sale of the assets.

This was a procedural victory for the Caires, but the court noted that it did not affect the fact that the corporation had terminated, calling this "absolute death," and was to be wound up for the benefit of the stockholders. Essentially, with this ruling, both parties were in the same position they had been in when the litigation began in 1912. As Ambrose Gherini noted with satisfaction some time later, the ruling "settled all of the law involved."[64] Based on their mother's gift of Santa Cruz Island Company shares in 1910 and their brothers' inadvertent nonpayment of the corporation tax in 1911, Amelie and Aglaë's legal team had achieved its goal and dismantled the Santa Cruz Island Company forever.

Was this the moment for both sides to have called a truce and found a way to negotiate, probably by a division of the island? Many of the principals in the original litigation were now dead. P. C. Rossi had died in 1911, Goffredo Capuccio died in 1915, and after years of poor health Amelie Caire Rossi died in 1917, resolutely refusing to the last to reconcile with her mother who was now in her late eighties. It was left to the younger generations to make approaches at negotiation. In August 1919, Edmund Rossi visited Arthur to seek a way to end "this costly litigation," but by now both sides were well entrenched, and the issue of legal fees began to dominate the thinking on both sides. At their meeting Arthur forced Edmund to admit that his legal team was working on a fee basis that was contingent on their victory. Arthur told Edmund that only with the cessation of all the lawsuits could there be a consideration of negotiation. This clearly would have been unacceptable to Gherini and Freidenrich, the lawyers for Rossi and Capuccio. They had undertaken many thousands of billable hours of work on behalf of their clients, in addition to the cost of co-counsel Orrin McMurray's fees. As McMurray was one of the top legal professionals in the state, these fees would have been considerable.

As the legal expenses mounted it was natural that the principals on both sides should seek a solution that did not involve lawyers, but from the start it had all been too personal. When it came to motives, for most of the Caires it was simply a question of their parents' legacy, of respect for family loyalty, and of family values betrayed. For the Rossis and Capuccios, Ambrose Gherini had masterminded a legal strategy of minority shareholder rights, with an overarching sense of injustice legitimized by the codicil to Justinian Caire's will. Arthur Caire speculated that, at the outset, Gherini and Capuccio had assumed that the threat to break up the family holdings and public scandal of a lawsuit between family members would be enough to persuade the Caires to part with a large sum of cash. When they were rebuffed, they resorted to litigation in an effort to save face, and then the legal strategy took on a life of its own, incurring costs that only an outright victory would satisfy.[65]

This would now be a fight to the finish, with no quarter given or taken. As one of the Caire attorneys, Frank Deering, told Gherini, "They [the majority Caires] would rather pay their attorneys than their sisters and in-laws."[66] The Caires felt that they had natural justice on their side, but Ambrose Gherini had a more pragmatic view of what really mattered before the law.

In 1919, the California Supreme Court concurred with the ruling of a lower court, holding that when the corporation had died, the rights of the shareholders to receive the corporate assets became "vested." They became an ownership interest that could not be taken away afterward, because at the time that the corporation lapsed there was no statute that allowed for its revival.[67] This judgment drove a spike into the heart of the Caire strategy to force their sisters back into the revived corporation. It set the stage for the other theater where their downfall would be acted out, in the courtrooms of Santa Barbara, within sight of the island that lay at the heart of the controversy.

Here the two sides divided along predictable lines, with the plaintiffs arguing that they were entitled to a share of the island assets of the dissolved corporation and the trustees arguing that the reinstated corporation owned the assets rather than the individual shareholders. The case was heard in

Santa Barbara Superior Court. In September 1920 the court found for the plaintiffs, a judgment that predictably wound its way up to the California Supreme Court where it was upheld in 1922.[68] This meant that the Rossis and Capuccios were legally entitled to a distribution of the corporate property.

Given the likelihood of a costly survey and partition of the island, the expense of which would have to be borne by all parties, approaches regarding negotiation were made again. Gherini met Frank Deering sometime in 1922 and tabled an offer to sell his clients' interest in the island for $500,000 [$6.4 million], or slightly more than 18 percent of the most recent valuation obtained by Arthur. The year before, Gherini and his law partner, David Friedenrich, had negotiated with their clients for a nearly one-third interest of their island shares in lieu of fees. This settlement would have meant a half share of a $165,000 windfall for Gherini, plus any further legal fees. The Caires rejected this offer out of hand. The bemused Gherini later recalled his surprise that they had not responded with a counter offer.[69] In this he continued to misread the motives of the majority Caires. The aged yet still imperious and unbending ninety-one-year-old Albina refused to countenance any dealings with her treacherous offspring who had betrayed the memory and expressed intentions of her husband. Her sons felt they had no choice but to accede to her wishes.

To Albina and the sons and daughters who stood by her, negotiation with the two rebellious and unstable daughters, or those who encouraged them, was tantamount to surrender to blackmail. Their resistance was a defense of basic principles and values, even if it meant that the Caires lost everything in the process. For Gherini and his clients, it was a simple matter of negotiation to find the right amount that would satisfy them. Referees were appointed by the Santa Barbara court to make the survey of the island, a prerequisite for partitioning. They prepared to go to work in spite of various appeals and motions by the Caires.

The Caire family might have been brought low, but for the other side in the litigation there was also a price to be paid. Ownership of the inheritance for which they were ostensibly fighting began to slip from the hands of the Rossis and Capuccios. From the outset, they had been unable to pay anything toward the substantial fees that accumulated year by year in pursuing the legal actions masterminded by their brother-in-law. In 1921, with the end game in sight and no possibility of paying off their legal bills, negotiations took place between Edmund Rossi (negotiating for both the Rossis and Capuccios) and the legal team of Gherini and Freidenrich. In a consequence that will hold no surprise for those familiar with the perils of protracted litigation, the two lawyers emerged as owners of almost a third (four and one-half) of the fourteen shares left by Albina to her two married daughters in 1910.[70] This ownership share would expand over the next eleven years of continued litigation and negotiation until the entire portion of the island for which the Rossis and Capuccios had fought for two decades was in the hands of the Gherini family.

Far from the troubles of the courts, in the postwar years the Main Ranch retained its air of immutability. Looking westward from the Sur road, the track parted the acres of vines that swept up the hills on either side. A mantle of fog might sit beyond the upper portion of the valley at Portezuela, as the family compound lay concealed within its grove of trees and flower-filled gardens planted decades before. In the other direction, the road leading eastward out of the Main Ranch was lined with the windbreak eucalyptus trees planted in the days of Justinian Caire, where a rail fence kept the cattle out of the vines and hay crops. On the road to La Playa, one could see the tracks made by the narrow wheels of one of the horse-drawn carts or carriages mixing with tire tracks (truck and Model T), crisscrossing the stream that flowed toward the harbor. In the nearby fields, two tractors were used for plowing and reaping, but much of this work was still done with horse-drawn implements. In the vineyard, the workers in their collarless shirts and broad-brimmed hats moved slowly along the rows, tending the vines.

There was often abundant entertainment as the Caires welcomed friends from San Francisco and Southern California who arrived on the schooner *Santa Cruz* or on their own yachts. Vera Eaton, the daughter of Ira and Margaret Eaton, who managed to patch up their relationship with the Caires and establish their resort at Pelican Bay on the island coast facing Santa Barbara, describes an elaborate lunch in 1919 for the guest of honor, John Barrymore. Served with no small ceremony by two maids, it was one of several occasions that the Caires entertained the most famous actor of his generation.[71] The summer of 1919 was also enlivened by a visit from the U.S.

Navy's destroyer *Hart*. After a formal lunch at the Main Ranch, Lily Caire, in a full-skirted dress, white shoes, fancy straw hat, and parasol, and Fred Caire, in riding boots, trousers, jacket, shirt, and fedora, were welcomed on board by a Captain Jones, who showed them around the vessel. It was this vision of Fred as old-fashioned California grandee that moved Barrymore to tell the Santa Barbara paper that Caire was one of the men whose lifestyle he most admired.

Throughout the 1920s the Caires continued the policy of welcoming to the island researchers from Stanford, the California Academy of Sciences, Mills College, the Santa Barbara Botanic Garden, and the Santa Barbara Museum of Natural History. These scholars specialized in various fields, notably geology, biology, and archaeology, and were often guests at the Main Ranch for weeks at a time. Fred Caire also carefully collected some specimens himself, which were proudly displayed in the family house.

The Caires felt that the ongoing lawsuits constrained them from extensive investing in and upgrading their operation, lest in the continuing legal actions a court rule that these were an improper exercise of their authority as trustees. Despite this, 1917, 1918, and 1919 all showed a substantial profit, and while there was still hope for a positive outcome in the courts, the family continued to plow resources into the various ranches, including Scorpion Ranch.

With the prohibition amendment working its way through the Congress and then the state legislatures, the Caires were looking at a bleak future for one of their main income streams. For the moment, things were on an even keel and they even experienced a spike in income as they liquidated their wine inventory with buyers seeking to lay in supplies in anticipation of the demand that would rise after the Volstead Act took effect. Wool sales too were especially strong in these years, as adequate rainfall in the winters of 1916–17 and 1917–18 coincided with wartime demand to help raise income. But in 1920, when scant rainfall combined with the first full year of Prohibition, the Santa Cruz Island Company plunged into loss for the first time in many years. The Caires watched their vineyard income fall by almost 90 percent, from $37,000 to $4,000 [$398,000 to $43,000], as they struggled to sell their grapes on the local market.[72]

As if to underscore the anxiety that they were feeling, Fred gave up his management role in Justinian Caire Company to focus full time on the Santa Cruz Island Company. When the superintendent was dismissed in 1924, he took direct control of the day-to-day ranching operations. The decline of the ranching business brought on by the constraints of the lawsuits was accentuated by labor shortages following the war, the changing nature of the California economy, and the lack of capital for investment. The Caire livestock numbers were also reduced by regular illegal forays by fishermen who supplemented their diet and income by shooting sheep and cattle in remote canyons and bootlegging the carcasses in ports like San Pedro. There were occasional exchanges of gunfire with island employees, but because of the rugged island topography, positive identification was extremely difficult and few prosecutions resulted.[73] The cumulative effect of these pressures began to be noticeable in the daily life of the ranch. There was little Fred or Arthur could do to arrest the decline except to try to eke out a profit wherever they could and cooperate with the court-appointed surveyors and agricultural consultants.

As the years passed after the death of Justinian Caire, his sons continued the management of the businesses he founded, "with as little change and alteration as possible," but in this lay the seeds of their downfall. Inevitably, the economy of California grew and developed in ways completely unforeseen by Justinian and his pioneer colleagues. By the early twentieth century, on the California mainland, the days of the open range were long gone, the wine industry was almost completely consolidated by the California Wine Association, and the balance of transport swung more and more toward land-based shipping. Yet the Caire operation, largely because of geography, but also because of the limitations imposed by the lawsuits, continued for the most part as it had in the nineteenth century. Though partly successful attempts were made to limit the spread of the sheep through fencing, the vertiginous canyons with which the island is scored were perfect hiding places for the increasingly wild herd, undisturbed by the annual corridas. And although there was diversification into wine and walnuts, these products would never provide the economic salvation of the island enterprise, increasingly deprived of capital investment, especially in the 1920s with loss of income resulting from Prohibition and the costs of the island's partition. On the mainland, the large land holdings of ranchers in a similar situation as the Caires at the turn of the century found profitability through mixed agriculture, rail and road access to markets, and land sales to an urbanizing California population. The Santa Cruz Island Company, perched beyond the continent's edge, remained wedded to the old ways that had prevailed in the previous century—open-range livestock management and sea transportation. The simpler, more flexible business operation of Vail and Vickers again provides a contrast: it was able to prosper in the face of changing costs, markets, and tastes.

At the end of 1924 the court-ordered surveyors delivered their findings in the partition suit. Combined with the 1922 inventory and value analysis by the Symmes Agricultural Surveyor Agency, the surveyors and referees recommended the division of the island into seven tracts, one tract per shareholder in the Santa Cruz Island Company at the time of the lapse of the corporate charter in 1911. In terms of land area, the majority Caires retained the western 90 percent of the island, including the Main Ranch, central valley, Prisoners' Harbor, and all the land west of a line running roughly from China Harbor on the north coast to Sandstone Point on the southern coast. The surveyors wisely took advantage of the natural physical barrier of the transverse range, the Montañon, to separate the two factions. The Capuccio, Rossi, and Gherini interests were allotted the eastern 10 percent of the island, including the ranches at Scorpion Harbor and Smugglers Cove. The surveyors' fees and expenses totaled $54,000 [$680,000], for which the Caires were liable for 86 percent, based on their shareholding percentage.

In spite of Gherini's objections, the referees' recommendations were upheld and the island was now effectively two properties. The Caires ran the western bulk of the island, and Ambrose Gherini took on the mantle of owner and operator of the eastern 10 percent. In the spring of 1927, the opposing parties divided up the livestock of the island. Gherini kept all of the sheep located on the east end, but prior to the division Fred Caire supervised the final shearing of all island sheep in May. The clip, now fallen to 234 sacks weighing 82,000 pounds, was packed and stored in the warehouse at Prisoner's Harbor, where it was divided, with 14 percent allocated to Gherini and his clients.[74] The story of Santa Cruz Island now effectively divides into two.

Idyllic summers continued for the younger generation. But as the 1920s began with the island's grazing lands suffering from two of the driest winters in memory, the winery closed by order of the Volstead Act, and with their vineyard income drastically cut, the grim reality of their financial situation forced the elder Caires to explore other possible sources of income. For

Family house at the Main Ranch, 1926.
Built in 1913, it was destroyed by fire in 1950. Justinian Caire granddaughter
(*seated*) and unidentified friend. *Caire Family Archive.*

about $100 per week [$7,500], the island became a favored location for the
Los Angeles–based producers of the burgeoning movie industry, who saw
the advantages of exotic locations nearby. Ira and Margaret Eaton, with their
concession at Pelican Bay, just to the west of Prisoners' Harbor, provided
readily accessible dormitory and catering facilities for movie crews working
on films such as *Pearls of Paradise* (1916), *Diamond in the Sky* (1917), *Male
and Female* (1919), *Peter Pan* (1924), and *The Rescue* (1928).[75] The producer
Henry Otto made a series of films, most with a nautical theme, featuring as
many as fifty diving girls. Additional income was secured from selling rock
to the city of Santa Barbara for its new breakwater, and almost a quarter of
a million tons were blasted from the cliffs above Fry's Harbor.

As the litigation wore on, the majority Caires looked for financial salvation from outside investors who would follow the lead of the Eatons and lease
part of the island for recreational purposes or possibly buy their entire parcel.
These negotiations were always complicated by the continuing lawsuits and

Prisoners' Harbor, 1928, disguised as a South Sea village
for a movie, *The Rescue. Caire Family Archive.*

the different requirements demanded of potential buyers by each side. In the end they came to nothing. There were also reports throughout the 1920s of a high level of interest by the state of California or the federal government in acquiring the island. The state acquisition story rumbled on through the decade, but with the stock market crash of 1929 and the ensuing Depression, the state and federal governments turned their attention away from recreational land purchase and toward more pressing concerns.[76]

The Caires' financial situation was becoming increasingly untenable. Ultimately they were humbled by the legal triumphs of Ambrose Gherini. His tenacity and greater grasp of what was essential under the law brought victory to him and the descendants of Justinian Caire he represented. The Caire majority had defended their principles and their holdings for as long as was possible through the courts, at immense financial and emotional cost. They could do no more. Their situation was made worse by their struggle to keep the island operating through the progressively deteriorating agricultural conditions that prevailed throughout the 1920s. The Caires were hampered by a lack of investment capital and court-enforced prohibitions against capital improvements through the years of litigation. With their livestock declining in the quality of its meat and wool, and prevented from realizing any income from their winery due to Prohibition, they found themselves in hard times. They had a property that was potentially worth a large sum of money, but they were strapped for cash to pay the operating costs month by month, let alone consider investing in the desperately needed tractors, livestock, upgrading of the schooner, and a host of other suggestions made in the Symmes Agricultural Surveyors Report of 1922. Their losses mounted, from $5,600 in 1929 [$70,000] to $6,800 in 1930. But the Caires' trials were about to significantly worsen. The Capuccio and Rossi families had paid the fees of Gherini and his partner David Freidenrich for the San Francisco–based litigation with more than a third of their patrimony. Now it was time for the majority Caires to pay for the legal fees associated with the partition suit.

It was 1932 and the vortex of the Great Depression, now in its third year and showing no signs of bottoming out, began sucking down the strong along with the weak. Winemaking had resumed on the island after the repeal of Prohibition, but as one agricultural analyst later wrote, "With strong outside competition and apathy on the part of the owners . . . wine inferior in quality to that previously produced was turned out and the industry failed to fully revive."[77] A wine historian notes, "The habit of drinking wine, never very firmly established in America, had been quite lost in the fourteen years of Prohibition. . . . On Santa Cruz Island the feeling may have been that winemaking was now more trouble than it was worth."[78] Given this background and their focus on trying to sell the property to any serious buyer, it is unlikely that Fred and Arthur had the inclination, energy, or resources to invest in wine production. The sheep business continued as it had, but as the number of wild sheep grew in proportion to the tame flocks, the island began to appear overgrazed. The family returned to the island for the corridas and shearing, which now took place only in the spring, and marketed the sheep and wool at prevailing dismal Depression prices.

In order to survive the adverse agricultural conditions of the previous decade, the Caires had borrowed to pay the fees in the San Francisco accounting action, and they had borrowed to keep the island going. In the absence of the ailing Judge Crow in Santa Barbara, Judge Collier from Los

Angeles set the fees awarded to Gherini at $75,000 [$1.2 million]. The sum was contested but upheld by the California Supreme Court as reasonable, given the nature and amount of work involved, the protracted litigation, and the great value of the property.[79] The Caires were liable for 86 percent of the fees, plus interest on the time taken for the appeal, a total of $69,700.

This was the final straw in this twenty-year legal, ethical, and emotional saga. Conceivably, in more temperate circumstances, there would have been negotiation about financing the fee payable to Ambrose Gherini over time, allowing the Caires to find a way out of their financial morass. But these options were not on offer, and the gloves had long since come off in this fight to the finish. Gherini insisted that they would have to find the entire sum immediately, and if that meant the Caires borrowing it at 6 percent in the depths of the Depression, then so be it. Adding to their financial woes, in 1932 the Justinian Caire Company showed a loss of $16,500 [$260,000].

It was the end of the road. To pay Gherini, the Caire brothers took out a mortgage on the island for the first time in the history of the Caire ownership. Although they toyed with the idea of negotiating a $250,000 loan [$3.75 million] to pay off their obligations and to seek investment capital for restocking and renewing the vineyard and winery, the appetite for risk-taking in such an adverse economic climate by the seventy-three-year-old Arthur and the sixty-seven-year-old Fred was gone. Ambrose Gherini settled into his role as master of the east end of the island, and the Caires began the long search for a private buyer of this trophy property that had been the cherished possession of their family for more than half a century.

The Capuccio and Rossi families had already begun to cede ownership of their shares of the island in lieu of payment to their legal team in 1921, and in October 1926 Aglaë Capuccio sold the remainder of her island holding to the Gherini interests. In the same month that he finalized his acquisition of the Capuccio holding, Ambrose Gherini began managing the two parcels as one ranch, operating through a shell company called the National Trading Company, which he had trumpeted in the local press the year before.[80] As of December 31, 1927, Gherini and his wife together controlled just short of 40 percent of the company, while eight of Maria's siblings owned the remainder.[81]

Gherini's first strategy was to form a partnership with resort developers as a way of cashing in on his newly acquired property, "to make it the show place of southern California . . . a resort that will rival Catalina."[82] The owners of Santa Catalina, the Wrigleys, need not have worried. The realities, including a lack of water and no direct access to or from the mainland, rendered this ambition impossible, particularly after the courts rejected his petitions to grant him or his clients the use of the wharf at Prisoners' Harbor. At the same time, Gherini was beginning to experience some of the challenges of running an agricultural enterprise separated from its market by twenty-five miles of open sea. The first year of operation, however, brought him an income of $4,992 [$62,000] and $1,171 to each of the other shareholders, for a total profit of more than $14,000. Gherini also received $2,584 [$32,000] as commission for his management services.[83]

But in the years that followed, Gherini lamented the underutilization of the potential of the east end of the island, noting that "the number of sheep with relation to the size of the range shows clearly that far from the maximum return is being obtained. It is much like operating a factory far short of its capacity. The building up of a worthwhile flock upon the present unsatisfactory basis is a very difficult task." He also reported on "the meager means available and all of the difficulties inherent in the property." In closing the report for 1929, Gherini complained that his "assumption of responsibility of management" had resulted in his being paid "absolutely nothing . . . it is now two and a half years that this work has been carried on by the writer with absolutely no cooperation or assistance from the co-owners of the property. Such a situation is too unjust to need further comment."[84]

These setbacks and difficulties did not deter his ambition to be the owner of the entire east end, and by June 1932 Ambrose Gherini and his wife, Maria Rossi Gherini succeeded at this, having bought out the interests of all her siblings. Maria owned two-thirds of parcels six and seven and her husband owned the remaining third, making the east end of the island officially the Gherini ranch.[85] They had fought for twenty years for this outcome, but the reality turned out to be somewhat less profitable and enjoyable than they had hoped.

Scorpion Ranch was the headquarters of the east end of the island, with substantial buildings and facilities dating back to the 1880s, but in the early 1920s, with the writing on the wall, the Caire family had scaled back on maintenance of the Scorpion and Smugglers Ranches. More importantly, there were no all-weather loading facilities for animals or cargo at either ranch. In the Caire era, cargo for the east end of the island was lightered to and from the schooner anchored in Scorpion harbor, and livestock was driven overland to Potrero Norte and Prisoners' Harbor for shipment to the mainland. The difficulties posed by sea travel remained a challenge throughout the entire Gherini tenure at the east end.

After their initial resort development plans came to nothing, the Gherinis had to face the same challenges that had confronted ranchers and agriculturalists over the previous seventy years, particularly on the smaller islands in the chain. The inexperienced Gherini found that he had taken on an undercapitalized, somewhat dilapidated ranch, with a flock that was too small to generate enough income to cover costs, let alone return a profit. With the country nose-diving into the Great Depression, he tried running the ranch at minimal cost, with his sons Pier and Francis providing much of the labor and his wife doing the books.[86] Although at one point in 1931 the sheep headcount spiked to 5,182, the average count hovered around 2,500. Sales of sheep and lambs ranged from five hundred to fourteen hundred annually. The Gherinis sheared the sheep in the spring only, the best time being April and early May before the still-green grasses seeded.[87] They had no boat to provide dependable transportation and had to rely on a patchwork of arrangements with local fishermen, and even, from time to time, the Caires. The Gherinis struggled to build a wharf at Scorpion, only to see it destroyed repeatedly in winter storms.

Small wonder that shortly thereafter Gherini told his son Pier that he was fed up with the island. In 1936, the fifty-eight-year-old attorney suffered a severe stroke that left him partly paralyzed, and active management of the east end of the island passed to his wife and four children, in particular his sons Pier and Francis.[88]

The Gherini family soldiered on through the 1930s, selling one thousand to fourteen hundred sheep a year, eventually transporting them in their own boat, a former Alaska fishing vessel that they christened the *Natco*. There would usually be two or three permanent employees on the island, supplemented by casual labor to help out with corridas, and by family members in the summer holidays. The dream of cashing in on the island by developing their holdings as a resort remained tantalizingly out of reach.

After the war, the overall impression of the Gherini ranch was that of a shoestring operation with an emphasis on making do with minimal investment and maximum ingenuity. A regional drought in 1948 forced the Gherinis to remove and sell 2,240 head of their herd, resulting in a lowering of stock levels for a number of years, with consequent financial setbacks. The balance sheet for 1948 saw the year ending with only 450 sheep, and there were fewer the following two years. The ranch saw little or no profit during the early 1950s. The year before he died, Ambrose Gherini wrote to his son Pier of his dissatisfaction with "the situation" on the island. "As it is, all we are doing is to load expenses upon ourselves and operate the place for the benefit of the hands. That simply does not make sense." In 1952, only 150 sheep were counted on the Gherini property, and the numbers only gradually increased to their former levels by 1956.[89]

Like almost everyone who spent time on Santa Cruz Island, the Gherini descendants developed a deep appreciation of the island's rugged charm that went hand in hand with its isolation and physical challenges, even as they struggled to keep it viable economically.[90] One possible reason for the Gherini family's persistence with sheep ranching in these conditions is that it was perhaps encouraged by the widowed Maria Rossi Gherini after her husband died in 1952. Profits, if existing at all, were never considerable, and labor expenses grew. The grandchildren of Ambrose and Maria Gherini continued to work on the ranch through the 1970s. The National Park Service study summarized this period thus:

> In essence the Gherinis did not live on the island but made occasional income from its operation; they kept the structures in fair condition although they rarely spent much time and money on building projects. . . . One could surmise that the sheep ranching operation, never a big profit-maker, was not seen as a long term use of the land and so the existing buildings were kept only in a state of preservation for day-to-day utilitarian uses.[91]

As the years passed, and the family continued to run its small sheep operation to cover costs, the dreams of turning the east end of the island into a profitable resort never completely went away. In 1963 the Gherini family hired architect George V. Russell to develop a conceptual plan to combine residential, commercial, and recreational development, with a marina for 150 boats, five hundred residential lots, hunting lodges, horse trails, and a predicted population of three thousand people.[92] The public hearings on the plan, conducted by the Santa Barbara County Planning Commission, brought out advocates for both the private development of the island and the preservation of public access to open space within the county. The commissioners reflected the prevailing conservative property rights ethos and gave a generally positive response to the Gherini proposal. Conservation groups, notably the Sierra Club, countered this, seeing the scheme as a threat to preservation of the unique island ecosystems. In the background was the National Park Service, which had been flirting with the idea of incorporating Santa Cruz Island into a Channel Islands National Park since the 1920s.

The Gherini position was that the federal government could step in at any time and make a bid for their holdings, but in the interim the National Park Service could not prevent the family from pursuing its own commercial interests. Opponents of the development scheme charged that the Gherinis were merely talking up the asking price that they would eventually have to accept from the government when the inevitable park was authorized. In 1966 the planning commission approved the Gherini development plan in the face of vigorous local protests.

This decision was upheld by the county board of supervisors, but times were changing, and one of the long-lasting outcomes of the tumultuous 1960s was a heightened environmental awareness. This new outlook put the autocratic tradition of island land management on a collision course with both public sentiment and the state and federal governments. The general concern for the fragility of the local marine environment was thrown into sharp relief in the aftermath of a major oil spill in the Santa Barbara Channel in January 1969. It coated the coastline with thick tar and wreaked a great deal of damage to wildlife and the recreational tourism assets of the Santa Barbara area. The spill, emanating from a platform operated by Union Oil, became a potent catalyst for a groundswell of public opinion that would strongly influence legislative action regarding the Channel Islands in the coming years.

The future of the island was sealed in the California 1972 general election, when voters passed the California Coastal Zone Conservation Act, creating the California Coastal Commission. This body had jurisdiction over land-use planning for sensitive environments such as Santa Cruz Island, making "any development on it difficult if not impossible," as Ambrose Gherini's grandson John Gherini writes.[93] Over the protests of the owners, the Coastal

Commission's plan substantially increased the minimum parcel size on the island from 10 acres to 320 acres. When applied to the Gherini holdings, this meant that no more than twenty-one dwelling units would be allowed, instead of the five hundred units approved in the previous decade. The commission also forbade any oil development on the island, initiating years of litigation from the Gherinis, but public sympathy was on the side of conservation and not private property rights. In addition to the immense investment needed to overcome the inherent shortcomings in water resources and infrastructure, which had doomed earlier schemes, the new legislative environment meant that the Gherini family's development dreams finally faded and disappeared.

This was the end of the road for the Gherinis. They returned to sheep ranching, an occupation they leased out to a colorful character named Pete Petersen in the 1970s. However, dissatisfied with the returns from this solution, they turned to catering to hunters in search of the thrill of stalking wild boar and sheep in the 1980s. Always hovering in the background was the shift from the primacy of private property to the growing awareness that these were environments too special to be left to the commercial whims of private owners.

A new era was beginning, a time of preservation and restoration of ecologies impacted by over a century of land and animal husbandry. By now the seventy-six-year-old Pier Gherini was in failing health (he would die in 1989), but his brother Francis, two years his junior, and two sisters, continued negotiations with the National Park Service to achieve the highest possible return on their family's seventy-one-year investment. A conclusion was finally reached after seventeen years on February 10, 1997. The Park Service now owned the east end of Santa Cruz Island in full. The last holdout, Francis, accepted a court-awarded $12.9 million, plus interest, for his quarter share in 1999, more than three times that of his siblings, but his triumph was short-lived. He died on April 28, 1999, aged eighty-four, just days after the verdict was announced, followed less than a month later by his wife.

The NPS now faced the costs of removing the Gherini's semi-wild horse herd and almost ten thousand sheep. Animal rights concerns ruled out shooting them on the island, and their capture and transfer to the mainland took almost two years and more than $2 million. The last sheep on the island, perhaps descendants of the first flocks taken out there by Dr. Shaw in 1852, were finally removed by the end of 1999. This severed the final link with the agricultural legacy of Justinian Caire, but in its buildings, design, and layout, the Scorpion and Smugglers Ranches still give ample testimony to his vision of nineteenth-century land husbandry.[94]

— ▸ • ◂ —

At the western end of the island, in the lingering years of the Great Depression, it took the Caires from 1932 until 1937 to find someone of sufficient means who was interested in this unique piece of real estate. This was Edwin Stanton, one of a new breed of Southern California entrepreneurs, whose wealth came from oil and manufacturing investments. He sold one of his automotive factories to raise the cash to buy the Caire family's property. Stanton made a down payment of $250,000, and signed a note for the remainder of the purchase price of $750,000 [$10.8 million] to complete the purchase.

Anxious to win over local opinion, Stanton called a lunchtime press conference in Santa Barbara to announce the completion of the transaction and his intention of "maintaining the island property as a great, typical, old-fashioned California ranch."[95] At the same time he declared his willingness to invest in restocking the island's herds of sheep and cattle, to overhaul the schooner *Santa Cruz*, and to build an airstrip on the island to facilitate a quick commute between his office in Los Angeles and the island. Also at the press conference was Nick Liatas, a Santa Barbara realtor who confirmed that the sale of the island was not only the most lucrative deal he had ever put together, but that he also believed it to be the single biggest realty transaction, in terms of both acreage and money, in Santa Barbara County history.

Stanton was as good as his word. In October the first of ten thousand head of sheep were shipped aboard the schooner *Santa Cruz* and the *Vaquero*, hired from the Vails of neighboring Santa Rosa Island. Twenty-five carloads of sheep, purchased in Arizona and temporarily corralled on Punta Gorda Street in Santa Barbara, were herded onto Stearns Wharf by "two expert sheep dogs of the island, Spot and Shep," to be ferried over to the island as quickly as possible.[96]

The changes continued. Although with the repeal of Prohibition the Caires had tried to restart their winery business, selling varietal wines in bottle to local customers like the Arlington Hotel, Stanton did not see

Ed Stanton, 1937, the year he bought the island from the Caires.
Courtesy of Santa Cruz Island Foundation.

profitability in this.[97] When he was advised that the twenty-six thousand gallons stored in the winery were gradually spoiling, he instructed one of his employees to empty the vats, and thousands of gallons of wine, along with the proud history of winemaking on the island, drained into the dust of the Camino del Este.

Unfortunately, the plan for making the island herd more docile by the introduction of ten thousand domesticated sheep came to nothing, as the newcomers headed for the hills to join their wild cousins, adding to the degradation of the rangeland. In 1939 Stanton ranch hands began to round up sheep for shipping to packinghouses on the mainland, collecting about thirty-five thousand. Over the next decade professional hunters killed some twenty thousand more, but the sheep continued to multiply and populate the island's ranges. According to one of the hands working for Stanton, "They were everywhere you looked. . . . They had multiplied and multiplied—due to the fact that you couldn't catch them very well, and they didn't have fences enough to get them down into small pastures where you could control them. The island was overrun with them. In fact, they were just denuding the island. . . . We estimated that there were probably around at least 30,000 head of sheep on the island at one time."[98]

The focus of the Stanton operation shifted to less-labor-intensive cattle-raising in the boom of the postwar period, though the challenges of ranching in Southern California hit home in the drought years of 1948 and 1949. As was the case with their island neighbors, lack of rainfall required the evacuation of the entire herd in 1948. The cattle operation was resumed in 1949, and that winter was notable as one of the few recorded times when the central valley was completely blanketed in snow. The Stantons reorganized the layout of the island operations to accommodate cattle, and although there were complications associated with running a ranch "in the sea," like the Vails they found that the advantages of isolation from predators, noxious weeds, and diseases resulted in healthy cattle that commanded a good price at market.

Along with the transformation of the herd, the physical legacy of the Caires gradually faded as more and more of the structures on the island underwent modifications—either deliberate or accidental—over the ensuing decade. At the Main Ranch, the Caires had made do with kerosene lanterns for domestic lighting, but the Stantons decided to move with the times by installing generator-powered electricity. In 1950, an overheating ice-maker on the back porch of the wooden family residence caught fire. The blaze quickly spread to the house, burning it to the ground. Sparks borne on a westerly wind ignited the roofs and contents of the nearby winery buildings, including the huge oak vats, barrels, carts, tools, and winemaking apparatus. There was, of course, no fire department to call for help, and the small number of ranch hands could only look on and try to keep the conflagration from spreading to the superintendent's house, the comedor, and bunkhouses. When the fire at last died down, all that remained of the Main Ranch compound to the east of the superintendent's house were the brick walls of the winery. The rest was a smoking ruin. Across the valley, Justinian Caire's diminutive brick chapel, which had taken pride of place among the vines at its dedication fifty-nine years before, now stood forlornly alone, surrounded by a few overgrown Blackwood acacias and vulnerable to earthquakes and weather.

After the fire, Stanton immediately hired a well-known Los Angeles architect, H. Roy Kelley, to design a contemporary two-bedroom ranch-style dwelling, appropriately named Phoenix House, to replace the old family house. At the same time, perhaps disheartened by the setbacks, he listed the island for sale at fifty dollars per acre, or $2.7 million [$33 million]. There were no takers for this "outstanding cattle ranch, lending itself ideally for a large colony or subdivision."[99]

At Prisoners' Harbor, the adobe house that had stood there for almost a century began to suffer severe damage due to flooding from a creek that had changed its course over the years. After a number of years in dilapidated condition, the house was dismantled for safety reasons early in 1960.[100] And it was on the rocks at Prisoners' Harbor at the end of the same year, with a Santa Ana wind blowing out of the northeast, that the schooner *Santa Cruz* was wrecked. Having served the owners of the island faithfully, and having survived the waters and hazards of the Santa Barbara Channel for sixty-seven years, the *Santa Cruz* was a total loss, and another physical remnant of Santa Cruz Island history disappeared.

The island's cattle operation continued through the 1950s, more or less breaking even. An exploration lease granted to the Richfield Oil Company in 1954 brought in welcome income but led to no oil findings. The abandoned sheep became feral, and in 1957, with Ed Stanton in failing health, his surviving son Carey took over the management of the island, charged by his father with the task of keeping it profitable. The younger Stanton had completed his medical education at Stanford just after the war and then had practiced pathology and internal medicine for about ten years. He later characterized his move to the island as his being "overtaken by good sense. . . . It was . . . the wisest decision of my life."[101]

The quiet, intensely private life on the island suited Carey Stanton perfectly. With his scholarly interests, Stanton enjoyed meeting scientists and students who regularly visited the University of California Santa Cruz Island Reserve, which he made possible in the mid 1960s. UC Santa Barbara (UCSB)

Carey Stanton, 1939, with his mother, Evelyn, watching from behind the gate.
Courtesy of Santa Cruz Island Foundation.

held a summer geology class on the island in 1963. It was such a success that the next year the quarters were moved from tents to semi-permanent buildings. In 1966 UCSB established the Santa Cruz Island Field Station about one-half mile to the west of the Main Ranch, where it still stands today.

Carey Stanton took the responsibilities of island land husbandry seriously, striving to maintain the memory of the previous century of human habitation while working with his trusted foreman, Henry Duffield, to keep the cattle operation functioning. Hired by Ed Stanton in 1960 to run the island's cattle business, Duffield did so for a quarter of a century. Paralyzed from the waist down by polio at a young age, Henry was known as "the cowboy in the red jeep with hand controls, never without his rifle in a scabbard, his flask of Ancient Age Bourbon in his glove box, and his several dogs at his side."[102]

As for Carey Stanton, a visitor from the Santa Barbara Historical Society presents an image of him from those years. After a pleasant day on the island, as she and others pulled away from Prisoners' Harbor at sunset, "There stood Dr. Stanton, short of stature and mild-mannered, alone on the pier waving to the group as the huge island loomed behind him."[103]

In the 1960s Stanton also saw an opportunity to cater to Southern California hunters who wanted more than the usual challenge in terms of rugged terrain and wily and powerful prey. Starting in 1966, for almost twenty years the Ventura-based Santa Cruz Island Hunt Club (Santa Cruz Island Club) operated as a partnership between Stanton and two other entrepreneurs. The club began as a sheep- and pig-hunting enterprise, with both a rifle season and an archery season, and in 1981 it expanded to include summer recreational visits. In 1966 a two-day hunt cost $100. For this sum, a customer received round-trip airfare, guides, meals, lodging, two trophy animals, and one lamb. Some twenty years later, the club cost per person had increased to $600. The Santa Cruz Island Company received 25 percent of the club's gross receipts. By its last year of operation, this was amounting to about $250,000 in income. In the end, plagued by insurance problems and by the desire of Stanton's new partners in island ownership, The Nature Conservancy, to eliminate the feral sheep, the Santa Cruz Island Club ceased operating at the end of December 1985.

The Nature Conservancy entered the scene in 1976 as part of complex negotiations undertaken by Carey Stanton in circumstances that mirrored the intra-familial litigation of the Caires. The deaths of Ed Stanton in 1963 and of his wife ten years later had triggered estate duties that were paid out of securities they had set aside for that purpose. Upon Evelyn Stanton's death, the Santa Cruz Island Company was reinstated, with two-thirds of the stock controlled by Carey Stanton and one-third going to his nephew, thirty-two-year-old Edwin Stanton III, the son of Carey's older brother (Edwin Jr. had been killed in World War II). Carey had been enjoying his modest but pleasant lifestyle on this unique property, conserving it as he saw fit and as his parents intended, but there had been little income that could be shared with the other principal shareholder.

The younger Stanton saw himself as one-third owner of a potentially very valuable piece of real estate from which he was deriving no income or benefit, but he kept his dissatisfaction to himself until after the death of his grandmother. At the start of 1976 he filed suit against his uncle to dissolve the Santa Cruz Island Company and submit to an accounting. As Carey was uncomfortably aware, his nephew's goal, like that of minority shareholders Amelie Caire Rossi and Aglaë Caire Capuccio sixty-four years before, was to dismantle the company and claim his inheritance after its sale.[104] The charges of mismanagement and a lavish lifestyle would have been very difficult to prove, given the income of the company and Carey's financially conservative and parsimonious nature, but at its core the suit echoed the same complaint that the two married Caire daughters made in 1912. They and Eddie Stanton were part owners of a valuable asset from which they were not benefiting to the extent they deemed appropriate.[105]

Carey Stanton's dilemma was similar to that of the Caires in that he felt he had natural justice on his side, but he knew from the Caire history that protracted litigation would be costly and would threaten his preservation efforts and control of the island he loved. He was desperate for a solution that would allow him to retain control of the property and provide cash to buy out his nephew. The only viable solution on offer was that of The Nature Conservancy. It cost the organization a little over $2.5 million to complete the transaction, but while it solved the immediate problem of Stanton's nephew, a number of the terms of the accord would ultimately cause friction between the two parties. One of the clauses, a conservation easement over Stanton's holdings, put the Conservancy on a collision course with the Santa Cruz Island Company and its lucrative hunting club. It gave the Conservancy the right to forbid activities that would degrade the natural flora and fauna, and to enforce the restoration of impacted areas. Inexact phrases like "selective reduction of or elimination of feral animals" and "selective control techniques as heretofore conducted" would provide a field day for legal minds on both sides of what would become a very fractious relationship.[106]

Against this backdrop of uncertainty and rising tension, in 1985 Stanton established the Santa Cruz Island Foundation as an organization devoted to preserving the history of the California Channel Islands. He hoped negotiations with The Nature Conservancy would guarantee a physical presence for his foundation on the island, but he became alarmed and depressed by the maneuverings of the Conservancy's legal team, which indicated no firm undertakings to support the foundation. In early 1986, his great friend and ranch manager Henry Duffield suffered a stroke that paralyzed his upper left side. Disconsolate at the thought of no longer being able to take an active part in the management of the ranch, Henry shot himself at the Main Ranch on November 23, 1986, and he was buried in the island's cemetery.

The loss of his great friend and the continued pressure he felt from The Nature Conservancy was making Stanton's life miserable. Unhappy and alone, he died suddenly on December 8, 1987, aged sixty-four, in the old superintendent's house on the island, from complications brought on by medications. Carey Stanton was buried in the family plot adjacent to his chapel at the Main Ranch. The Stanton portion of Santa Cruz Island land passed to The Nature Conservancy and Carey Stanton's personal estate was left to the Santa Cruz Island Foundation, his enduring island legacy.

Under the auspices of The Nature Conservancy, and after the NPS acquisition of the east end, a new chapter in the preservation of Santa Cruz Island was about to be written. Within a few weeks, the Stanton ranching operation was closed down and its cattle shipped off the island. Twentieth-century sensibilities regarding ecological systems and habitats now came to the fore. The Caires had tried to "civilize" the island according to their understanding of contemporary agricultural and conservation practices. The Stantons employed their own ideas about preservation. For The Nature Conservancy, the island represented a unique opportunity to attempt a comprehensive, science-based plan to restore an island's ecology to its natural state, which had been dramatically changed by more than a century of intensive land husbandry. From the point of view of the Conservancy, the first essential task was the elimination of the thousands of feral sheep and pigs. Despite the best efforts of nineteenth- and twentieth-century owners at controlling these populations, these sheep and pigs had caused serious damage to the island flora, and their removal was a top priority, begun even before the sudden demise of Carey Stanton. The sheep were removed by the late 1980s, but the pigs were adept at hiding in the steepest, most inaccessible parts of the island. A group of professional hunters from New Zealand finally destroyed the last of them in 2006.

The programs for the restoration of the natural environment of the island have demonstrated the complexity of the task (and more than once the law of unintended consequences), but the removal of feral pigs and sheep is now allowing native vegetation to reclaim the island. Formerly rare plant species such as Island buckwheat, Santa Cruz Island live-forever, and Santa Cruz Island silver lotus are now almost commonplace. Oak woodlands and bishop pine forests are expanding, and native bunchgrasses are returning. The Conservancy and its partner, the National Park Service, are facilitating the return of indigenous flora by eliminating invasive, non-native weeds such as the non-indigenous wild fennel that spread vigorously after the disappearance of sheep and pigs. Oak seedlings are flourishing for the first time in 150 years. Seldom-seen endemic plants are now sprouting across the island's hills and valleys. Island foxes—the endangered, cat-sized descendants of the mainland gray fox—are back in strong numbers after the removal of the non-indigenous golden eagles. After being reintroduced under the auspices of the Conservancy, bald eagles, which had been victims of DDT and trophy hunting, are once again soaring above the island and successfully hatching young for the first time in half a century.[107]

Island research continues to flourish under the auspices of the Park Service, The Nature Conservancy, the University of California, the Santa Barbara Museum of Natural History, the Santa Cruz Island Foundation, and other institutions. Recent activities include studies of vegetation change, native shrub recovery, fennel and feral pig eradication, and prescribed burns of exotic plants, as well as specific studies of stream fauna and individual plant and animal species. Investigation and documentation of the island's archaeological sites, historic structures and landscapes, and museum collections continue, particularly on behalf of the Park Service.

And so, after almost 150 years, with the Southern California mainland altered beyond all recognition, the goal of the various custodians of Santa Cruz Island is to restore the natural functioning of the island's ecosystems to something approximating their condition under the dominion of the Chumash, while at the same time preserving the historical and archaeological record of its nineteenth- and twentieth-century inhabitants.

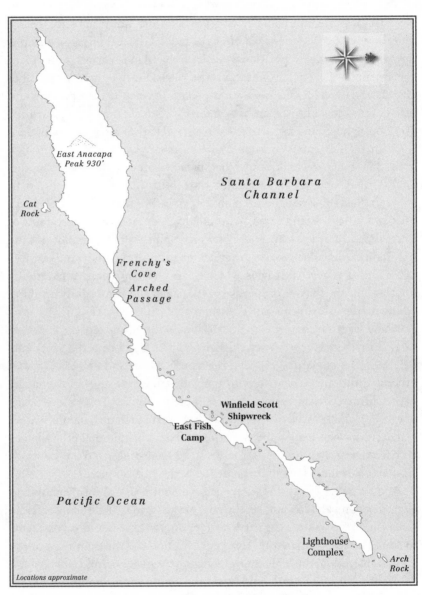

East Anacapa Peak 930'

Cat Rock

Santa Barbara Channel

Frenchy's Cove

Arched Passage

Winfield Scott Shipwreck

East Fish Camp

Pacific Ocean

Lighthouse Complex

Arch Rock

Locations approximate

Anacapa Island.
Map by Gerry Krieg.

CHAPTER 6

Anacapa Island

Approximately five miles of open water separate Santa Cruz Island from its neighbor to the east. Eneepah, meaning "ever-changing" or "deceptive" or perhaps "mirage" to the Chumash islanders, was turned into Enecapa for the first time on the charts of George Vancouver in the 1790, finally becoming Anacapa on a U.S. Coast and Geodetic Survey map of 1854. It is the only one of the California Channel Islands to retain its Indian name. With the play of light, wind, and fog in the Santa Barbara Channel, several of the northern Channel Islands often change their appearance from the coast eleven miles away and from the water, but Anacapa is probably best suited for this evanescent description. Its three small islets can appear through the fog like a dimly seen humpbacked sea creature. At other times they are a substantial presence on the horizon or perhaps seeming to float above it. A visitor in 1890 saw it as a mirage. "First it became a balloon, then a dragon ... next a turreted fortress, then a medusa, and lastly a devil-fish, with antennae writhing, and crouching like a great sea tarantula for a spring."[1]

At first, easy to dismiss as three large lifeless rocks, Anacapa surprises the visitor with its rugged beauty. Like its sister Santa Barbara Island to the east, it lacks subsistence essentials such as freshwater and fuel for fires, though its position, rich intertidal marine resources, and the existence of almost two dozen kitchen middens attest that it was attractive for seasonal habitation by the Chumash. There is also a bit of Chumash oral history that claims that eight families fled to Anacapa after a civil war on the mainland, settling on the landward side of the middle island. Eventually they were said to have moved to Santa Cruz and from there populated all the other islands.[2]

The waters surrounding the island are teeming with life. Anacapa contains the largest colonies of Western gulls and brown pelicans on the Channel Islands. The pelican colony on West Anacapa is the only major nesting site of this species left on the Pacific coast.[3]

Anacapa is predominantly composed of highly weathered Miocene volcanic rock, pushed up by faulting rather than volcanic activity in the epoch between 23 million and 5 million years before the present, so its rocky core is older than its neighbors, Santa Cruz and Santa Rosa. Along with the three other northern Channel Islands, the trio of islets that are East, Middle, and West Anacapa represent a visual and geological extension of the Santa Monica Mountains on the northern side of the Los Angeles Basin. Rising sharply from deep water to a height of 930 feet on West Anacapa, the island shows the interaction of tide, wind, and weather in its rugged sea caves, blowholes, and the natural bridge of Arch Rock. The tides have worked on the volcanic rock for eons, forming caverns, columns, and arches. A visitor in 1920 described the working of the tides and the caves: "Many of the caves are beneath or just on the surface, and are constantly hissing like living things, spouting water in great jets with tremendous force of compressed air."[4] The lower elevations and smaller size of the East and Middle islets puts them in the rain shadow of their larger sister, giving them an annual rainfall under ten inches, which makes their terrain technically desert.

Few early European explorers made much mention of Anacapa. The records of the navigator of the Cabrillo expedition talk of passing the island, giving it more notice than the records of Vizcaíno or Cermeño. The sea contingent of Portolà's expedition called it Las Mesitas, "Little Tables," while Portolà's captain Miguel Costansó referred to it as Vela Falsa, "False Sail." The descriptive images of tables or illusory sails served to ratify the shifting description of Anacapa attributed to the Chumash.

Like several of the other Channel Islands, Anacapa has never had a private owner. From being an unassigned part of Mexican territory, it became subject to the jurisdiction of California under the terms of the 1848 Treaty of Guadelupe Hidalgo. With the arrival of California statehood in 1850, its title went to the U.S. government. Three years later, it was surveyed by the U.S. Coast and Geodetic Survey to determine the need for a light to aid in navigation.

One outcome of the government survey of Anacapa was an illustrative engraving prepared by twenty-year-old James McNeill Whistler. In it he showed an elevation drawing of East Anacapa and its distinctive Arch Rock. Dissatisfied with its stark appearance, he added two flocks of seagulls. This artistic license lost Whistler his draftsman job. Not long thereafter, he moved to Paris to continue his artistic training, and over the next forty-eight years he acquired international fame and fortune. His portrait of his mother, *Arrangement in Grey and Black*, first shown at the Louvre in Paris in 1872, is one of the most widely recognized images in Western art of the time.

The wreck of the coastal steamer *Winfield Scott* in December 1853 gave urgency to the task of building an aid to navigation in the Santa Barbara Channel. The *Scott* was a 225-foot side-wheeler owned and operated by the Pacific Mail Steamship Company, making the run from San Francisco to Panama. It was just before midnight on December 2 when she went aground on Middle Anacapa in dense fog. Eight hundred panicky passengers scrambled ashore in the darkness, anxiously aware of the proximity of towering cliffs and crashing breakers. They spent an uneasy night on an offshore rock and in the light of dawn were transferred by the ship's boats to the nearby beach on the islet proper. The next day the northbound *California*, alerted by a signal from the *Scott*, plucked the *Scott*'s women and children—and the ship's cargo of gold—off the beach. A week later the *California* was back on her southbound run to rescue the remaining passengers and carry them on to their destination of Panama. The crew of the *Scott* remained with the wreck to try to salvage what they could, but the ship itself was a write-off. Remnants of the wreck are still visible to divers in the shallow waters off the aptly named Survivors' Camp on Middle Anacapa.

At least two clichés of sea lore can be observed in this incident. Not only were the women and children accorded their first place among the rescued, but many of the ship's rats left the sinking vessel, and without any natural predators they prospered on Anacapa, with highly damaging results to the local ecosystems. More than 150 years passed before they were successfully, if controversially, eliminated by the National Park Service.[5]

The year after the wreck of the *Winfield Scott*, the island was set aside by executive order of President Franklin Pierce for lighthouse purposes, to be administered by the Lighthouse Bureau, an arrangement that lasted until

1938, although it was not until 1911 that the first navigation aids, an acetylene-powered light and a whistling buoy, anchored off the extreme east end of the island, were brought into operation.

Although it was title-holder throughout the latter half of the nineteenth century, the federal government, with its many distractions, maintained a light touch regarding the possession and use of Anacapa, leaving the island coves and beaches open to exploitation by seasonal seal hunters, fishers, Chinese abalone hunters, and others not particularly scrupulous about title holding and property rights of the tablelands above. They were the usual collection of risk-taking islanders whose names are prominent in the story of almost all the Channel Islands at this time.

One of the first to raise sheep on the island, sometime in the 1850s or 1860s, was Captain George Nidever, whose name runs like a thread through the histories of Santa Rosa, San Miguel, and San Nicolas Islands, as well as early navigation along the coast. In 1869 a "sale" of the islands of Anacapa by William Dover to Louis Burgert and W. H. Mills was recorded for $1,500 [$25,000 in 2011 equivalent]. It was sold again in 1872 to the Pacific Wool Growing Company, a consortium that ran sheep on San Miguel and San Nicolas as well. Ten years later, two brothers named Elliot quit-claimed the island, the default method when ownership was deemed to be murky. Their proprietorship appears to have lasted fifteen years, until 1897, when Frenchman Louis Le Mesnager bought their interest for $8,000 [$217,000]. It was during the tenure of Le Mesnager that the federal government began to take a more active interest in the island, officially leasing it to the Frenchman for grazing and farming. Under the terms of the lease it was formally acknowledged that the government held title to Anacapa, and the tenant was directed not to "erect any permanent buildings upon any part of said island."

At the expiration of the Frenchman's five-year lease, its ownership went to a Ventura businessman, Herman Bayfield (Bay) Webster. Long familiar with the island, Bay Webster had made his first visit in 1884, hunting seals for their pelts and oil, but he had found the returns very poor, and a few years later he sold his last skins to a glue factory for seventy-five cents [$18] per hundred pounds and the oil, locally used in place of linseed oil, for twenty cents a gallon. At that point, seals and otters were no longer found in commercial numbers on the Channel Islands, and Webster turned his attentions

Anacapa Island Light, built 1912.
Courtesy of Channel Islands National Park.

Herman B. Webster (*white beard on right*) and family, ca. 1901.
Courtesy of Santa Cruz Island Foundation.

to sheep-raising. When he took over the lease of Le Mesnager in 1907 he also took on the Frenchman's approximately fifty sheep. To augment this small flock, Webster purchased another 250 sheep from his neighbors, the Caires of Santa Cruz Island.

Centered at Sheep Camp on Middle Anacapa, a rough and ready operation focused on selling wool rather than meat from its flock. The animals were moved from islet to islet on Webster's boat, the *Ana Capa*, as circumstances dictated. They were roped and bound and bundled aboard the boat, then untied and thrown over the side to swim to their new home. Webster imported shearers from the mainland in the season. Although his herd suffered from poaching by fishermen, the numbers increased to approximately five hundred head, only to decline precipitately in years of drought that made water and feed scarce.

Webster's Anacapa holding was hand-to-mouth and was centered on his five-shack residence on the middle island. This was in the same location as the Elliots from the 1880s, today marked by a small stand of eucalyptus trees. The Webster family spent summers and two winters on the island, and in

1911 Bay Webster hired a tutor and governess for his two sons and erected a tent to be their schoolhouse. Clearly a committed islander, he tried to renew his lease for twenty-five years when it expired in 1917, even though it now excluded East Anacapa. Since 1911 this had become the location of the Coast Guard–operated lighthouse. But to extend the lease for a period of more than five years would have required an act of Congress, and with the country at war, there was little question of Congress finding the time to pass such an act. Even worse for Webster, he lost his bid for the lease to Captain Ira Eaton.

Eaton, the leaseholder of land at Pelican Bay on Santa Cruz Island, where he and his wife Margaret ran a resort that catered to sailors, fishers, and film crews, held the Anacapa lease for ten years, until 1927. It provided handy storage for the bootlegged liquor that he ran into various ports on the Southern California coast after the start of Prohibition in 1919. Anacapa was near enough to his legitimate operation at Pelican Bay but at the same time out of the sight of his disapproving wife. Eaton also augmented his income by renting locations to fishermen who acted as suppliers to the Larco Brothers, operators of a Santa Barbara fish company and well-known members of the island fraternity.

After Eatons' lease expired, there were no official tenants at first, but the vacuum was quickly filled by Raymond (Frenchy) LeDreau, who moved onto West Anacapa. A native of Brittany in western France, he had studied for the priesthood, become disillusioned with the church, and gone to sea. He is said to have joined the U.S. Navy and then the U.S. merchant marine. While on leave from a merchant ship in California, he met a local woman and they had three children. She died in the 1918 flu pandemic, and in his grief Frenchy sank into a life of reclusive drinking and fishing. During Prohibition, Frenchy's income seemed to have derived mostly from bootleggers and rumrunners who used the caves of the islet or even Frenchy's chicken coop for storing their product. With his fondness for drink, Frenchy was a natural partner for the local alcohol suppliers, often taking partial payment for his services in the product itself. After the repeal of Prohibition, Frenchy stayed on, living in the largest of four board-and-batten shacks that lined the bluffs of the cove on West Anacapa that had acquired his name. These had been built in 1925 by Ventura promoters with ideas of developing a sport-fishing club on Anacapa. Frenchy made his shack more comfortable by using magazine pictures for insulation, and he created a lifestyle that suited his simple tastes. Although often short of water, which he would cadge from passing yachts or, when necessary, from a brackish seep in a nearby cave, he got by with pet cats for companionship. He had handy access to his skiff, lobster traps, and fishing gear, which ensured him a constant supply of food. Frenchy became widely known by Pacific Coast fishermen as an agreeable and welcoming recluse who enjoyed company and was always ready to trade some fresh lobster for water or something stronger to drink. A local historian writes, "In his customary red flannels and a [with] three-day stubble on his face, Frenchie would be stoking the fire from a wood pile that housed his colony of semi-wild cats. Beer and wine would be passed around. The sea stories would start and so would another day in Frenchie's Cove."[6]

Another visitor to Anacapa in 1950 saw him as a hermit who enjoyed company, saying, "We invaded his privacy.... This seemed to please him rather than perplex him. From the first he was friendly and helpful. He greeted us with all of the expressions of happiness of which a Frenchman is capable short of kissing us on the cheek. He made us feel that we had been long expected and that he was glad we had arrived."[7]

Even after the creation of the Channel Islands National Monument by president Franklin Roosevelt in 1938, LeDreau's friendliness and local knowledge allowed him to remain as the unofficial guardian of Anacapa. He lived alone for almost thirty years, rarely absenting himself from the island, and only departing permanently at the age of eighty after suffering injuries in a fall.

In the intervening years Congress had passed a statute dealing with "unused" federal properties, which included Anacapa Island. In 1939 the Lighthouse Bureau, which had nominally controlled the island since the 1850s, went out of existence, and its responsibilities were transferred to the Coast Guard. The East Anacapa lighthouse, the last new light station established on the California coast by the Lighthouse Bureau, was staffed by crews from the Coast Guard using facilities that had been constructed between 1930 and 1932.[8] The challenge of the perpendicular cliffs of East Anacapa had been overcome through the use of a heavy-lift boom, which raised a supply boat approximately thirty feet above the waterline to a custom-built cradle. It was a unique solution to the supply problem and took some getting used to. One keeper's wife, who experienced the terror of having the launch's

Frenchy LeDreau and H. Bay Webster in front of Frenchy's house, ca. 1940s.
Courtesy of Channel Islands National Park.

winch malfunction with the boat in mid-air, refused to use it again, denying herself shore leave until she left the island for good.[9]

The Coast Guard lighthouse complex eventually began to resemble a small neighborhood. A central road was flanked by stucco Mission Revival houses with red tile roofs and gardens that were set off by rows of white-painted rocks and neat fences. The usual complement was six men, some with families, on a two-year tour before moving on to another assignment. There could be between fifteen and twenty-five residents at one time. When they were not working, they occupied themselves with fishing, hunting rabbits, or searching for Chumash artifacts. Television arrived on the island in 1951, at about the same time that it arrived in most U.S. neighborhoods.[10]

In spite of the island's relative proximity to the coast, those who worked and lived on Anacapa had to be largely self-sufficient, at least for everything besides fuel and water. Three two-thousand-gallon tanks of fuel were stored in the "oil house" that formed part of the settlement. For freshwater

Boat hoist.
Courtesy of Channel Islands National Park.

storage, the Coast Guard constructed a building to protect the two large redwood water tanks that might otherwise have been vulnerable to vandals, rodents, and weather. With tall, arched windows, an arched doorway, and a circular window in a protruding gable, it was disguised as a chapel. A thirty-thousand-square-foot cement catchment basin was built behind the tank house to funnel rainwater down to the tanks. The flat surface was effective at catching rainwater, but it also proved popular with gulls and other seabirds. Because of the amount of guano they generated, the basin was only used occasionally.[11]

The two Channel Islands that made up the National Monument, Anacapa and Santa Barbara Islands, were administered from Sequoia National Park until 1957, then from San Diego for ten years, after which headquarters were established in Oxnard. During that time the Park Service flirted with the idea of opening the island to the public using a concessionaire, but in the end discussions came to nothing. In a pilot study in 1959, Frenchy's camp on West Anacapa functioned as a temporary headquarters for the Park Service, and it opened to visitors with seasonal ranger service in July. Visitor numbers rose dramatically, with people arriving on private boats and ones operated by Island Packers, the first transportation company to function as a Park Service concessionaire. With the removal of Coast Guard personnel from the light station, there was an opportunity for the NPS to take over the remaining houses, with the benefit to both government agencies. In 1962 a plan was adopted to automate the Anacapa light station. Work went ahead, and in the first phase several of the houses and other redundant facilities were demolished. The remaining houses were slated for demolition as well, but the change in custody of Anacapa found a new use for them.

Early in 1970, an agreement was reached for joint custody and use of the East Anacapa wharf and hoist facilities. After some rehabilitation work, Park Service personnel took up residence, managing the property that is owned by the Coast Guard, which continues to maintain the automated navigation aids on the island to complement their facilities at Point Mugu on the mainland.[12]

During the 1950s a series of proposals were made to the Park Service to develop Frenchy's Cove and build facilities for the public enjoyment of the island's natural features. In June 1959 the area was cleaned up and the

Coast Guard station, ca. 1950s.
Boat hoist lower left; water catchment and storage upper right.
Courtesy of Channel Islands National Park.

Coast Guard station, with east end of Santa Cruz Island in the distance.
Courtesy of Channel Islands National Park.

decades-long accumulation of debris removed. The worst of the shacks was dismantled and serviceable timber from it used to build an outhouse. The next month saw a surge in visitors, and the area showed continuous popularity thereafter, though in 1960 Anacapa still had only a seasonal ranger. In the mid-1970s the Park Service began a concerted cleanup operation and installed the first permanent ranger on the island.

As the island closest to the mainland, connected by scheduled boat trips for much of the year, Anacapa retains its popularity. Its hiking trails, visitor center, exhibits, campground, and picnic area offer opportunities for fishing, diving, snorkeling, watching the colonies of gulls and pelicans, and observing the seals and sea lions that breed on the island.

The craggy island that has beguiled small numbers of hardy residents in the past is now available to the public. Its pristine tidal pools, its carpet of spring flowers, its richly populated kelp beds, and its splendid views of the mainland and neighboring Santa Cruz Island are part of Channel Islands National Park. The "ever-changing" islets of the Chumash, with their rugged charm, provide for many visitors a welcome antidote to the crowded modernity of the mainland.

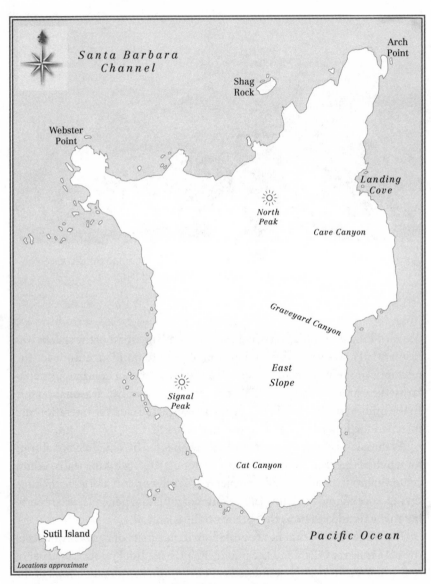

Santa Barbara Island.
Map by Gerry Krieg.

CHAPTER 7

Santa Barbara Island

Progressing generally eastward down the chain of Channel Islands from Anacapa, roughly midway between the northern and southern island groups, thirty-eight miles from the coast, is Santa Barbara Island. This somewhat triangular sea-girt mesa, the smallest of the eight islands, rises steeply from the ocean to two modest peaks. At 635 feet and 562 feet, they give Santa Barbara Island the appearance when approached by sea of a high, rounded dome. A few narrow rocky beaches are exposed at low tide, with caves, rock bridges, offshore pillars, and spray-spouting stacks creating a dramatic maritime landscape.[1] The rest of the island is edged in steep cliffs, though once scaled these open out in rolling slopes with a wide saddle between the two peaks, sometimes described as camel humps. In season it is green, with the broad grassy terraces ending abruptly at the encircling escarpment, with the sea below.

Santa Barbara Island is thought by geologists to be younger than some of the other Channel Islands. Like its neighbor Anacapa, it was formed by volcanic activity and subterranean pressures rather than the faulting along the edges of the Pacific and North American plates that characterizes its other neighbors to the northwest. Santa Barbara also differs from the northern Channel Islands in that it was never connected to the mainland or to any other island. Colonization by plants and animals began in recent geologic time—within the last several hundred thousand years. In spite of its small size, with an area of one square mile, it played an important role for Indigenous people, probably owing to the centrality of its location along the islanders' trade routes.

Situated twenty-four miles northwest of Santa Catalina, about midway between that island and San Nicolas, it appears that Santa Barbara Island was used as a convenient stopover point for inter-island travel and trade. There are archaeological indications from a number of sites that it was occupied seasonally. With average rainfall less than twelve inches a year, the island lacks basic subsistence components, such as firewood and a reliable supply of drinking water, that would make long-term settlement possible. But the rich marine life of fish, shellfish, and sea mammals would have seasonally drawn the southern island neighbors to its shores, with recent studies indicating that this first began happening at least four thousand years ago.

Santa Barbara Island got its Western name from the explorer Sebastián Vizcaíno in winter 1602, referring to the saint whose feast day is December 4. The island was seen from his ship but not visited, so we have no eyewitness confirmation of Indigenous activity there. As no grant of ownership of the island was issued by the Mexican authorities during their period of governance, title to Santa Barbara Island devolved to the U.S. government under the terms of the Treaty of Guadalupe Hidalgo of 1848. It was surveyed by the U.S. Coast and Geodetic Survey in the early 1850s, but the government did not begin actively leasing the island until early in the twentieth century.

In the meantime, fishermen and seal hunters squatted on the island at various times, building semi-permanent structures as circumstances dictated. A large feral goat population, source unknown, was said to be present by 1846, and feral house cats were abundant by the late 1890s and persisted on the island for at least half a century. One of the most noteworthy squatters was H. Bay Webster, who lived in a shack near the northwest point that today bears his name. Like others of his ilk, he was at home in the rugged circumstances that characterized the smaller islands, ready and willing to try whatever it took to eke out a living.

Most were unsuccessful. A visitor in the late 1890s noted what appeared to be the remnants of a series of failed enterprises:

> A narrow shelf where a crayfisherman has built a hut of lath and canvas, . . . a wooden trough and trying pot of cemented stone about which hangs an odor of seal oil. . . . The result [of overhunting of the pinniped population] is that the animals are now so nearly exterminated that the industry is practically abandoned. The writer saw scattered skulls and hooves of sheep, the remnants of a herd that throve until the arrival of a dry year and the grasses disappeared.[2]

As a result of government inquiries about lighthouse sites on the Channel Islands, it was discovered in 1903 that the federal government held title to the island, and at the urging of the Lighthouse Board, President Teddy Roosevelt issued an executive order in 1905 reserving the island for lighthouse purposes. Then the government set out to lease the island, with the provisos that any lease would be for five years and could be revoked by the secretary of commerce and labor and there could be no subletting. The request for sealed bids for the island lease was advertised in coastal newspapers. The winning bid, at $26 per year [$643 in 2011 equivalent], was J. G. Howland's in July 1909.

Howland was an islander born and bred whose father had run sheep on Santa Catalina during the Civil War, and he perceived opportunity in the islands. The month after he took the lease on Santa Barbara, he took an identical lease on San Nicolas Island for $151 per year [$3,580]. Although he was enjoined from subletting any part of the island, in October he accepted $125 from a Mr. C. B. Linton of Long Beach, who had a scheme for using abalone to propagate pearls. Stretching the terms of his lease even further, Howland also took money from Japanese and Chinese fishermen for rights to fish from the island. A legal controversy between Linton and Howland over the killing of a sheep on San Nicolas alerted the government to the various subletting deals negotiated by Howland, and when his lease expired on Santa Barbara Island in 1914 it was not renewed. It would appear that he only used the island lease for its fishing rights and ran no sheep on the island.

That year the government put public notices in post offices from San Francisco to San Diego, fired off a communiqué to various land companies, and published advertisements in coastal newspapers announcing the availability of a five-year lease of the island. Despite all this publicity, there was only a modest bidding contest, in which Alvin Hyder of San Pedro outbid T. D. Webster of Carpenteria, besting his rival's offer of $225 with a bid of $250 [$5,600].

Even by the extreme standards of hardworking islanders, Alvin Hyder was a standout. One of twelve children born in a log cabin in Missouri, Alvin was young when his father died, and in 1892 his mother joined the great migration to Southern California, settling in newly founded Huntington Beach. When he was fourteen Alvin went to sea, and by twenty-two he and a brother had a small boat that followed a fixed route around the lobstermen's

Alvin Hyder's boat, *Nora II,*
loading wool, ca. 1920.
*Courtesy of Santa Cruz Island
Foundation.*

camps on the islands, picking up their product for sale on the mainland. In 1904 he built a sixty-five-foot boat, the *Nora I,* using it to transport sheep among the islands and to haul fish for coastal canneries. After the *Nora* was accidentally destroyed by fire, Hyder had a new one, *Nora II,* built by a Wilmington shipyard, and he equipped her deck with sheep pens. It was the next step in his island ambitions.

On a rainy morning in January 1916, Alvin and Annie Hyder and their two children, Nora and Buster, set sail in *Nora II* for Santa Barbara Island with all the household goods they would need to build an island life, including lumber to construct a house. They started their existence there in a humble two-room structure above Landing Cove constructed the year before by Alvin and two of his brothers. Anchored to the ground by cables to prevent it blowing off the cliff, it was home to two families, with Alvin Hyder's family in one room and that of his brother Clarence in the other. They built a barn and chicken houses close by. The Hyders devised a wooden sled and track

that ran from the cove to the top of the hill where supplies were destined to be used and stored. The hauling power was supplied by their horse, Old Dan. The sled tracks were attached to the rock by metal spikes set in hand-drilled holes filled in with cement. They can still be seen along the hillside between the cove and the location where the Hyder buildings once stood.

During the Hyder years, the island population exploded, with up to fifteen people living in two houses and adjoining tents, probably the largest settlement on the island since the demise of the Indigenous population. In the first two-room house lived Alvin and Clarence, their wives, and six children. They were joined by a third brother, Cleve, who lived with his wife in the nearby second house. Another couple and a hired man who worked with the Hyders lived in tents.

Freshwater was a perennial problem, solved to a degree by the Hyders with three small reservoirs—one next to the house, a second above Cat Canyon at the south end of the island, and a third on the west side near Webster

Loading sheep on the gear sled, ca. 1918.
Courtesy of Santa Cruz Island Foundation.

Point. They used the *Nora II* to transport water from the mainland, 1,250 gallons at a time in fifty-gallon drums, pumped up to the house reservoir through a pipe that ran from the cove up the hill. The Hyders relied on rainwater to fill the other two reservoirs, though this water would be fouled by bird droppings and become less and less palatable as the dry months wore on.

Undaunted by these challenges, the Hyders put their backs into any kind of labor that would facilitate their survival. Years later, Buster Hyder described his father's work ethic: "The ol' man got up with a lantern and went to bed with a lantern. Eight hours was just getting started. He worked all the time. He was a hard working man who never knew when to stop."[3]

Using two horses and two mules pulling plows and scrapers, as well as cutting by hand, the Hyders cleared areas of ice plant and coreopsis where they could raise crops. Without the use of any motorized vehicles, they cultivated several acres of potatoes on the upper west slope near Webster Point and planted a crop of barley hay for three years toward the southern end of the island. Heartbreakingly, the potato crop failed because of excessive nitrogen in the soil from the guano of the sea birds. Then one of these hay crops was cut, baled, and sent to mainland buyers who promised to inject some cash into the Hyder economy, only to have the customers go bankrupt and fail to pay. The experiment was not repeated.

On their arrival the Hyder family found cats and mice the only animals present in enough numbers as to be pests. They had probably been introduced by fishermen and wrecked ships. The family raised domesticated farm animals such as chickens, turkeys, geese, pigs, goats, and sheep. The chickens in particular proved vulnerable to the high winds that often rake the island, and a number of them were lost when they were blown off the island and out to sea. Another food source for the family was gulls' eggs, though they took care to remove only one egg per nest so as to not threaten the gull population. Margaret Hyder took charge of schooling the six children, though she often had break off lessons to join her husband at lobster fishing.

In 1915, it appears that the war-fueled boom in the wool market led the Hyders, like their predecessor on Anacapa, Bay Webster, to purchase approximately three hundred sheep from the Caire ranch on neighboring Santa Cruz Island. The lack of a fencing requirement or maintenance on their island domain was clearly an advantage, and sheep-raising became central to their enterprise. The roundup was accomplished on foot and on horseback, gathering up the sheep along a wooden-wing fence that led them to the ranch complex. Here they were sheared and the wool packed into burlap sacks for transport to the mainland. The sheep that were to be sold were tied up and placed in the wooden sled for the precipitous trip down the hill to the cove. From there they were loaded on the *Nora II* for voyage to the mainland. In 1918 the Hyders turned some two thousand Belgian hares loose to forage, with the intention of creating a local food source, but many fell victim to the resident feral cats. Within a short time the hare population was greatly diminished, and they disappeared almost completely prior to the outbreak of World War II.

The Hyder lease expired in 1919 and the family was unsuccessful in its bid to renew it. In spite of this, the Hyders stayed on for another three years. After eight years of unremitting hard work and frustration they finally left the island in 1922. They honored the terms of the lease by tearing down their buildings and removing the lumber. They also removed all their animals to their homestead in the Cuyama Valley north of Santa Barbara, with the exception of the hares, a few sheep, and a mule, later said to have disappeared, presumably eaten by fishermen.

Cleve and Margaret Hyder's house, ca. 1918.
Courtesy of Santa Cruz Island Foundation.

The Hyders remained connected to island endeavors, but it only led to tragedy. In 1936, Alvin and Buster were loading wool bales on San Nicolas Island when a swell rolled the boat, killing Alvin. Buster eventually moved to San Pedro where he established a successful sport-fishing business, dying at the age of eighty-seven on the land homesteaded by his father decades before in the Cuyama Valley.

With the expiration of the Hyder lease, Santa Barbara Island was again advertised by the government, which sought another tenant. Two bids were received, one for $25.50 per year [$338] and the other for $1,250 [$16,300]. The latter, initially accepted, was from a group of individuals from the Venice Chamber of Commerce who revealed a plan to develop the island for public use—camping, fishing, and construction of an aquarium and biological station. Clearly this would involve considerable expense, and in return the chamber requested a twenty-five-year lease for their $1,250. The request was

Landing stage with gear sled leading up hill to the right, ca. 1940s.
Courtesy of Channel Islands National Park.

denied, no rent was paid, and the lease was revoked. Several years passed, and in 1929 a fourth lease was granted to two men, Arthur McLelland and Harry Cupit, for grazing livestock. Their enterprise did not prosper, and they only made one rent payment. In 1932 their lease was canceled. Thereafter no other leases were issued, so that in 1937, when the Channel Islands National Monument was being planned, there were no outstanding grazing leases as an impediment. The island became part of the national monument in 1938, along with Anacapa Island.

Two parcels of land on Santa Barbara Island were reserved for access to the two automated lighthouses serving shipping into and out of the Port of Los Angeles. This was now the principal West Coast port, having surpassed San Francisco in total tonnage a few years before. The first of the Santa Barbara beacons was constructed in 1928 on northwest side of the island, and in 1934 the second was built on the southwest corner. They were serviced

Funicular gear sled used by the U.S. Navy, ca. 1940s.
Courtesy of Channel Islands National Park.

at first by the Lighthouse Board and then by the Coast Guard beginning in 1939. The original wooden northwest tower was replaced by a steel structure in the 1980s, with a solar-powered beacon.

In the panic that accompanied the outbreak of World War II, after Japanese submarine attacks on shipping near Los Angeles and firing on the Ellwood Oil Field near Goleta, the two lights were extinguished as part of a general coastal blackout. From 1942 to 1946 Santa Barbara Island served as a military outpost. As jittery nerves gradually subsided, the beacons were relit in 1943. For the enlisted men assigned to the navy's Coastal Lookout Station on the island, it was an easy assignment. They served two weeks of duty on the island, followed by a week of shore leave. The men fished and tended lobster pots, and they kept chickens and rabbits, adding to the island's existing rabbit population. There was not enough water for a garden, though the navy had constructed a water tank that was filled by pumping up from supply boats. "It was a good life," one of them recalled thirty-five years later, "an enjoyable experience."[4]

Throughout the war various military buildings, barracks, and a boat-landing facility were constructed, including facilities for housing a link in the new top-secret coastal radar system. Some of these structures were removed at the end of the war, and the remaining ones became the target of extensive vandalism by casual visitors from the mainland. By the mid-1950s some of the buildings had been demolished and others were severely damaged. A fire in 1959, which burned two-thirds of the island, razed some of the remaining structures. In the 1960s the navy established a photo-tracking station as part of the Cold War militarization of the government-controlled islands. When the navy left the island in the middle of the decade, a Quonset hut remained, along with photo pads, generators, and a Jeep road. The hut was repurposed as a ranger residence for a number of years, housing personnel of the Channel Islands National Park, created in 1980, but it was replaced by a new ranger residence and visitor contact station in 1991.

The Bureau of Lighthouses had first suggested transferring Santa Barbara and Anacapa Islands to the newly formed National Park Service in 1932. Four years later the NPS responded affirmatively, and two years after that Santa Barbara Island became part of the new Channel Islands National Monument. The NPS set to work evaluating the island's resources and developing a management plan. They made various recommendations, including using the Coast Guard to patrol the islands and adjacent waters and removing the hordes of feral cats that were threatening the endemic bird and mammal populations. The need to protect the islands was further illustrated in the report of their survey trip, where NPS personnel described their encounter with an armed group of visitors who professed ignorance of the new status of the island—though the yachtsmen promised they would not go hunting there again. The authors of the report commented, "In former years, considerable slaughter of sea-lions has taken place in this vicinity and the animals need just such a sanctuary as Santa Barbara Island affords." The report further noted the results of overgrazing—the destruction of native vegetation, introduction of large numbers of noxious weeds, soil erosion, and scarring. There was also mention of high-powered-rifle shells found on the cliffs above the sea lion rookeries.[5]

After the war the monument boundaries were extended to include the offshore areas of the two islands, thereby protecting the rocky beaches, kelp beds, and offshore rocks. In 1961, a twenty-year war began to stop the depredations of the rabbits, perhaps descendants of the Belgian hares introduced by the Hyders in the 1920s and the New Zealand red rabbits introduced by Coastal Lookout Station personnel in the 1940s. Guns, traps, and poison were used, with the last being ultimately the most effective, notably delivered in the form of poisoned carrots dropped from aircraft over the island. The feral cats were also eliminated, and both the vegetation and the bird populations showed an almost immediate improvement, though it was too late for the Santa Barbara song sparrow, an endemic bird once found only on the island, now just a memory.

Vandalism, theft, littering, and illegal hunting continued through the 1950s and 60s. Park Superintendent Bill Ehorn arrived in 1974 and found the island in poor condition, without a dock, with few trails, and generally lacking amenities. With appropriate resources to clean up the island, new trails were opened, and an inventory and monitoring of the island was begun. Developments through the 1980s and 1990s included building of a residence for the island ranger, a museum, a campground, a bunkhouse for NPS staff or researchers, and interpretive exhibits of bird and submarine life. In recent years a new trail system was instituted to guide visitors around the island.

With the end of agricultural activities, visitors to this tiny remote corner of California can now see the recovery of much of the vegetation that once covered the island. Winter rains bring a vibrant palette of color to the wide saddle between the two peaks. The tree sunflower, coreopsis, endemic Santa Barbara Island live-forever, buckwheat, and chicory all add their touches of

Coast lookout and
communications tower,
early 1940s. *Courtesy of
Channel Islands National Park.*

color. Eliminating the rabbits has allowed the ground cover to spread, providing shelter for ground nesting birds. The removal of non-native predators, feral cats, has allowed those same birds to flourish. Though several endemic species of birds have been lost forever, many other populations are making a strong comeback. Today there are fourteen species that nest annually here. Of these, the horned lark, orange-crowned warbler, and house finch are subspecies that are found only on this island. Seabirds have benefited as well from the recovery of the island, and it is now one of the most important nesting sites within the Channel Islands.

The steep cliffs of Santa Barbara Island are ideal for endangered brown pelicans' nests, and they share the cliffs with three species of storm-petrels, one of the largest colonies of Xantus's murrelets, and three species of cormorants. There are eleven nesting species of seabirds here, including thousands of western gulls, some of whom make their homes alongside the six miles of trails that traverse the island. Marine mammals—sea lions, harbor seals, and northern elephant seals—are much in evidence on the shoreline. They feed in the rich kelp forests, and there are several excellent overlooks from which to view the colonies. For those who want a closer look at marine life, snorkeling in Landing Cove rewards the swimmer with the sight of brilliant orange garibaldi fish, spiny sea urchins, and colorful sea stars at home in some of the warmest and clearest waters in the park.

Like the other islands in the Channel Islands chain, Santa Barbara, through its relative isolation from the inexorable changes that have transformed mainland Southern California, has created its own special history and a singular cast of characters who felt a remarkable attachment to this tiny, cliff-girdled speck on the edge of the continent.

CHAPTER 8

San Nicolas Island

B reasting the Pacific swells sixty-one miles from the edge of the continent, wind-besieged San Nicolas Island is the farthest removed of California's seaward outliers. Its closest island neighbor, twenty-eight miles to the northeast, is tiny Santa Barbara. The constant pounding by the wind, weather, and waves has created an island that is relatively flat-topped, with a mesa-like profile on the horizon, punctuated by Jackson Hill's elevation of 907 feet.

Although it is has had almost seventy years to recover from the destruction wreaked by grazing sheep, much of the island is still sparsely covered by vegetation and extremely eroded. The southern, ocean-facing side of the island is a giant escarpment that rises from the seabed to seven hundred feet within a mile of its shoreline. The northern, coast-facing side of the island is defined by cliffs that rise as wave-cut terraces to the mesa level about four hundred feet above the sea. The island's appearance is dominated by these terraces and by grassy slopes.[1]

San Nicolas's bedrock of uplifted sandstone with very few volcanic components dates to the time of the emergence of the first "modern" mammals in the Eocene, about fifty-six to thirty-four million years ago. Strata of sediment from later periods overlay this. The intensely faulted and gently folded island features marine sedimentary rocks forming terraces composed of sandstone, shale, siltstone, and other conglomerates. Along the central portion of the island are fourteen marine terraces. Pleistocene marine shells can be found in the higher reaches, eloquent testimony to the rise and fall of sea levels with the advance and retreat of ice sheets over the millennia. San Nicolas's

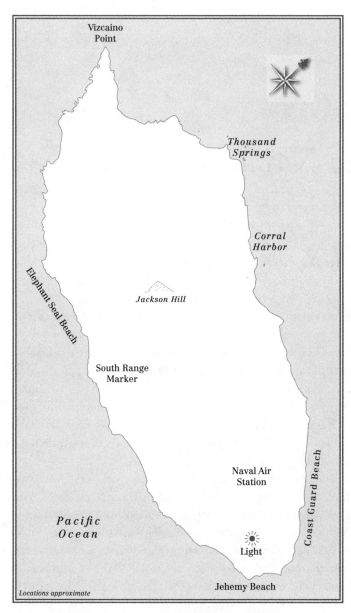

Vizcaino
Point

*Thousand
Springs*

*Corral
Harbor*

Elephant Seal Beach

Jackson Hill

South Range
Marker

Naval Air
Station

Coast Guard Beach

*Pacific
Ocean*

Light

Locations approximate

Jehemy Beach

San Nicolas Island.
Map by Gerry Krieg.

annual average rainfall is just over eight inches, giving the island a generally arid outlook and desert conditions.

For more than eight thousand years this island was home to a people generally referred to now as Nicoleños. Though they traded with the Chumash island people, they were not related to them, speaking the language of a different family, more common to the Great Basin, the Southwest, and central Mexico than coastal California. Their connections ran to the south—Santa Catalina and San Clemente Islands, and on to the Palos Verdes Peninsula. Language differences did not prevent the Nicoleños from exchanging goods based on their highly developed skills in stone and wood sculpting. The islanders also created elaborate sandstone carvings of considerable complexity, discovered in one of the most interesting archaeological sites on all the islands, the Cave of the Whales, near their settlements on the south side of the island. In this narrow sea cave that extends to a depth of about fifty feet, reproductions of at least nine killer whales in both horizontal and vertical positions were carved on stone walls, two sections of which are now among the collections of the Autry National Center in Los Angeles. Artifacts of whales and other fish carved from steatite (soapstone from Santa Catalina), including bowls and other vessels found on the island, attest to the Nicoleños originality and creativity.

Several nineteenth-century archaeologists worked on San Nicolas and removed an unknown number of artifacts to various museums. Population estimates range from two hundred to three hundred Nicoleños, although records are less complete than on the other islands because of the distance of the island from the mainland. More than five hundred archaeological sites have been mapped on the island, and the general dearth of Spanish-American artifacts leads to the conclusion that there was little or no trade with Spanish explorers or settlements.

The first historical mention of this ocean-bound twenty-two square miles was in the log of Bartolomé Ferrer, who had taken control of Cabrillo's expedition after his commander's death in January 1543. Ferrer's ship passed the island on its way southwest in February of that year, though fifty-nine years then elapsed before the island was given an official name by Sebastián Vizcaíno. This Spanish explorer and soldier of fortune happened on it in his launch, *Tres Reyes*, on December 6, 1602. Following the custom of naming locations after saints' days, it was named for Saint Nicholas of Myra.

Although San Nicolas escaped official notice of Spain, Mexico, and even the missionaries for more than two centuries, the island population did not evade the attentions of early-nineteenth-century American and Russian hunters of the much-valued sea otter. In 1814 a vessel owned by the Russian American Company, the *I'lmena*, brought a group of Kodiak hunters from Sitka. The Nicoleños were no match for the well-armed northerners doing the bidding of their Russian masters. In one of the more bloodthirsty episodes in this unsavory chapter of island history, after one of their number was killed by a Nicoleño, the Russian-led Kodiaks retaliated by slaughtering all the islanders they could lay their hands on.

Spanish authorities attempted to assert their rights over the sea otter trade in 1815, arresting the Russian Boris Tasarov for hunting in their territorial waters, but by that time he and his Aleut minions had taken almost one thousand otters, largely destroying the local population. The Alaskan otter and seal hunters had brought down the curtain on one of the key constituents of the local fauna and put an end to approximately ten thousand years of island human civilization in the bargain.

The year 1812 saw the beginning of the Mexican revolt against their colonial overlords, which culminated in Mexico's independence in 1821. The Spanish Crown had been the main protector of the California missions, whose extensive landholdings were eyed enviously by local landowners. The change in government brought about the secularization of the missions and the stripping of much of church's lands. During the heyday of the missions, between 1763 and the early nineteenth century, Franciscan missionaries enticed local Indians into their compounds, and many islanders followed suit. This semi-voluntary emigration combined with the ravages of introduced diseases, which spread even more quickly when large numbers of Indians were forced to live in close proximity within the missions, worked to largely depopulate the islands. The Indigenous populations of San Miguel, Santa Rosa, and Santa Cruz were removed to Mission Santa Barbara, and those of the southern islands—San Clemente, Santa Catalina, and San Nicolas—were taken to the pueblo of Los Angeles and Mission San Gabriel. As on the northern islands, the earthquake of 1812 convinced many Native people that they should make the move to the mainland. The island inhabitants, whose reasonably complex way of life was for the most part sustainable and communitarian, were caught between the arguably benign intentions of the Franciscans, whose mission was the saving of souls, and the markedly commercial aims of the hunters and smugglers of the modern era of globalized trade, whose sole aim was profit. The result for the Nicoleños was disaster. Of the hundreds living on San Nicolas from time immemorial, fewer than two dozen remained in the second decade of the nineteenth century.

The Franciscan holdings on the mainland were in much-reduced circumstances by 1835 when the Franciscans became acquainted with the plight of the few remaining Nicoleños. Most sources tell us that the Franciscans chartered the schooner aptly named *Peor es Nada* (Better Than Nothing) to bring the last remaining islanders to the mainland and the "civilizing" influence of the mission. Captain Charles Hubbard and his crew managed to convey to the Indians that they should leave their home and go to the mission where they would find safety and plenty to eat. Seemingly the entire population—now greatly reduced—took up the offer, though the crew reported that one lone woman and possibly her child had remained on the island. This set in motion the legendary story of "The Lone Woman of San Nicolas."[2]

Shortly after removing the population of San Nicolas to the mainland, the *Peor es Nada*, with a cargo of timber for San Francisco, foundered off the Golden Gate. According to George Nidever, the pioneer hunter, trapper, and sailor, whose name figures in the history of several of the islands, after the loss of the *Peor es Nada* several vessels called at the island but did not find any Native people. Nidever gives voice to the local assumption that the woman had fallen victim to disease or predatory hunters. The years passed and interest waned, though the story never died, and in 1850 a Franciscan of the Santa Barbara Mission offered a reward of $200 [$5,760 in 2011 equivalent] to a local man, Tom Jefferies, to find the woman and her child and bring them to the mainland. Nidever and his ilk continued their hunting and fishing activities on the islands, including San Nicolas. One day in 1853 on a trip when they had dedicated themselves to searching the island, they found on the west end of the island a windbreak made of whale ribs and sticks, covered with brush. A woman was inside, clothed in a dress of skins and feathers. She offered them some wild onions she had roasted. With their encouragement, she gathered her few possessions and followed them down to their boat. After completing their otter-hunting endeavor, they conveyed her to Santa Barbara where her appearance caused a local sensation.

Nidever took her into his house, where she lived and was available for the curious and interested to observe, entertaining visitors with singing and dancing. The woman from San Nicolas was the talk of Santa Barbara, given new clothes that she accepted with enthusiasm, and communicated with sign language and pantomime, because after eighteen years, no one could be found who could speak her language, which was very different from that of the Santa Barbara Chumash. This gave rise to later speculation that she might have arrived on San Nicolas as a result of a shipwreck or been left behind there by Aleuts, and that she was not a native Nicoleña. Unfortunately, her motives for remaining on the island can only be speculated upon. She exhibited a childlike delight in foods and sights that were completely unfamiliar to her, such as people on horseback. In a throwback to the days of the initial Aztec encounters with the horses of Cortez, she is said to have first seen them as immensely tall four-footed men. Her enjoyment of new foods was to prove her undoing. After almost two decades of subsisting on birds, eggs, fish, abalone, and seal blubber, she lasted but seven weeks with her new diet of fruit, meat, and vegetables before her system was unable to cope. According to Nidever she took sick from eating too much fruit and succumbed to some internal disorder. Given the name Juana María by the Franciscans after her death, she was buried in the Santa Barbara Mission Cemetery, where it could be said that she finally joined the rest of her island family.

The story of "The Lone Woman of San Nicolas" was almost immediately wreathed in legend. Her dress was exhibited to the public in San Francisco and from there was said to have been sent to the Vatican Museums, though there are no records showing that it was ever received there. Other artifacts were sent to the California Academy of Sciences, where they were displayed to much popular interest, but they were later destroyed in the earthquake and fire of 1906. The story of Juana María continued to be told over the decades, fueling the public's continuing fascination with the general theme of the castaway on a desert island.

It was the first instance of a popular focus on the more romantic aspects of the islands of California. The island setting, as a stereotype of an unspoiled paradise in which castaways are forced to become self-sufficient and create a new society, demonstrated its hold on the popular imagination. Islands have been the setting for fiction and drama for almost one thousand years, and this tradition continued throughout the nineteenth and twentieth centuries as semi-fictionalized accounts of Juana María appeared at regular intervals in popular magazines. Scott O'Dell's 1960 novel, *Island of the Blue Dolphins*, which was made into a Universal Pictures film of the same name (1964), has perpetuated the theme, acquainting generations of children with the legend of Juana María.

This interest in the "Lone Woman" also sparked scientific interest in San Nicolas Island. From the 1860s onward the island was visited by French and American archaeologists who noted the evidence Indigenous civilization and collected a large number of artifacts. They published their findings in the scientific journals and popular press of the day, like the *Overland Monthly*, whose readers were treated to the following description of Nicoleño burial practices.

> The mode of burial on this island is different from that previously investigated. The bodies rest in distinct graves by themselves, lying on their backs, feet drawn up, and arms folded over the chest. . . . The skeletons, as a rule, were facing the east, although other directions were observed. Some show signs of having been buried in matting coated with asphaltum. Most of the skeletons and implements are laid bare by the winds.[3]

Natural historians noted the native island fauna, including night lizards, snails, and island foxes. Others reported on the sunflowers, buckwheat, and a species of box thorn now possibly extinct. Today, after decades of extensive sheep grazing in the nineteenth and twentieth centuries, almost half the plants found on the island are ones that were introduced—a higher percentage than that found on any other Channel Island.[4]

In 1857, about four years after the "rescue" of Juana María, Nidever returned to San Nicolas to shoot the feral dogs that had been her companions. The removal of these descendants of animals kept by the Native inhabitants was judged necessary to make the island safe for stocking with sheep.[5] There is no record of Nidever actually introducing sheep onto San Nicolas, however, although, as we have seen, a few years later he was running flocks on San Miguel.

In 1858 Captain Martin Kimberly filed a claim for 160 acres in the vicinity of Corral Harbor on San Nicolas, which he marked with several white-pine posts, an adobe house, and a corral. Kimberly was the first of a series of ambitious stockmen operating under various claims to the island but without actual title. As with Santa Barbara, San Miguel, and Anacapa Islands, ownership of San Nicolas resided with the federal government, which turned something of a blind eye to activities there until the twentieth century. The

Corral Harbor, 1922.
Courtesy of U.S. Navy.

net effect of animal husbandry on this dry windswept island was the same as on the others. As early as the 1870s a visiting archaeologist wrote, "The vegetation on the island is like that of San Miguel, ruined by overstocking it with sheep, which are here found in like starving condition.... The shifting sand has almost buried the adobe house, and its old inmate, the superintendent of the [Pacific Wool Growing] Company."[6]

Presumably the superintendent avoided being buried alive, but twenty years later botanist Blanche Trask reported, "There is an old house built of stones yet standing, half snowed-in by sand, at Corral Harbor. At the east end there are a cabin, a barn, shearing sheds, a cistern, and a platform which drains its rainwater into a reservoir. All these improvements are due to the once ambitious ranchmen who seem now to have abandoned the sheep; about 500 are occasionally seen."[7]

With the coming of the twentieth century, the government began to take a more businesslike approach to the island, leasing it in five-year terms to various individuals, some with the aim of placing fishermen on the island, others to attempt vague development plans. In 1919 the lease went to Ed Vail. As we have seen, the Vail family removed most of the sheep from Santa Rosa

Old ranch buildings gradually being buried by sand, 1930s.
Courtesy of U.S. Navy.

when they bought the island ranch there in 1901–1902. But Ed Vail was ready to have a go at sheep ranching on San Nicolas, petitioning the Lighthouse Bureau administration at one point to allow him a twenty-five-year lease to justify a major investment, a request that was turned down. This was just as well because by 1930 little more than 40 percent of the original fourteen thousand acres remained covered by vegetation. Today the island's flora consists of grasses, shrubs, and some introduced trees. San Nicolas is the least diverse of the California islands, ecologically and biotically. Lack of diverse habitats, distance from the mainland, and its small size are all contributory factors.[8]

In 1930, the decades-long antagonism between the sheep ranchers of the islands and fishermen sailing out of San Pedro and other Southern California ports exploded into fatal confrontation. Ranchers and island owners were convinced that fishermen were rustling sheep from remote locations on the islands and selling them at the same time they landed their marine catch on the mainland. On San Nicolas a young ranch hand, eighteen-year-old Milton Prentice, spied a Yugoslav immigrant fisherman in the distance and was convinced that he had caught a criminal in the act. Taking aim with his rifle, Prentice got Steve Seremenko in his sights and shot him. Prentice was

(*above*) Ranchers, 1926.
Courtesy of U.S. Navy.

(*left*) San Nicolas Light, 1934.
Courtesy of U.S. Navy.

(*opposite*) Ranching families, 1933.
Back, left to right: Margaret and Roy
Agee, Edna and Lyman Elliott,
Agnes Mundon, Ed Rucker,
unidentified friend, teacher
Winona McAllister; *front, with
dogs*: Shorty Daily and Frances
Agee. *Courtesy of Santa Cruz Island
Foundation.*

arrested for murder. Ranchers from other islands testified for the defense
at the murder trial, and there was a large dossier in the hands of the Santa
Barbara County sheriff with complaints from other islanders about illegal
plundering of their herds. The trial judge heard mitigating testimony from
the owners of San Miguel and Santa Cruz Islands about the losses they
had suffered from "Austrian" fishermen. (The territory that would become

Yugoslavia had until recently been part of the Austro-Hungarian Empire.)
Nevertheless, Prentice was found guilty and sentenced to San Quentin, but
he later received a pardon from the state governor.

Just before the end of Vail's third five-year lease, the navy (which had
taken over administration of the island on executive order of president
Hoover) constructed an airfield and a weather station. Vail relinquished
his lease in 1934, but his successors, Roy Agee and L. P. Elliot continued to
run sheep until 1941, when the navy revoked the agreement. During World
War II, San Nicolas Island was designated a naval auxiliary air station and
was used to train carrier air support units and specialized airfield construction units (ACORNS) for the island war in the Pacific. The facility boasted
a six-thousand-foot runway and a complement of more than four hundred
officers and enlisted sailors. San Nicolas was considered as a possible test
site for the Manhattan Project, which developed the first atomic bomb, but
fortunately lost out in favor of White Sands, New Mexico.

In the new age of guided missiles after the war, the navy decided on a
West Coast location for much of its testing of pilotless aircraft and missiles.
For its command and control center it chose Point Mugu, sixty-five miles

Members of the McWaters and Agee families
with Roy Agee's truck-frame, four-horse wagon, ca. 1937.
Courtesy of Santa Cruz Island Foundation.

northwest of Los Angeles. The distinctiveness and remoteness of San Nicolas Island were a major factor in this choice. The distance from the coast made it an ideal location for the placement of radar and telemetry equipment to observe test firing of the weapons launched from Point Mugu. Initially the navy spent $5 million upgrading its island facilities, and on October 1, 1946, San Nicolas became an auxiliary landing field of Point Mugu.

Today, after an investment of tens of millions of dollars, San Nicolas is an integral part of the Naval Air Warfare Center Weapons Division. In the intervening years, the runway has been improved and extended to ten thousand feet, capable of landing planes as big as the C-5 air transport. The base, now home to approximately two hundred personnel, boasts the recreational assets of any mainland navy base, with courts for tennis and racquetball, a gym, Jacuzzi, movie theater, and bowling alley. Besides radar and telemetry facilities, the island also has one target site used in missile testing. The navy appreciates that because of its isolated environment and shoreline characteristics, San Nicolas Island is also ideal for conducting littoral warfare tests as well as providing an excellent setting for classified operations far removed from public scrutiny.[9] The island is closed to the public, though limited scientific access is permitted with prior clearance.

In the twenty-first century, whether the navy is writing the island's epitaph or preserving San Nicolas for posterity is an open debate. A pessimistic assessment was made by island expert Adelaide Doran in the 1980:

> While California and the rest of the nation have grown and developed phenomenally in two hundred years, little San Nicolas has ironically seen the opposite trend. Gone are the otter, gone is most of the plant life, gone are the Indians. White men, sheep, wind and snails have inflicted multitudinous wounds. Now only the Navy, maybe the little fox, the white-footed mouse, the sand lizard and our winged friends can give a future accounting of "Dying San Nicolas."[10]

On the other hand, the reintroduction of the otter in 1987 illustrates a more positive view. Recognizing that marine mammals found the distant shores of San Nicolas congenial, and with the aim of safeguarding the California sea otter population, the U.S. Fish and Wildlife Service decided that a backup population of otters should be created on the island, safe from the threats of mainland pollution. Shortly thereafter, between 1987 and 1991, 139 otters were transported to San Nicolas, provoking a storm of complaints from local abalone and lobster fishers, whose livelihood was now threatened by the crustacean-loving mammals. An unforeseen complication was that most of the otters disdained their new neighborhood in favor of returning to their original habitat on the Central California coast. Eight years later only about 10 percent remained on the island, but they were reproducing, raising hopes that they will reestablish the colony that thrived there for thousands of years before the arrival of globalization in the form of hunters supplying the Asian market for luxurious furs.[11] The hopes seem well placed, as there are now over fifty otters seen regularly around the island.

Another recent bit of good news concerns the successful effort to eradicate the feral cats that were threatening the local populations of cormorants, gulls, and an endangered species of night lizard native to only three of the Channel Islands: San Nicolas, Santa Barbara, and San Clemente. After many months of planning, it took a year and a half to humanely trap all the cats on the island, a process completed by the end of 2011. The operation involved six government agencies, biologists, a team of researchers, and a retired bobcat hunter. It required 250 custom-built padded restraints with sensors that flashed computer alerts to researchers when they were sprung by unsuspecting felines. Ultimately the traps caught sixty-three cats, which were then airlifted to a specially prepared refuge near San Diego. At an ultimate cost of $3 million, these descendants of navy household pets cost in the region of $48,000 each to remove, but from the San Nicolas perspective of protecting endangered species, the money, most of it from private sources, could be judged well spent.[12]

The marine habitat around the island meanwhile seems healthy. In the waters surrounding San Nicolas, divers continue to enjoy exploring the thick kelp forests, which are home to a typically diverse Channel Islands mixture of southern warm-water fish, northern cold-water fish, and sea mammals. On balance, it seems that the navy has been a good steward of its island kingdom. In the 1990s, it undertook a massive cleanup operation, disposing of tons of waste that had been deposited in the years of its tenure on the island. So, in spite of the depredations of decades of livestock-raising and weapons testing, the remoteness of San Nicolas continues to make it a site of special scientific and evolutionary interest and a haven for wildlife, with much to teach us about the interaction between humans and nature and the capacity for recovery of isolated island environments.

(above) Final sheep removal, 1943.
Courtesy of U.S. Navy.

(below) Testing Nike-Deacon rocket, 1957.
Courtesy of U.S. Navy.

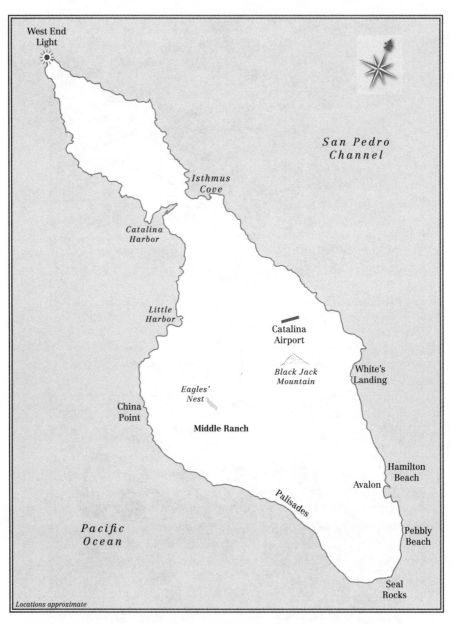

West End
Light

*San Pedro
Channel*

*Isthmus
Cove*

*Catalina
Harbor*

*Little
Harbor*

Catalina
Airport

*Black Jack
Mountain*

White's
Landing

*Eagles'
Nest*

China
Point

Middle Ranch

Hamilton
Beach

Avalon

Palisades

*Pacific
Ocean*

Pebbly
Beach

Locations approximate

Seal
Rocks

Santa Catalina Island.
Map by Gerry Krieg.

CHAPTER 9

Santa Catalina Island

Fabled in song and story, Santa Catalina is, after Alcatraz, probably the best known of all California's islands. Of the southern Channel Islands, it is closest to the coast and has the most visitors, with daily ferry and air service from the Southern California mainland to the towns of Avalon and Two Harbors. The former has a permanent population of nearly four thousand, slightly more than the highest estimate of the pre-contact Native population, making Catalina by far the most populous of all the islands. Avalon is the only urban development on any California Channel island, and as many as ten thousand visitors may arrive there on a busy summer day, part of almost a million visitors a year the island hosts. Some islanders differentiate Santa Catalina as the safety valve of the Channel Islands, absorbing visitors who want a sophisticated and accommodating island experience without the challenges of the more isolated, largely unpopulated islands. Santa Catalina is tied to the mainland in a way that the other islands are not—very much a part of Los Angeles County, whose sheriff, fire, and building inspection departments provide their services in Avalon, working with the local mayor, city council, and city manager.

There is much about disembarking in Avalon that is like stepping ashore into a California beach town of the 1940s or 1950s. And though there is plenty that suggests that Catalina is moving with the times, there is also a generous helping of the charm and graciousness that has delighted visitors from the first days of tourism—from the boat harbor, enclosed by the semicircular corniche, and the beach-town architecture of the 1930s, to the dominant rotunda of the casino at the far end of the bay. But Avalon is not all of Santa Catalina—it is more like its sunny, welcoming face presented to the casual visitor over from Los Angeles or Orange County for the day or the weekend. With an average rainfall of about twelve and a half inches per year and summer temperatures in the seventies and winter temperatures in the sixties, Catalina is defined by the sea that creates this moderate version of the Southern California mainland climate. The island is ten or more degrees cooler in summer than the nearby mainland, and it is warmer to about the same extent in winter. This has made Santa Catalina a popular destination with yachters, fishers, and vacationers for more than a century. Catalina Harbor, on the island's south side, one of its eighteen bays and coves, is the only natural, deep, all-weather harbor between San Diego and San Francisco.[1]

The island was created more than one hundred million years ago when the small Farallon Plate slid eastward toward the North American Plate. In a slow-motion collision beneath the sea, the North American Plate rose as the Pacific Plate drove the Farallon beneath it. The debris scraped off by the collision formed what would become Santa Catalina Island, a twenty-one-mile-long ridge of mountains extending from northwest to southeast, varying from a half mile to eight miles wide. About twenty million years ago the last of the Farallon Plate slipped under the North American Plate. Five million years of fiery volcanic and hydrothermal activity followed. The final geological stage in the process of island building ended about five million years ago. The block of the earth's crust on which Catalina rests moved about 156 miles north from its location near the current Mexican border while being subjected to vertical movement and changes in sea level. The end of the last ice age saw the island shoreline contract to near where it is today, but a mile or more seaward from the island and eighty feet beneath the surface is the evidence of an ancient shoreline—a large wave-cut terrace with valleys once carved by streams. The violence of the island's birth created rock of character and beauty, visible on Santa Catalina today, and on the face stones, sourced from island quarries, of some of Los Angeles's early landmark buildings.[2]

As with the other Channel Islands, Santa Catalina's marine climate and proximity to the mainland has created a special ecosystem—a living laboratory demonstrating a changing tapestry responding to variations in climate, introductions of animals and plants, extinctions of native species, and conservation efforts. The seas around the island comprise a transitional zone where the cold, nutrient-rich waters of the California Current mix with warmer southern waters to support a startling diversity of marine life, with kelp beds that provide a home to a variety of shallow-water sea creatures, skates, rays, and game fish. There are also sizable populations of seals and sea lions and several species of cetaceans—whales, dolphins, and porpoises. These last often race out to meet incoming ferries and accompany them back into Avalon Bay, regularly enough to make visitors think they are on the payroll.

Santa Catalina has been a Mecca for more than 150 years, not only for tourists but for scientists, archaeologists, botanists, and anthropologists as well. Among the first was Thomas Nuttall, who travelled on the Boston-based *Pilgrim*. Richard Henry Dana, who was working on the ship, noted that the crew "christened Nuttall, 'Old Curious,' from his zeal for curiosities."[3] This first naturalist was followed by a parade of scientific collectors. In the nineteenth century two of the foremost were the historian, publicist, and big-game fisherman Charles Frederick Holder and the "scientific discoverer" Luella Blanche Trask. Holder played a formative role in the early development of Catalina tourism, and the formidable Mrs. Trask, who made her home on the island for several years, performed extensive field work in the 1890s and 1900s, though the principal exhibits of her work were destroyed in the San Francisco earthquake and fire of 1906. It is reported that on a number of occasions she walked from Avalon to the isthmus and back in the same day, a distance of thirty miles, presumably gathering specimens in her travels, though people who know that road are inclined to be a bit skeptical.[4]

One of the great scientific attractions of the island has always been its variety of flora and fauna. Among the Channel Islands, Catalina has a diversity of land animals only equaled by Santa Cruz Island. The cause is the proximity of the outflows from the Los Angeles, San Gabriel, and Santa Ana Rivers. In the heavy floods occurring every three to five decades on the mainland, there is an increased probability of lizards, snakes, or small mammals rafting to the island on debris carried down to the ocean. Of the eight Channel Islands, snakes are found only on Santa Catalina, Santa Cruz, and Santa Rosa Islands, with Catalina distinguished as the only island with a rattlesnake.[5]

A total of 606 identified plants have been found growing wild on Santa Catalina; 421 are indigenous, and 185 were introduced.[6] The native plants present today are likely to have arrived by over-water dispersal, as the geology of the island indicates total submergence sometime during the Pleistocene (ca. three hundred thousand years ago).

Much of the plant life of Catalina Island is special—rare and of biological importance. Although many types of flora that grow here are also found on the other Channel Islands, eight exist only on Catalina. Highlights are the Catalina manzanita, Catalina live-forever, and Catalina mahogany. More than 10 percent of the native flora is very rare, having not been recently observed or collected.

A simple six-mile hike starting on the western headlands takes one through distinctively diverse plant communities, from maritime desert scrub to moist oak woodland, by way of coastal sage scrub, grassland, and chaparral environments. This concentrated version of habitats found on the mainland offers unusual and sometimes unique species and subspecies, at home in the cool, moist, Northern California–like climate. Having been ravaged by imported animals, chiefly goats and pigs in the nineteenth and twentieth centuries, the grasses in particular are now staging a strong comeback with the encouragement of the Catalina Conservancy.[7]

As on the other Channel Islands, Santa Catalina flora and fauna give us a glimpse of the past and a chance to understand how ecosystems and evolutionary processes operate. The example of the destruction of the island's otter colony by hunters in the early nineteenth century demonstrates the interconnectedness of marine communities. With the decline of the local otters came a rise in population of their principal food source—sea urchins. The sea urchins' food—kelp—decreased. Fish and other creatures that lived and bred in the kelp faced an impaired habitat to which they were forced to adapt.

On land, fauna like harvest mice, deer mice, and Catalina island foxes (whose greatest threat is now cars) show how animals' size and coloring adapt and mutate in island environments. Other examples of unexpected consequences of the introduction of exotic fauna, from ants to bison, all point to the difficulty of managing a fragile island ecosystem, but recent decades have shown how protecting it is extremely worthwhile.[8] The exotic herbivores left on islands, such as sheep, goats, burros, and rabbits, undergo population explosions in the absence of their natural predators and diseases. The result is overgrazing of the island's vegetation, causing the extinction not only of plant species but also of the birds and mammals that depend on them.

Though the origin of some of the more intrusive grazing animals is identifiable, the arrival of goats on Catalina is uncertain. It now appears that they were first brought to the island early in the nineteenth century by traders who avoided paying full import duties in California by leaving a portion of their cargo on Santa Catalina, returning later to smuggle the rest of it, untaxed, to the mainland. Well established by the middle of the nineteenth century, with a population high in the twentieth century of twenty thousand, these four-footed eating machines have destroyed or altered much of the original island vegetation. Currently the number of goats is down to near one thousand in the canyons and ravines near Avalon.

A bison herd is the legacy of the filming of the 1924 John Ford movie *The Vanishing American*, based on the novel by Zane Grey, when fourteen of the animals were brought over for the filming. The herd is now kept at a level of about five hundred and can be seen in locations around the island. Wild pigs were introduced in the 1930s, ostensibly to curb the rattlesnakes, and they have added to the damage caused by goats and bison. Large feral populations are still present, numbering about three thousand in the area around Avalon. They are said to have been instrumental in the disappearance of forty-eight indigenous and eighteen introduced species of the island's flora.[9] Bald eagles were wiped out in the 1950s, a victim of DDT, but reintroduced in the 1980s, and they are now much the presence they once were when Eagle Reef, Eagle Rock, and Eagle's Nest were named.[10]

Some parts of Santa Catalina Island were inhabited by ancient cultures as many as 6,800 years ago. The people of recent prehistory we now call the Tongva (or Gabrieleño, associated with the Mission San Gabriel Arcángel, founded 1771) were encountered by the Spanish explorers in mid-sixteenth century. Like their neighbors on San Nicolas and San Clemente, the islanders were related to the Shoshonean peoples widely scattered throughout the Southwest and to the Tongva people of the Los Angeles Basin who were present on the mainland about five hundred years ago. The distinct island culture crystallized about five hundred years before the arrival of the Spanish explorers. At Avalon, the Isthmus and Little Harbor were major villages containing as many as five hundred people each. Smaller village sites near sources of water were scattered across the island. Population estimates for the whole island vary between five hundred and twenty-five hundred.[11] Using their local version of the lashed plank tomol, called a *ti'at*, they navigated back and forth between their villages and the mainland coast. In good conditions it was said that they could make the crossing in four hours. Early Spanish descriptions recall the "graceful, easy style" of the local fishermen. This skilled and handsome people survived and prospered on a diet of plant and marine foods. For necessities not present on their island, they traded objects with the mainland and other islands, such as the bowls, jars, and ornaments made of island soapstone, at which they excelled in carving.[12]

The first contact between the Gabrieleños and the Spanish was in the fall of 1542, probably on the broad protected beach that is now known as White's Landing, northeast of Avalon. The Gabrieleños called the island Pumu or Pemú'nga and referred to themselves as Pimungans or Pipimares.[13] A contemporary account recalls the first contact. "As the boat came near, there issued a great quantity of Indians from among the bushes and grass, yelling and dancing and making signs that [the Spanish] should not be afraid." There was the predictable gift of "beads and little presents," and then the Spanish sailors "went ashore and were secure, they and the Indian women and all."[14] "Secure" seems a euphemism for what is likely to have transpired, given the welcoming nature of the island Indians and the fact that the Spanish had been at sea for some time.

After the customary ceremonies of greeting between Cabrillo and the Gabrieleño chiefs, the bemused locals were informed that they were now subjects of the king of Spain. From the Natives' point of view, this encounter with the wider world had the benefit of supplying metal tools, which they incorporated into their soapstone carving, but they had no way of knowing that accompanying the superior technology of the pale-skinned sailors on their white-winged boats were the diseases that would tip their culture into crisis.

Cabrillo, having noted that the climate was "*delicioso*," departed northeastward, sighting other islands, but the exact course of his journey after his encounter with the Native people of Catalina is subject to some debate. It is known that he died after a shattered shinbone suffered in an accident in late December 1542. Although he has a monument on San Miguel, and traditionally he is said to have overwintered there, a growing body of opinion holds that he actually chose to stay on Santa Catalina in the winter of 1542–43.

Cabrillo is given credit for discovering Catalina for the Spanish and gave the island its first Spanish name, San Salvador, the name of his flagship. From time to time in his log he referred to both Catalina and San Miguel Islands as Isla de Posesión, giving rise to an apparent misinterpretation of where his accident and subsequent death occurred.

More than ten years passed before the island was again mentioned in the log of one of the yearly Manila galleons commanded by Sebastían Cermeño. Although he did not stop, Cermeño managed to obtain food from the Gabrieleños on the island. No Europeans are recorded landing there for another sixty years after Cabrillo, though it is assumed in some quarters that the yearly trans-Pacific Manila galleons must have made occasional contact with the islanders. When Sebastián Vizcaíno arrived on the feast day of Catherine of Alexandria in 1602, following the custom of the time he gave her name to the island, Santa Catalina.

Santa Catalina did not play a part in the colonizing efforts of the Spanish that began in 1769, but the indirect influences of new diseases and the destruction of their hunting, fishing, and trading way of life led to the demise of the Native population. Plans for a mission on the island were abandoned after a measles epidemic killed two hundred Gabrieleños. Scarce freshwater and lack of government support doomed the idea. In addition, the local otter colony had attracted the unwelcome attentions of heavily armed Aleut hunters transported on Russian ships. Fears for the islanders' safety provided another motive for their removal to mission San Gabriel, although records show only a few arrivals from the island. In any event, between social disruption of their way of life, the ravages of disease, and the aggressive Aleuts, it seems that there were no Gabrieleños left on the island by the end of the mission period in 1832.[15]

During the Spanish and Mexican periods, 1769–1848, Santa Catalina was noteworthy largely as a center for smuggling. According to Richard Henry Dana's memoir *Two Years before the Mast*, American traders and even upstanding naturalized Mexican citizens like Don Abel Stearns would avoid the payment of customs duties by hiding their cargoes on the island, paying tax on a small amount of goods that they landed at Los Angeles and then reloading the cargo and proceeding up the coast to the bigger markets of Monterey and San Francisco Bay. In the case of Stearns, there was even a building on Santa Catalina that functioned as an adjunct to his warehouse at San Pedro. Catalina was also a handy place for Boston sailors to salt down the hides they had bought from the Californios.[16] This tradition continued after California achieved statehood, with Santa Catalina used to hide various sorts of contraband, including Chinese immigrants in the 1850s and liquor during Prohibition—in the 1920s and early 1930s.

Little is known about the first island residents who followed the Gabriele-ños at end of the mission period, other than the fact that there were a series of squatters who called it home at various times. One of the best known was Samuel Prentiss, who built a house at Johnson's Landing in the mid-1820s and made a living fishing, hunting, and selling firewood for the next thirty years. Early California pioneer George Yount searched for gold on Santa Catalina in the 1830s, responding to persistent rumors of a mother lode, but like many others he went away empty-handed.

The last Mexican governor of California, Pío Pico, ceded the island in 1846 to Thomas Robbins of Santa Barbara, allegedly in exchange for a fast horse on which to flee from advancing U.S. troops. The title to the island changed hands many times during the following years. There was a gold rush centered on the isthmus in the early 1860s, a fever that was cooled by the establishment of a U.S. Army garrison there. Its barracks building still stands as the home of the Isthmus Yacht Club. Only small amounts of gold were ever found. One of the officers of the garrison reported that the population of the island was about one hundred, about half of them miners who "entertain highly exalted views of the vastness of [Santa Catalina's] mineral wealth." Lt. Col. James Curtis, in command of the garrison, estimated the sheep population at fifteen thousand and the number of goats at eight thousand.[17]

Four years after his "purchase" of Catalina, Robbins sold the island to Jose María Covarrúbias for $10,000 [$297,000 in 2011 equivalent].[18] Covarrúbias in turn sold it to Albert Packard of San Francisco in 1853. A series of owner-ship changes and divisions ensued until James Lick, a Pennsylvania manu-facturer and philanthropist, began buying up the various interests in 1864. By 1867 he was the single owner of the island, and before he died Lick created a trust that held title to the island.

In 1887 the Lick trustees sold the island to George Shatto, a land specu-lator from Michigan, for $200,000 [$4.9 million]. He created an echo of the real estate boom that was roiling in Southern California, subdividing an area of Catalina on a charming bay where its principal city would be located. Shatto laid out streets and auctioned lots for between $150 [$3,660] and $2,000 [$49,000]. Residents of the burgeoning city of Los Angeles were encouraged to buy tent sites and lots for summer cottages. The summer of 1888 kicked off with Shatto's two steamers shuttling passengers between the mainland and the island. His newly built, luxurious Hotel Metropole became a gathering place for a growing class of wealthy Angelenos, setting Catalina's course to become a world-renowned retreat for the wealthy and celebrated in the 1920s and 1930s.[19]

But what to call the town that was rising quickly around the bay? After running through a series of names—the Indians had called it the Bay of Seven Moons—Lick had given it the name of Timm's Landing, after an early settler who lived there. George Shatto was inclined toward Shatto City, but fortunately it was finally called Avalon at the suggestion of his sister. She had been much moved by Tennyson's recently published story of the legend of King Arthur and felt that such a beautiful place deserved a more lyrical name than Shatto City. To the relief of residents then and since, Avalon it became.[20]

While the Southern California land boom kept pace with Shatto's large investment costs, his finances were reasonably secure, but when the depression of 1892 caused the stream of new investors and visitors to dry up, Shatto was unable to service his debts. The Lick trust foreclosed in 1892 and resold the island to William, Joseph, and Hancock Banning. These were the sons of the stagecoach king, the dashing Captain Phineas Banning, who made his fortune connecting Southern California with Northern California and other states of the Southwest. The Bannings paid almost $129,000 for the island [$3.3 million] and transferred the title to the newly formed Santa Catalina Island Company. By the turn of the century Avalon hosted a summer population of around three thousand and a permanent population of around one hundred. A decade later, the summer population had more than tripled to ten thousand, and the permanent population had increased fivefold. Young upper-middle-class Angelenos of the era remembered Avalon as a golden part of their youth. The young men enjoyed elaborate encampments, and after days spent sport fishing or hiking the trails to pristine beaches, they joined their girlfriends for dancing at the pavilion by the beach, under the glow of Japanese lanterns.[21]

The Bannings expanded the Hotel Metropole and the steamer-wharf, and, encouraged by Charles Holder—island publicist, writer, and sports

Swimmers, 1890s, with Little Sugarloaf Rock in background.
Courtesy of Catalina Island Museum.

fisherman—built an aquarium, created the Pilgrim Gambling Club (for men only), and improved the standard of Avalon's beach by erecting a seawall and adding covered benches or "spoonholders." They built a bathhouse, added new steamships to the island run, and set up close to one hundred tents throughout Avalon Canyon. These tents were part of a democratic spirit: if the expense of a hotel was too much, a visitor could rent a tent for as little as $7.50 per week [$207]. To this day, many homes in Avalon are the possession of the descendents of the owners of tents that stood on those spots over a century ago.[22]

Although the Bannings' main focus was Avalon, they undertook plans to open up the rest of the island to the public. They made the first dirt roads into the island's interior, where they built hunting lodges; and they led stagecoach tours, making Avalon's surrounding areas (Lovers Cove, Sugarloaf Point,

Tent tourism, Avalon, ca. 1900.
Courtesy of Catalina Island Museum.

and Descanso Beach) accessible to tourists and goat hunters using a mode of transportation that was fast disappearing from western roads with the advent of the automobile.

The stagecoach tours were not for the faint-hearted, skirting mountain ridges, plunging cliff tops, and precipitous canyon rims. The hairpin turns were taken at a full gallop—as near to flying, said Charles Holder, as anything on the ground could be. By 1904 visitors could travel from Avalon overland to the isthmus. For the adventurous, there was a package excursion that included an overnight stay at Eagle's Nest Lodge in Middle Ranch Canyon, built by the Bannings in 1894 and named for an eagle's nest in a nearby cottonwood tree. For the less daring, an exploration of the "undersea gardens" of Avalon Bay was a must. Glass-bottom boats dated from the early

1890s, when a local abalone fisherman discovered there was much more money to be had showing visitors where the abalone lived than in prying them off the rocks, one success of many trumpeted by Holder, which led to much copying and the foundation of a mini-industry. Not long after, the tradition of sightseeing cruises to view flying fish was established, quickly becoming another popular attraction.

The Bannings built two homes, one near the beach at the opening of Descanso Canyon and the other in what is now Two Harbors. Today the latter is the only hotel in Two Harbors. The construction ambitions of the Bannings were still unsatisfied. They built a funicular railway to give visitors a birds'-eye view of the Capri-like blue waters of the Bay of Avalon, and a Greek amphitheater bandstand nearby. Avalon now boasted a theater featuring minstrel singers and players performing nightly in the summer, as well as "the latest in Big Photoplay Pictures." Happy fishermen posed on the pier with giant sea bass they had caught, and visitors queued for a trip in the popular glass-bottom boats for a view of the underwater wonders. Shops selling the recently invented Kodak cameras, film, and print developing sprang up in several locations of the city.

The Bannings' "magic isle" was on the rise, and they had even more plans. But in the background was family dissension, which would become their undoing. Based on arguments about business decisions, exacerbated by the drinking habits of Joseph Banning, the brothers and their wives took sides on almost every issue regarding island management and development.[23]

By 1908, Joseph and Hancock Banning were only communicating through their lawyers or through their brother William. Rumors of the sale of the island cropped up in the newspapers from time to time, linking Santa Catalina to the president of the Southern Pacific, E. H. Harriman, and the president of the Great Northern Railroad, James J. Hill. Avalon residents organized and voted in 1913 in favor of incorporating their city. Now they had a voice and a legal entity that could take on the Bannings and their monopoly on transportation between the mainland and the island as well as their control of liquor sales.

The ambitions of the majority of the Catalina Island Company directors were nevertheless undaunted as negotiations between the city, the Freeholders Association (a group of property owners in Avalon), and the Bannings gave cause for optimism. With peace just about reached by mid-1915, there

Stagecoach driven by Captain Banning, 1905.
Courtesy of Catalina Island Museum.

was hope that better relationships would bring in more business and an
increase in general prosperity. But on November 29, 1915, just as the Catalina
Island Company was preparing for construction of the new luxurious Hotel
Saint Catherine, such hopes received a severe blow. A fire of mysterious
origin ripped through Avalon, razing half the town. Landmarks like the
Hotel Metropole, the Bath House, the Tuna Club, and the Pilgrim Club were
reduced to smoking foundations. In spite of this setback to their plans and
finances, the Bannings refused to sell the island and hoped to rebuild the
town, starting with a new luxury hotel, the St. Catherine. The hotel would
be located on Sugarloaf Point, at the north end of Avalon Bay. The Bannings
borrowed $850,000 [$12.8 million] to pay off debts and have capital to invest
in the new hotel. Expensive blasting of the cliffs to create a roadway was

Sport fishers, Avalon, 1908.
Courtesy of Catalina Island Museum.

begun, and costs began to mount. The Banning brothers fell out again over the direction the company was heading. Plans were modified to situate the hotel near Hancock Banning's family home in Descanso Canyon, and the Sugarloaf rock was blasted away to make way for the first Sugarloaf Casino. The St. Catherine Hotel was completed just in time for the start of the 1918 season, but the impact of the fire and the negative effect on tourism of World War I, which the United States had entered in 1917, brought a slump in revenues. In addition, the younger generation was less inclined to vacation in one place as their parents had done. They now had new destinations on the mainland—and the cars and roads to take them there.

The directors of the Island Company split over what strategy to take going forward, with Hancock Banning on one side, hoping to borrow enough money to reinstate the island as it had been, and the other directors,

Glass-bottom boat, Avalon Bay, with incline railway
in background at Lovers Cove, ca. 1910.
Courtesy of Catalina Island Museum.

including his brothers William and Joseph, getting serious about selling the island. In 1919, with Catalina's future teetering in the balance, the directors' hand was forced by the appearance of a small consortium of investors led by the chewing-gum magnate William Wrigley, Jr. His ready cash would provide the Bannings an escape route from their financial morass.

One of the great American business success stories began when William Wrigley, Jr., ended his formal education at the tender age of twelve in 1873 and started work in his father's Philadelphia soap factory. Not long after, he hit the road as a salesman for the company. In 1891 he moved to Chicago and went into partnership in another soap company that before long diversified into baking powder. One of their sales drives included an innovation: "Buy one can of baking powder—receive two packages of chewing gum, free." It soon became clear that the gum was more popular than the baking powder, and the restless, endlessly enthusiastic Wrigley made this the focus of his investment and took his new product to national market domination by 1910.[24]

The ubiquitous Wrigley brands, Spearmint, Juicy Fruit, and Doublemint, were the foundation of a significant fortune and meant that when he was in his fifties Wrigley could take a more measured approach to life, combining business and pleasure. Like many other wealthy Americans in the pre-income tax days before the ratification of the sixteenth amendment in 1913, Wrigley and his wife began to spend their winters in Southern California. He bought a mansion on "Millionaires Row" in Pasadena in 1914, which is now the headquarters of the Pasadena Tournament of Roses organization. Two years later he purchased a controlling interest in the Chicago Cubs baseball team, who would now play their home games in Wrigley Field, as Cubs Park was renamed.

Wrigley's love affair with Santa Catalina began almost sight unseen, when, after viewing some postcard pictures of the island, he closed the 1919 deal to invest as part of a real estate consortium after just three hours of negotiation. Wrigley had thought that his original investment of $3 million [$30.7 million] would be a profitable short-term venture. But the story goes that on his first visit to the island with his wife Ada, she got up in the morning, looked out the window of their suite in the new St. Catherine Hotel, and excitedly called out to him, "I should like to live here!" Wrigley continued the story: "I joined her at the window. The sun was just coming up. I had never seen a more beautiful spot. Right then and there, I determined the island would never pass out of my hands." By the end of the year he had bought out all the Bannings' and his partners' interests, and he was sole owner of Santa Catalina. It was the beginning of a new era. Wrigley had the energy, enthusiasm, and, most importantly, the deep pockets to write a new chapter in the history of the island. He started with a belief: "There is to be nothing of the Coney Island flavor about Santa Catalina. It would be unthinkable to mar the beauty of such a spot with roller coasters and the like." Wrigley not only had very fixed ideas about what he did not want, he also had some firm notions of what he did want: "to put within the reach of the rank and file of the United States—the people to whom I owe my prosperity—a playground where they can enjoy themselves to the utmost, at such a reasonable figure of expense that all can participate in its benefits." With this philosophy, Wrigley set to work to make Santa Catalina Island in his image. By 1924, he had spent $2.5 million [$27.4 million] to achieve his dreams.[25]

One of his first concerns was to strengthen the transport links with the population centers of Los Angeles. With the aim of opening the island to the masses, Wrigley purchased the SS *Virginia* in 1920. Built as a Lake Michigan steamer, he renamed her the SS *Avalon,* to join the existing two steamships that served the island. Another, the SS *Catalina*, was launched in 1924. Each of these new ships could carry more than fifteen hundred passengers in comfort and style. The Catalina Island Steamer Terminal was linked with the Pacific Electric Red Street Car line that served Wilmington and downtown Los Angeles. Wrigley's gleaming white steamers (each with a W logo on the smokestack), their bevy of uniformed couriers, and their dance bands became an iconic representation of travel to the island, particularly when they were met by the high-powered Miss Catalina speedboats zooming out on the steamers' approach to Avalon Bay.

Wrigley developed the day-trip concept for Catalina, in which the customer paid only for transportation, with many of the island activities and attractions free. Visitor numbers soared. By 1930, the annual number of visitors to Santa Catalina was equal to 60 percent of the population of Los Angeles, as customers responded in droves to the Wrigley blandishments: "The Price You Won't Remember—But the Trip You Can't Forget."[26]

Communications between the island and the mainland were also upgraded. The first high-speed links had been via carrier pigeons, which in 1894 could get a message to downtown Los Angeles in forty-five minutes. Their place was taken in the following decade by the telegraph, and in 1920 the Pacific Telephone Company inaugurated a radiotelephone system. It had seventy-five island subscribers who had the convenience of communicating with the mainland, but with the drawback of having their conversations audible to anyone in Southern California with a radio receiver. So in 1923 cables were laid between San Pedro and Santa Catalina, with a manual switchboard that remained in service until 1978.[27]

In the first flurry of activity after the island's acquisition, the Hotel Atwater, named for Wrigley's daughter-in-law Helen Atwater Wrigley, rose on the beachfront during the winter and spring of 1919–20. Ready in the nick of time for the 1920 summer season, it was adjoined by a cafeteria, said to be the biggest in the world, capable of serving a thousand meals a day. The following year Wrigley had a home built for himself on the mountainside on the southern end of Avalon Bay. Conceived in the popular "Georgian colonial"

Chicago Cubs spring training, Wrigley Field, Avalon, ca. 1920s.
Courtesy of Catalina Island Museum.

style, it was named Mount Ada in honor of his wife, and it overlooked both
the town and the Chicago Cubs spring training camp, where each spring for
the next thirty years the team prepared for the coming baseball season. In
deference to his wife's love of the view and the Catalina light, the Wrigleys
made sure that Mount Ada caught the first of the sunrise and the last of the
sunset every day. In this house were welcomed presidents and celebrities of
the era. Calvin Coolidge, Herbert Hoover, and the prince of Wales enjoyed
the Wrigleys' hospitality.[28] Images of the broadly grinning Hoover with a
big fish on his line and the less-than-amused Coolidge with a large macaw
on his shoulder capture the mood of the times.

Mirroring the outlook of its owner, a spirit of progress and optimism
pervaded the Wrigley world of the 1920s. The editor of the island newspaper
captured the character of those days on Catalina:

Old buildings began to disappear and new ones were erected. Streets were torn up for sewers, water mains, gas lines and other public utilities. New steamers and a pier were built. . . . Old glass-bottom boats . . . were replaced by models of greater speed, safety and efficiency. . . . Better streets, more comfortable homes for employees, cheaper food products, adequate entertainment, and hotel accommodations for visitors. Various kinds of industries were started. New school buildings were erected.[29]

His views on natural beauty notwithstanding, Wrigley encouraged large-scale mining for silver, zinc, and lead to help pay for his investments in island infrastructure. The local mining industry behind Pebbly Beach and on Mount Black Jack was joined by furniture and ceramics plants, and the island population grew in response to these manufacturing activities. With a peak output of between ten thousand and fifteen thousand pieces per week, ceramics production lasted for ten years. Now highly sought by collectors, Santa Catalina decorative tiles and pottery sold all over the world, including to the White House of Franklin Roosevelt. To educate the children of the island workers, a new elementary school and high school were built in 1925.

One of Wrigley's first priorities was to cater to the craze for dancing that was sweeping the country by creating a new and improved dance pavilion for the island's visitors. Before the Banning brothers sold the island, part of the large rock at the northwest end of Avalon Bay, Sugarloaf Point, had been blasted away to start the construction of the Hotel St. Catherine, though in the end the hotel had been built in Descanso Canyon. Wrigley completed the job, demolishing most of the remaining rock to build the first dance hall, which he named Sugarloaf Casino. It served as a ballroom and Avalon's first high school for several years, but its time as a casino was short, for it proved too small for Catalina's growing tourist population.

In 1928, the casino was dismantled to make room for the Casino Ballroom and Motion Picture Theater, with a dancing capacity of three thousand and theater seats for almost twelve hundred. The remainder of Sugarloaf Rock was dynamited to enhance the view of the ocean. With dancing also available on the ferries going to and from the mainland, 1930s weekenders or day-trippers so inclined could spend the majority of their time on the dance floor, moving to the latest rhythms of the day, with bands led by Buddy Rogers, Kay Kyser, Bob Crosby, and Benny Goodman.

A new Avalon was emerging from the outlines of the old. The unpaved streets laid out by the Bannings in the 1890s were shaded by now-mature eucalyptus trees planted at the time, and scores of "bungalettes" were built along streets like Descanso Avenue that had once been lined with rental tents. For a total price of approximately $500 [$6,500] one could purchase one of these modest cottages, so that Wrigley could fulfill his policy of offering clean and attractive lodgings in all price ranges. From those early days, the connection with wealthy Pasadena also meant a constant demand for more luxurious accommodation. So many Pasadenans stayed in the hotels or boardinghouses of Avalon that the Pasadena *Star News* kept a correspondent on Catalina all summer to report on island doings for those remaining at home. One of the first Pasadenans to promote Catalina was Charles Holder. A naturalist, relentless booster of Southern California, and founder of the Tournament of Roses, in the 1890s he turned his considerable energies to proclaiming the glories of Santa Catalina. Holder had one of the first glass-bottom boats constructed and he was instrumental in founding and publicizing the Tuna Club, whose honorary members included Teddy Roosevelt and Herbert Hoover and where for many years Holder held the record for the biggest tuna landed with rod and reel. Other early buyers into the Catalina dream were the family of General George S. Patton. His father was on the board of the Island Company in the days of the Bannings, and the boy who would become one of the most famous generals of World War II spent several weeks of every summer of his youth on the island, hunting, swimming, and developing a love of the great outdoors.

Also drawn to the balmy summer climate and the opportunities for deep-sea fishing was the writer Zane Grey, who in 1924 built his distinctive Southwest pueblo-style home overlooking Avalon Bay. At the time, Grey was making more than $100,000 a year from his writing [$1.3 million] and he cruised the world seeking the challenge of the biggest fish. A photograph from 1926 shows a large crowd assembled on the Avalon Pleasure Pier to admire a giant broadbill swordfish he had just landed. Winston Churchill and Herbert Hoover led the list of political leaders drawn to the island by the challenge of fighting the big fish, but for Grey, "It is an environment that means enchantment to me. Sea and mountain! A place for rest, dream, peace, sleep."[30]

This was not the experience of all the residents of Santa Catalina. From the 1890s on, much of the manual labor on the island, as in the rest of

Southern California, was provided by the local Mexican American population. On the island they faced the same level of casual discrimination that they encountered on the mainland. They were not permitted to speak Spanish downtown, and they were not allowed to swim from the beaches or sit on the walls, though they were permitted to add local color by diving for coins thrown by arriving steamer passengers. They lived in four small barrios, largely removed from the sight of visitors.

Under the island ownership of William Wrigley, Jr., Mexican American living conditions improved markedly. He conceived of a "Mexican village" for the working people and their families on Tremont Street. Old shacks were replaced by more-permanent stucco-and-tile structures housing family and bachelor apartments that rented at reasonable rates. A community hall was constructed to provide recreational activities. These measures showed an active and positive concern, but the separation of the Spanish-speaking community only began to slowly disappear with the return of their veterans after World War II.

The dawn of the movie industry sparked a search for locations that were near yet seemed exotic. The Channel Islands provided environments that could work as backdrops for filming and places where silver-screen celebrities could relax and play. John Barrymore was fond of sailing his yacht to call on the Caires of Santa Cruz Island, but none of the islands were as near to Hollywood as Catalina, spiritually as well as geographically. The 1912 arrival of the director D. W. Griffith on Catalina marked the beginning of a connection with Hollywood that has lasted to the present. In the roll call of the new Hollywood royalty, there were few who were unconnected with Catalina. John Barrymore, Tom Mix, Jean Harlow, Howard Hughes, James Cagney, Bing Crosby, David Niven, Judy Garland, Henry Fonda, Mickey Rooney, Marilyn Monroe, John Wayne—all of them had a strong association with the island in the '20s, '30s and '40s.

If Hollywood was still a film-industry "colony" in the teens and twenties, Avalon was its summer getaway of choice. Charlie Chaplin and Paulette Goddard, with their love of sailing and escaping to a place where they could slip out of their movie-star personas, were regulars in the yacht basin and the restaurants on Crescent Avenue along the waterfront. Errol Flynn, with his love of adventurous back-country pursuits, found the wild boar hunting in the hills of Catalina a great attraction. Tom Mix, star of *Riders of the Purple*

Sage and some three hundred other films, met the writer Grey on the set of *Riders* and soon followed him out to Catalina, buying a house not far from Grey's home in Avalon.

Beginning with silent films of the 1920s starring Harry Houdini and Buster Keaton, films shot on Santa Catalina included hits with Charles Laughton and Bela Lugosi and *Mutiny on the Bounty*, with Laughton and Clark Gable. In the 1943 film *Guadalcanal Diary*, William Bendix, Preston Foster, and a cast of thousands stormed ashore at Little Harbor. In the post-war period, Avalon continued to provide the backdrop for hits like *The Glass Bottom Boat*, starring Doris Day and Rod Taylor, and *All Ashore*, with Mickey Rooney. Several scenes from *Chinatown* (1974), starring Jack Nicolson and Faye Dunaway, were filmed on the island, which continues to provide locations for both movie and television productions today.

William Wrigley, Jr., threw himself into generating Catalina tourism with the same enthusiasm and energy he had shown for soap and gum salesmanship in his youth. The island entered a float in Pasadena's Tournament of Roses parade, featuring a "bathing beauty" on a boat decorated with Catalina holly branches and clusters of berries, taking first prize in its division. On the island there were Easter pageants and Fourth of July celebrations, with big community parades. The New Year's Eve dance was a popular fixture in the island social calendar. In January 1927 Wrigley launched the Wrigley Ocean Marathon—after all, it was twenty-six miles across the channel from the mainland. He offered $25,000 [$324,000] to the first man to swim the channel—and mysteriously $10,000 less for the first finisher of "the fair sex." Out of a field of 102 that plunged into the surf at Isthmus Cove, only a seventeen-year-old Canadian swimmer completed the distance to San Pedro, in a time of 15 hours and 44 minutes. The two women who came closest to finishing were awarded $2,500 each [$32,000].[31]

Toward the end of his first decade of ownership, looking down from his house Mount Ada, Wrigley could revel in the changes that his investment was bringing. To the west he could see the town growing. To the south the baseball diamond of the Cubs' spring training ground glowed like an emerald against the arid golden backdrop of the surrounding hills. The perennial problem facing Southern California—water—had been solved through a network of dams and pipelines, the largest private water development at the time, underwritten by Wrigley to the tune of more than a million dollars [$13 million]. Avalon, the isthmus, and the island's various coves could now be assured of an adequate supply of freshwater to guarantee their development.

Avalon Bay was now set off by what was to become its most famous landmark, the new Avalon Casino. The previous structure's dome had been taken down and reassembled in Avalon Canyon to serve as a huge birdcage, the cornerstone of another Wrigley landmark, the Bird Park. This institution, based on the avian passion of William Wrigley, Jr., housed thousands of birds from around the world. At the new casino, Wrigley commissioned John Beckman, who later designed sets for *Casablanca, The Maltese Falcon,* and *Lost Horizon,* to paint murals for the foyer and theater. The luxuriously appointed theater was the first specifically designed to present "talkies." With its reflective surfaces shimmering with colored lighting, its huge pipe organ, and its sixteen murals, the Casino Theater ably reflected the ambitions of its owner. At the same time as a film was being shown there, as many as three thousand dancers could be enjoying the Pavilion orchestra in the largest circular ballroom in the world, two floors above. Its cantilever design was an inspiration to architects and engineers from across the country. The finishing touch was the encircling fourteen-foot covered loggia, with its views of Avalon and the sea framed by exotic, slender Moorish-inspired columns. Opening night at the casino featured the newly released film *The Iron Mask,* starring Douglas Fairbanks, while in the ballroom "leading members of the motion-picture world" and others swayed to the music of Maurice Menge and the El Patio Catalina Orchestra.[32]

The glittering social life of Santa Catalina dimmed for a time in 1932 when flags at half-mast announced the death of William Wrigley, Jr., at his Arizona home. He was seventy years old and had set the direction of the island for the remainder of the century. The mantle passed to his son, Philip Knight Wrigley, who had accompanied his parents on their first visit to Avalon as a twenty-four-year-old in 1919. Quieter and less outgoing than his father, he nevertheless shared the elder Wrigley's business acumen and passion for baseball. Although nursing his own set of hobbies and interests, his love of the island was as strong as his parents'. Philip Wrigley had formally joined the family company when he was twenty and accomplished his first task of setting up an Australian subsidiary with a minimum of fuss. He became the president of the parent company in 1925. Wrigley was a man of few words but strong beliefs. Just after the war he circulated a memo entitled "Basic

Policies." In it, he encouraged his children and anyone else who cared to pay attention to turn liabilities into assets, do jobs thoroughly or not at all, to never try to get something for nothing, and to be fair and above-board.

On Catalina Philip Wrigley established El Rancho Escondido as a focus for his interest in horse breeding and training. It was his idea to import wild pigs from Santa Cruz Island in the early 1930s to help reduce the rattlesnake population. This the pigs doubtless did, but they added native island flora to their menu, doing great damage to the island's oaks and other endemics.

During World War II, like many corporations, gum manufacturers found their raw materials diverted to military use or heavily rationed. Making a virtue of necessity, the company pulled their top brands from public sale and produced them for military use only. At the same time they made sure that their customers would remember their public-spirited participation in the war effort with a successful advertising campaign. The Wrigley's island was also heavily affected by the war. In the panic that followed the attack on Pearl Harbor in December 1941, it was closed to tourists and used for military training facilities. The U.S. Maritime Service set up a training facility in Avalon, the Coast Guard had a training camp at Two Harbors, and the Army Signal Corps maintained a radar station in the interior. The Office of Strategic Services—forerunner of the CIA—trained at Toyon Bay, while Emerald Bay on the island's west end was used by the navy. The Catalina steamships were expropriated for use as troop transports, ferrying soldiers and war workers across San Francisco Bay.

The postwar period could be said to have gotten off to a flying start with the founding of Catalina Airlines and the opening in 1946 of Catalina's airfield, the "Airport in the Sky," at 1,602 feet above sea level. The 3,250-foot runway straddled two flattened mountaintops, with the rock from their demolition used to fill the canyon between them. Until the time of the airport's construction, the only air service to the island had been provided by seaplanes, which had enjoyed a proud history begun just a few years after the first flight of the Wright brothers.

In 1912, Glenn Martin flew his seaplane from Newport Beach to Avalon, completing the thirty-three-mile flight in twenty-seven minutes, the longest flight over water at the time. Martin's mother allegedly sent him off in his best suit saying, "If you crack up in that ship, I want you looking your best." The lure of running an airline serving Santa Catalina spanned most of the century following Martin's inaugural flight, as various consortia and individuals made the attempt. In the 1920s, the airline of Charlie Chaplin's half-brother Syd Chaplin was followed by Pacific Marine Airways, flying twin-engine Sikorsky biplanes. Then the route was taken over by the Wrigley-financed Wilmington-Catalina Airline in 1931. After landing at Hamilton Cove near Avalon, the airline's Douglas Dolphins required a turntable to position them to take off for their return trip. At the time it was the world's shortest and safest airline, flying the channel 38,000 times in ten years with no accidents or injuries.[33]

After the war, air service to Catalina was provided by DC-3s flown by United Airlines, of which Wrigley was a board director. In the 1950s and 1960s competition was provided by Avalon Air Transport's Flying Boats, which landed in Avalon Bay, avoiding the half-hour bus trip from the mountaintop airport.

In the postwar years, Catalina continued its accustomed way of life, which included accommodating thousands of visitors, celebrities, movie companies—and local characters like Leo Fishman, "the Duke of Catalina," who held sway on Avalon's beach as lifeguard, greeter, and friend to stars like Mickey Rooney and John Wayne. A gregarious fixture of Avalon life for decades, he joined a tradition of island characters. Before Fishman had come individualists like "Chicken Johnny," who had more in common with the semi-reclusive denizens of the other islands than with those who enjoyed elbow-rubbing in glossy and populous Avalon. Chicken Johnny lived up off Avalon Canyon in a spot now called Hermit Gulch. He seldom left his makeshift shack, infrequently going into town to barter eggs or vegetables for supplies he couldn't produce himself. Before him had come José (Mexican Joe) Presciado, brought to the island at age seven and remaining there for the rest of his life, who became famous for his knowledge of the island and its surrounding waters. Much sought by big-game fishermen in the late nineteenth century, Mexican Joe claimed, "If there is a tree on the island I do not know, it must have grown last night."[34] In the twentieth century the Cadmans, owners of the Avalon Fish Market, and Louie Crow, owner of the Hoover Grocery, were just a few of many who caught "Catalina fever." They came for a visit in their youth and stayed for a lifetime.

Catalina Island life must have felt reasonably well insulated from the explosive culture wars of the 1960s, but one of them came calling on the island in September 1972 when twenty-six members of the Brown Berets, a group of Chicano activists, traveled to Catalina and planted a Mexican flag, claiming the island for all Chicanos. As others had done on California islands before them—including William Waters on San Miguel in 1896 and American Indians on Alcatraz in 1969—they asserted that because the 1848 Treaty of Guadalupe Hidalgo between Mexico and the United States did not specifically mention the California islands, Catalina could be claimed as a separate nation in the name of all Mexican Americans. The well-behaved group camped outside of Avalon, and in a demonstration of the Catalina spirit they were given the status of a new tourist attraction. Mexican American islanders provided them with food after they used up their own supplies. Having made their point, when a municipal judge visited the camp after twenty-four days to ask them to leave, they departed peaceably on the Catalina ferry, just as they had arrived.

That same year, 1972, the Santa Catalina Island Conservancy was established as a private land trust to preserve the natural resources of the island. One of its chief supporters was Philip Wrigley, who had begun serious conservation efforts in 1964 with the donation to the University of Southern California of forty-five acres at Big Fisherman's Cove for a marine science center, including a library, classrooms, labs, and related facilities. Ten years later, the Santa Catalina Island Company guaranteed public access to virtually the entire island by granting a fifty-year open-space easement to Los Angeles County. In 1975, Philip Wrigley and his sister Dorothy deeded 88 percent of their Island Company shares to the Santa Catalina Conservancy that he had helped create. Today it protects nearly 90 percent of the island, including sixty-two miles of unspoiled beaches and secluded coves—one of the longest publicly accessible stretches of undeveloped coastline left in Southern California.

With a goal of being a responsible steward and balancing conservation, education, and recreation, the Conservancy is dedicated to preserving the habitats of more than sixty plant and animal species (including insects) found nowhere else in the world—a demanding role in light of the island's annual visitor population approaching a million. It is just one of the challenges facing the Conservancy and the Catalina Island Company as they confront the changing expectations and demographics of their visitor base in the twenty-first century.

William Wrigley, Jr., put forth his vision of Catalina early in the last century when he declared the island open to all the people who had helped him amass his fortune, no matter the size of their vacation budget. Now it is in the hands of the inheritors of that vision to make the island relevant and sustainable for a new generation of visitors. In 2008 the Santa Catalina Chamber of Commerce officially asked the Island Company to formulate a plan to take the island economy forward, to invest with them to create jobs and opportunities for Catalina in the new century. This is now taking place with new building, refurbishment, and establishment of new attractions that will fulfill the expectations of today's visitors.[35]

Meanwhile, on the vast majority of the island that is dedicated to preservation of Santa Catalina's natural and historical heritage, the Conservancy points with pride to its successes in protecting and restoring endangered species and their habitats—removal of invasive plants and animals and recoveries of the endangered island fox and bald eagle populations. With a delicate balance of preservation, education, and recreation, it aims to reach visiting adults and schoolchildren through activities at its botanic garden and two nature centers, as well as guided experiences across the island's rugged interior. Now in its fifth decade, the Conservancy sustains its three roles with programs to improve the natural health of the island, supported by activities in island ecology and biodiversity, to position Santa Catalina Island as a leading ecological and cultural destination. More than sixty thousand schoolchildren each year visit camps on Conservancy lands, becoming acquainted with aspects of a much older California and gaining appreciation of what has been lost and what has been preserved since the days when the excited Pimungans greeted stout Cabrillo more than four centuries ago.

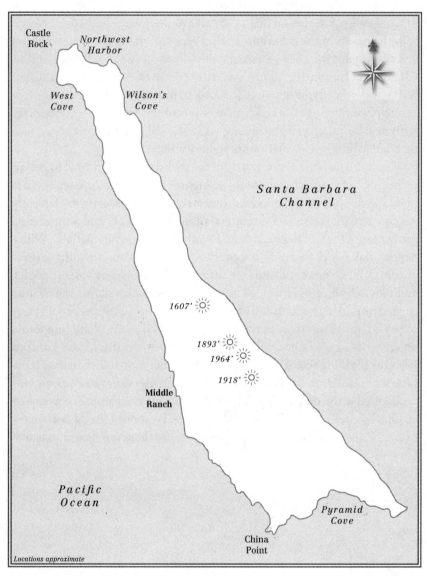

Castle
Rock

*Northwest
Harbor*

*West
Cove*

*Wilson's
Cove*

*Santa Barbara
Channel*

1607' ☼

1893' ☼

1964' ☼

1918' ☼

**Middle
Ranch**

*Pacific
Ocean*

*Pyramid
Cove*

**China
Point**

Locations approximate

San Clemente Island.
Map by Gerry Krieg.

CHAPTER 10

San Clemente Island

Closing the arc of the Channel Islands archipelago that defines the Southern California Bight is San Clemente Island, an uplifted structural block along the submerged San Clemente Fault. In contrast to Santa Catalina, defined by its mainland proximity, development, and population, the defining characteristic of San Clemente is its isolation. Forty-one miles from the mainland, it is almost as remote as San Nicolas Island, and like San Nicolas it is owned and controlled by the U.S. Navy, with no public access.

With a frost-free, semi-arid climate, it typically gets less than six inches of rain a year, with most of that arriving in storms between December and April. The island's aridity is somewhat mitigated by the humid influence of the surrounding marine air, though extremely limited supplies of fresh surface water have been a general condition of life on the island for millennia.[1] When approached from the sea, the island appears to be a long, relatively flat bench that gradually rises to an elevation of about 1,965 feet. The northern (mainland-facing) side of the island is low and flat, and on the ocean-facing southern side the landscape, dominated by a series of wave-cut marine terraces, ascends slowly to the high point known as Mount Thirst. The eastern face of the island drops from the elevation of Mount Thirst directly into the sea. The western side is likewise dominated by wave-cut terraces, perhaps the most dramatic on the Pacific Coast.

San Clemente's exposed, ocean-facing southern location make it wind-besieged, with the prevailing westerlies and northwesterlies sweeping across its rough surface, its wave terraces, and its four peaks. The general presence of volcanic rock on the island is typical of a location on the margin of two tectonic plates and speaks of its fiery birth in the Miocene epoch—twenty-three million to five million years ago. Strong testimony to the changing sea levels across the ages is written in the different heights of the marine terraces that mark the island's craggy coastline and in the marine fossils of sharks, whales, and seaweeds from the Miocene to the Pliocene periods in its upper reaches. Sharply defined canyons furrow the Pacific-facing coast, and the few sandy beaches are found principally on the southern part of the island. Rock islets dot the western shore, and at the north end are two of the biggest, Bird Rock and Castle Rock.

Sometimes referred to as a time capsule in the sea, remote San Clemente Island provides the historical outlines of a maritime-based cultural odyssey that began at least nine thousand years ago and probably considerably earlier—sea voyages reaching back in time nearly to the last ice age. For its size (fifty-seven square miles), San Clemente is one of the best documented archaeological settings in California, if not all of North America.

Called Kinipar by the island Indians, it was their home for more than nine millennia. Over twenty-five hundred prehistoric sites, spanning a time range from the Early Holocene to Spanish contact in the mid-sixteenth century are currently recorded on the island, locations where these ancient people lived and generated the detritus that sheds valuable light today on the details of their everyday existence. The prehistoric sites made San Clemente a rich environment for scientists and collectors of artifacts from the 1870s onward, though the island's remoteness saved it from excessive depredations of pot hunters and the like.[2]

Similar to their out-of-the-way neighbors on San Nicolas Island, the inhabitants of Kinipar spoke a language distinct from that of the northern island Chumash. Like the Nicoleños, it was closer to the Shoshonean dialects of the Los Angeles Basin and the Southwest, not that this would have excluded them from the lively inter-island and mainland trade, based on their mastery of the local version of the wood-plank craft that they called ti'at. Evidence has been found of trade materials from the northern islands and from the mainland, including Coso obsidian from the Mojave Desert. It has not been established what tribe the Clementeños belonged to, although the Tongvas, who are well documented as resident on neighboring Santa Catalina Island and in the Los Angeles Basin, are the most likely candidates.[3]

But what of their daily existence? The commonly accepted mythic condition of these early inhabitants—a generally easy-going circumstance of homeostasis with their island environment—has had to be modified by recent archaeological research. It would appear that the ancient populations were as prone to over-exploitation of the natural resources as those who followed them, significantly impacting their environment and with it their culture. By overfishing and otherwise inducing changes in resource availability, they shaped their society toward adoption of new technologies and new economic patterns. This was particularly true in terms of fishing and hunting tools and techniques, whether it was new methods of hunting sea mammals or the development of ever more sophisticated hooks and lures.

Likewise, these changes impacted labor patterns and demands, dietary quality, and susceptibility to disease. In their behavior, the Indians of San Clemente appear to have been doing what contemporary populations would probably do under similar circumstances when faced with the question of day-to-day survival versus long-range conservation of resources, "shaping robust patterns of cultural change, including the adoption of new technologies and new economic patterns."[4]

Over the millennia, San Clemente's prehistoric population had also learned to cope with cyclic changes in sea surface temperatures, but the islanders of about twelve hundred years ago had to contend with what climate scientists are calling the Medieval Climate Anomaly, a two-hundred-year period of unusual aridity, which as we have seen forced rapid cultural change across the entire region, including the northern islands. Water was perhaps the most important limiting resource for prehistoric human settlement, and the people of Kinipar apparently experienced a decline in population as they moved their settlements to different places on the island in search of sources of adequate drinking water.[5]

It now appears that in the centuries just prior to the arrival of the Spanish explorers the region was experiencing a level of drought leading to dramatic changes in demographics and settlement patterns, coupled with declining levels of health and rising instances of warfare.[6] As one archaeologist puts it, "Contrary to traditional models of coastal prehistory, which have often portrayed the proto-historic era as one in which coastal peoples achieved unprecedented levels of economic abundance and subsistence security, the late Holocene appears to have been a time of significant crises, including damaging droughts."[7]

At the same time, in the face of its cyclical aridity and its marine and climatic environmental cycles, the island clearly reflects a long-term pattern of successful human occupation, as these challenges were met by a variety of local survival strategies on the mainland and on individual islands, particularly the more remote ones like San Clemente.

It was into this changing and uncertain world that the Spanish explorers suddenly entered. The expedition of Juan Rodríguez Cabrillo sighted the island in 1542 without dropping anchor, and it is said that he called it Victoria in honor of one of his three ships. The island's Spanish name for Saint Clement was given by the mapping expedition of Sebastian Vizcaíno sixty years later as he saw it on November 23, 1602, but it was not until 1769, when the *San Antonio* of the Portolà expedition landed at Pyramid Cove on the island's southern end, that actual contact was made. The Native ti'ats skimmed out across the waters of the cove to greet the great vessel, and in the exchange of gifts the locals presented the Spaniards with two otter-skin robes.

The arrival of the Portolà expedition was a transformative event in the long history of the islanders. Sent out as part of the last expansionist gasp of the empire of Spain, the Franciscans and their mission system played a central role in the expedition. The news from Pyramid Cove doubtless alerted the well-meaning friars as to an indigenous population of souls to be saved, while the gift of the otter robes signaled the presence of a valuable commodity to the outside world. This would attract less-well-intentioned predators in the form of Aleut hunters, with their objective of feeding the demand of the Chinese ruling class for luxurious fur robes. Within thirty-five years the population of approximately 250 islanders had shrunk to 11, described in chapter 2 and in the diary of a visitor off the ship *Leila Byrd* in 1803. The portrayal of their lack of clothing in the cool weather and lack of cooking utensils or any of the civilized hallmarks of the island and mainland societies described by the first explorers is a measure of how far they had fallen.[8]

These final survivors of the island's Indigenous population were "victims of epidemic disease, shattered native cultural networks, and the persecution of violent outsiders."[9] The last Indian inhabitants of San Clemente Island departed about 1829, and with their exodus a San Clemente Island maritime cultural saga reaching back in time to the last ice age ended. The island population had been caught in the pincers of the arguably well-meaning motives of the Franciscans and the market-driven rapacity of the northern hunters.

Remnants of the island civilization are thought to have chosen to abandon their homeland rather than be forcibly removed by the missionaries. The baptismal records of Mission San Gabriel from 1776 to 1832 include those of some Indians who claimed to have come voluntarily from San Clemente Island. From this point, the history of the island would be Euro-American.

As on San Nicolas, Santa Barbara, Anacapa, and San Miguel Islands, no land was granted during the Spanish or Mexican periods of California history, therefore title to the island of San Clemente went to the U.S. government upon California achieving statehood in 1850. Though it was only a matter of four years before President Franklin Pierce reserved the entire island for lighthouse purposes, no actual lighthouses were built at the time. In later years structures to support navigational lights were built at North Head, Lighthouse Point, Wilson Cove, Jack Point, Pyramid Head, and China Point. The U.S. Coast and Geodetic Survey mapped San Clemente in the 1860s and 1870s, reporting the location of four good harbors or landing places. In the meantime, the faraway federal government had its hands full with other issues, and into the forty-seven-year vacuum after statehood stepped the usual cast of island characters—fishermen, hunters of sea mammals, ranchers, and the odd scientific explorer.

Early in the nineteenth century, whalers had used the coves of the island to process their catch, as noted in the 1835 log of the whale ship *Elbe* of Poughkeepsie, New York, whose crew was hunting sperm whales as far north as "St. Clements Island." This practice was still common a century later, with whaling ships anchored in Pyramid Cove to cut up whale meat for shipment, at thirty dollars a ton, to the Dr. Ross dog food factory in Los Angeles.[10]

In the latter part of the nineteenth century, the lack of water, particularly during the summer months, was well known to would-be stockmen but did not deter the likes of S. S. Hubbell, who brought sheep and goats for grazing on the island, and Walter Vail, who followed him, bringing out sheep and cattle for himself and others. The result is that no one knows now what San Clemente Island looked like two hundred or even one hundred years ago. The depredations of the sheep and goat populations cleared what were said to be forests of *Malva rosa* and other flora from what older literature implies was a verdant landscape.[11]

Early in the twentieth century, the federal government began to stipulate the same program of short leases to stockmen and the like on San Clemente as prevailed on the other islands to which they had title. Starting in 1901, the first and only official lessee was an organization known as the San Clemente Wool Company. It held the lease in four-year increments until 1909 when it got Congress to grant a twenty-five-year lease for $1,500 per year [$38,000 in 2011 equivalent] and a promise of $1,000 a year in improvements. This long-term tenure greatly added to the value of the company and it constructed several dams around the island for retaining water. At Wilson Cove it built an eight-room house, which announced itself rather grandly with a sign on the roof: Casa Blanca. This was adjoined by a bunkhouse, wool sheds, shearing pens and sheds, blacksmith shop, barn, and a small wharf. Rainwater was carefully collected from the roofs and funneled into six storage tanks. Other smaller houses and accompanying buildings, wells, tanks, and corrals were built at other locations. Fourteen miles of wagon roads were laid out, and a four-and-one-half mile fence was built down the middle of the island.[12]

The San Clemente Wool Company ran approximately twelve thousand sheep using a permanent group of about seven employees who were kept supplied by a company schooner. During the six-week roundup period each year, there might be as many as sixty-five men living and working on the island. The sheep were rounded up by the vaqueros on horseback and on foot, gathered from the south, and herded north to turning fences above Wilson Cove. Here the shearing took place and the wool was baled for shipment to mainland wool merchants.

The Wool Company's twenty-five-year lease did not go unchallenged. In 1909, the secretary of the Newport Beach Chamber of Commerce wrote to President Teddy Roosevelt, whose interest in the environment and public lands was well known:

> We thought it ought to be brought to your personal attention that some five or six years ago San Clemente Island was covered with a heavy growth of underbrush and trees. This [San Clemente Wool] Company in order to increase the grass area, burned over San Clemente Island from one end to the other three separate times, almost completely destroying the tree growth.... Our main objection to a lease of any longer period [than four years] is that as soon as the Panama Canal is completed [1913], this island will have additional value to the American people at large ... as a pleasure resort ... as now exists on Santa Catalina Island.[13]

Casa Blanca, Wilson's Cove, headquarters of the
San Clemente Wool Company from 1892 to 1913.
Courtesy of Santa Cruz Island Foundation.

Despite these serious charges, the protest was ignored and the San Clemente Wool Company held sway on the island for a quarter of a century, changing its name and ownership in 1918 to the San Clemente Sheep Company and carrying on business as usual for another sixteen years.

In 1934, the leasing policy of the U.S. government was discontinued and sheep operations terminated. The only remaining evidence of the activity is to be found in the three reservoir areas and a line of fence posts at the southern end of the island. Because the ground was too hard for postholes, the fence posts were supported by piles of rock held in place by wire baskets. A few foundations from one of the smaller sheep ranch installations can be found in the area of Middle Ranch, but there is no trace of Casa Blanca at Wilson Cove.

The administration of San Clemente was transferred to in 1934 to the U.S. Navy, which began construction of a small landing field paved with crushed rock and shell in the center of the island, to be used by both the navy and the marines. An asphalt road connected it with the navy's new training facility at Wilson Cove. In the late 1930s the facility was upgraded to include three-thousand-foot and two-thousand-foot runways and a hangar.

Casa Blanca ranch buildings and Wilson's Cove, ca. 1900.
Courtesy of Channel Islands National Park.

In 1942, just after the outbreak of the war, a marine unit operated from the airfield, and the runways were extended. San Clemente was included in the chain of top-secret early-warning radar installations along the Pacific coast and home to an army detachment of two hundred. The marines expanded their training establishment with an antiaircraft machine-gun training unit. The radar installations were made permanent in 1944, and the navy began using parts of the island for gunnery training. San Clemente now boasted three asphalt runways and a complement of almost nine hundred officers and enlisted personnel. The island was evaluated for blimp operations and was judged to be unsuitable because of high winds and fog, but by the end of the war records show that there were three dirigible landings a week from military bases at Santa Ana and Del Mar on the mainland.

The radar installations were in service throughout the 1950s, and the island was used extensively for shore and underwater missile and rocket research, development, and testing. In the early 1960s the military abandoned the old World War II facilities and constructed a new airfield on the north end of the island near Wilson Cove. The old airstrips were torn out but the associated buildings remain, still sometimes used in ground-warfare training exercises.

San Clemente Island is the navy's last ship-to-shore live-fire range. Since the terrorist attacks of September 11, 2001, training on the island has increased by 25 percent, and the Department of Defense began construction in July 2002 of a $21-million simulated U.S. embassy compound to train troops in hostage rescue. The San Clemente target ranges provide the U.S. Navy, U.S. Marine Corps, and other military services space and facilities that they use to conduct readiness training, tests, and evaluation activities. The island's remoteness from the mainland and its complete navy ownership make it ideal for fleet training, weapons and electronics system testing, and research and development.

Today San Clemente is home to about three hundred military personnel, of whom approximately one-third are women. For the purposes of navy records, time spent on the island is classified as sea duty. Most personnel are stationed at the main base at Wilson Cove, which includes a 9500-foot runway and accompanying facilities. Flights to and from San Diego are daily occurrences. Also found here are barracks, eating and recreation facilities, and structures housing operations, administration, and transportation services, along with a dispensary, barbershop, and market. At nearby Northwest

Harbor there is a Basic Underwater Demolition and SEAL Training (BUDS) facility, used for preparing Navy SEAL personnel to act as special forces. Under cover of darkness they practice climbing the steep slopes and planting explosives. The island itself is divided into three zones. The northern third of the island contains the main base, airport, and living quarters. The middle third is a buffer demarcated by two gates, and beginning at the southern-most gate is the Shore Bombardment Impact Area of the island, which is considered extremely hazardous, and access to it is highly limited.

In this last zone is a mock airfield, complete with nonfunctional fighter jets and dummy missiles. It is used for military exercises and as a test target for short-range missiles. It is said that San Clemente Island is the only location associated with the Pacific fleet where weapons that actually explode can be tested.[14]

Parallel with all this military activity, San Clemente has emerged as one of the most productive locales for Pacific Coast archaeological research. It is a long tradition. Led by Blanche Trask, the first botanist to study it in the 1890s, San Clemente Island has been the object of investigations and work by archaeologists, botanists, biologists, and other scientists through-out the twentieth century. The navy continues to encourage this work by maintaining a field station for approved research projects. In addition, as the island owner the navy has fulfilled its responsibilities to comply with environmental laws and regulations. Under the Endangered Species Act of 1973, feral cats and goats that were endangering the habitats of endemic wildlife were eliminated. Many of the island's archaeological sites are better preserved than sites located on the mainland coast, and they are less likely to be damaged or obliterated by the kinds of urban industrial expansion that continues to transform Southern California.

Preserving the flora of San Clemente Island from the introduced goats was particularly difficult, resulting in a twenty-year saga starting in 1973. At the beginning of the process it was estimated that there were approximately 12,500 goats on the island. Using herding, trapping, and sport hunt-ing, by 1978 most of the goats had been removed, but there were still 1,500 remaining. Still reproducing, they were becoming more difficult to catch. A plan of the navy and the U.S. Fish and Wildlife service to shoot them from helicopters ran into immediate opposition. Animal rights organizations filed suit and stopped the process, after which the Fund for Animals began a program of netting the goats from helicopters. About half the remaining

(*above*) Aerial view of San Clemente Island, looking southeast, showing the spread of sand dunes, 1930. Photo: U.S. Naval Air Station, San Diego. *Courtesy of Channel Islands National Park.*

(*below*) East End Camp, Pyramid Cove, 1933. The camp was established to keep fishers off the island. *Courtesy of Santa Cruz Island Foundation.*

Last sheep being shipped off in 1934 as the navy begins administration of the island. *Courtesy of Santa Cruz Island Foundation.*

goats were removed to the mainland, but the final holdouts were proving too difficult to trap because of the rugged terrain. The navy took over the process again, and by 1989 a total of nearly 29,000 goats had been removed, yet the remainder were still reproducing. Over the next two years the last of the wild animals were lured to their capture by tame female "Judas goats." Finally the process of flora recovery could get fully under way.[15]

Under the navy's stewardship, a level of success has been achieved in rescuing the endemic bird populations, such as the San Clemente Island loggerhead shrike. Its numbers have grown significantly, with the navy managing its live-fire training to minimize disruption during the breeding season. Biologists who have visited the island since 1991 have been impressed with the extent of the recovery of many island plant species, such as the San Clemente bush mallow, silver lotus, and Indian paintbrush.[16] At the same time the navy's use of San Clemente for target practice has impeded recovery of island vegetation, particularly that of the native grasses. With the end of close-cropping by goats, the island is now more likely to burn if set alight by live ordnance. Although periodic fires are a natural component of scrub ecosystems, frequent fires tend to eliminate native species in favor of nonnative grasses.

These are issues that merit continuous attention, and in the present era the navy is showing it is a good landlord by taking the lead in efforts to reduce the use of diesel fuel and to prevent harmful emissions, installing wind turbines that are providing an increasingly higher percentage of the island's power needs. The navy also hosts other military personnel, civilian government representatives, contractors, environmentalists, fishers, boaters, and members of civic organizations like the local Boy Scouts, which has an annual schedule of camping days on the island.[17]

Mysterious, arid, and distant, anchoring the southern end of the scattering of islands enclosing the Southern California Bight, the island of San Clemente by its very remoteness has become a noted cultural and biological laboratory of ecological recovery and of paleo-archaeological studies, where the latest theories of early continental settlement are being tested. These are leading to a hypothesis of coastal maritime migration—providing knowledge that puts this distant outpost of North America—and its island neighbors—in the center of the debate over the entry of humans into the Americas.[18] Thus, one of the last outposts of indigenous culture becomes a starting point for proto-historical and archaeological exploration, the ongoing gift of the Channel Islands of California.

Notes

CHAPTER 1. AN INTRODUCTION

Epigraph Source: Nicolson, *Sea Room*, 174. The Hebrides archipelago is located off the west coast of Scotland.

1. The factual information in this chapter is based on a number of key works that summarize the important research that has taken place on the Channel Islands over the last 150 years. See the bibliography.
2. The complex prehistory of the Channel Islands has been the subject of much study, especially in the last thirty or forty years. Three sources that I found particularly helpful were Jones and Klar, *California Prehistory*; Gamble, *The Chumash World at European Contact*; and Raab et al., *California Maritime Archaeology*.

CHAPTER 2. THE FIRST INHABITANTS

1. The Channel Islands have been the subject of intensive study by geologists, archaeologists, and anthropologists for more than a century, and the results of their research are available in a large number of scientific publications and anthologies. A good starting point for readers interested in the cultural pre-history of California is Jones and Klar, *California Prehistory*, which contains chapters by many of the leading experts in the field.
2. Harrington became a permanent field ethnologist for the Smithsonian Museum's Bureau of American Ethnology in 1915, a position he would hold for forty years, collecting and compiling a massive amount of raw data on native peoples, including the languages and technologies of the Chumash and Gabrieleño peoples. His vast archive is held in the National Anthropological Archives (NAA), Smithsonian Institution Museum Support Center, Suitland, Maryland.

3. Richard Hughes and Randall Milliken, "Prehistoric Material Conveyance," in Jones and Klar, *California Prehistory*, 266.

4. Crespi, *Description of Distant Roads*, 291.

5. Herbert E. Bolton, *Font's Complete Diary: A Chronicle of the Founding of San Francisco* (Berkeley: University of California Press, 1931), 253; quoted in Gamble, *Chumash World*, 118.

6. Crespi, *Description of Distant Roads*, 447.

7. Quoted in Daily, *California's Channel Islands*, 35.

8. Raab and Fagan, *California Maritime Archaeology*, 145.

9. Donald Johnson, "Episodic Vegetation Stripping, Soil Erosion and Landscape Modification in Prehistoric and Recent Historic Time, San Miguel Island, California," in Power, *California Islands*, 120.

10. Ibid.

11. Fagan, *Before California*, 356.

12. L. Mark Raab, in Raab and Fagan, *California Maritime Archaeology*, 197–211.

12. Quoted in White and Tice, *Santa Catalina Island*, 18.

13. Cleveland, *Voyages and Commercial Enterprises*, 194.

CHAPTER 3. SAN MIGUEL ISLAND

1. Donald Lee Johnson, "Episodic Vegetation Stripping, Soil Erosion and Landscape Modification in Prehistoric and Recent Historic Time, San Miguel Island, California," in Power, *California Islands*, 103.

2. Schoenherr, Feldmeth, and Emerson, *Natural History*, 261.

3. Livingston, "Channel Islands National Park, Historic Resource Study," 46. Hereafter referred to as Livingston, "Study."

4. Bown, *A Most Damnable Invention*, 157; Doran, *Pieces of Eight Channel Islands*, 219; Schoenherr, Feldmeth, and Emerson, *Natural History*, 60; Livingston, "Study," 44.

5. Torben, Erlandson, and Vellanoweth, "Paleocoastal Marine Fishing," 595–613; Schoenherr, Feldmeth, and Emerson, *Natural History*, 60.

6. Guthrie, Thomas, and Kennedy, "A New Species"; Daily, *California's Channel Islands*, 109.

7. Kelsey, *Juan Rodríguez Cabrillo*, 159–61; Schoenherr, Feldmeth, and Emerson, *Natural History*, 266–67.

8. Livingston, "Study," 47.

9. Dollar values in brackets throughout this book estimate the 2011 value based on the Consumer Price Index. "Seven Ways to Compute the Relative Value of a U.S. Dollar Amount: 1774 to Present," MeasuringWorth, www.measuringworth.com/uscompare.

10. Daily, *California's Channel Islands*, 118.

11. William Dall, *Coast Survey*, 1874, cited in Livingston, "Study," 54.

12. Livingston, "Study," 53–54, 55.

13. Diary of Minnie Waters, in Daily, "A Step Back in Time."

14. Cited in Livingston, "Study," which includes much of the detail of the Waters tenancy, 59–68.

15. Arklee Gillian Rawlins, "Life on San Miguel Island in the Year 1903," in Daily, "A Step Back in Time," 56–59.

16. *Daily News and Independent*, September 25, 1916, cited in Livingston, "Study," 66.

17. Doran, *Pieces of Eight Channel Islands*, 221–22.

18. Business statements on file at the Santa Cruz Island Foundation, cited in Livingston "Study," 69.

19. Horace Sexton, "The Wreck of the Cuba," *Noticias: Quarterly Bulletin of the Santa Barbara Historical Society* 5, no. 3 (1959). Reprinted in Daily ed., *Northern Channel Islands Anthology*, 134.

20. Livingston, "Study," 70.

21. Family details in this section from Roberti, *San Miguel Island*.

22. Roberts, *San Miguel Island*, 129.

23. Lester, *Legendary King of San Miguel*; Johnson, "Sweet Memories of San Miguel," *Ventura County Star*, August 24, 2008.

24. Roberts, *San Miguel Island*, 133–36.

25. Blanche Trask, *Los Angeles Times*, January 21, 1906, cited in Doran, *Pieces of Eight Channel Islands*, 219.

CHAPTER 4. SANTA ROSA ISLAND

1. William Carey Jones, *Report on the Subject of Land Titles in California* (1851), quoted in Doran, *Pieces of Eight Channel Islands*, 192; Holland, "Santa Rosa Island," 56. Holland cites Owen H. O'Neill, *History of Santa Barbara County* (Santa Barbara, 1939).

2. Jones to Hon. Charles Fernald, August 4, 1856, in "A County Judge in Arcady," 111, cited in Livingston, "Study," 153.

3. Thompson to Timothy Wolcott, June 12, 1857, Santa Barbara Historical Society, cited in Livingston, "Study," 153.

4. Hollister to Dibblee, Feb. 8, 1861, from the collection of the Santa Barbara Historical Museum.

5. K., "Shearing Time on Santa Rosa Island," *Overland Monthly* 21 (May 1893), 492–501; Holder, *The Channel Islands*, 285.

6. J. Ross Browne, "The Island of Santa Rosa," *Overland Monthly* 13 (September 1874), 209–13, cited in Livingston, "Study," 166.
7. K., "Shearing Time on Santa Rosa Island, *Overland Monthly* 21 (May 1893), 494.
8. Thomas M. Storke, *California Editor*, 1958, 80, cited in Livingston, "Study," 175.
9. Edward Lennox Vail to Agnes Vail, September 25, 1901, reprinted in Allen, ed., *Island of the Cowboys*, 103–105.
10. *Los Angeles Times*, December 3, 1906; unidentified Arizona newspaper in Santa Cruz Island Foundation files, cited in Livingston, "Study," 189.
11. N. R. Vail to E. L. Vail, February 13, 1918, Santa Cruz Island Foundation, cited in Livingston, "Study," 221.
12. Oral history interview with Diego Cuevas, July 26, 1993, by Will Woolley, Tape 7, Santa Cruz Island Foundation, cited in Livingston, "Study," 222.
13. Ibid.
14. Oral history interview with Margaret Vail Woolley by Ann Eggers Jones, March 10, 1994, Santa Cruz Island Foundation, cited in Livingstone, "Study," 233.
15. Ibid., March 2 and 10, 1994, cited in Livingstone, "Study," 235.
16. Interview with Al Vail by Dewey Livingstone, October 4, 1999; notes from interview with Al Vail, September 1992, by Jere Krakow; oral history interview with Al Vail, October 22, 1986, by Marla Daily, and with Margaret Vail Woolley, March 10, 1994, by Ann Eggers Jones, transcript 19–22; all cited in Livingstone, "Study," 214.
17. Oral history interview with Al Vail, October 22, 1986, by Marla Daily, transcript 15–16, Santa Cruz Island Foundation, cited in Livingstone, "Study," 198.
18. Oral history interview with Diego Cuevas, July 8, 1993, by Will Woolley, Tape 7, Santa Cruz Island Foundation, cited in Livingstone, "Study," 196.
19. Oral history interview with Margaret Vail Woolley, March 10, 1994, by Ann Eggers Jones, Santa Cruz Island Foundation, cited in Livingstone, "Study," 196.
20. Oral history interview with Diego Cuevas, July 26, 1993, by Will Woolley, Tape 7, Santa Cruz Island Foundation, cited in Livingstone, "Study," 199–201.
21. Ed Vail to commanding officer of U.S. Naval Amphibious Training Base, San Diego, June 22, 1944, Santa Cruz Island Foundation, cited in Livingstone, "Study," 249.
22. Michael Glassow, "Archaeological Research on Santa Rosa Island," cited in Allen, *Island of the Cowboys*, 162–64.
23. Hillinger, *Channel Islands*, 203.
24. Interview with Tim Setnicka, January 27, 2000, by Dewey Livingstone; Tim Setnicka to Al and Russ Vail, December 30, 1996; and various correspondences in file L30, Vail and Vickers Special Use Permit, CHIS (Channel Islands), cited by Livingstone, "Study," 262.

CHAPTER 5. SANTA CRUZ ISLAND

1. Fr. Estevan Tapis to Gov. Jose Arrillaga, 1805, cited in Livingston, "Study," 459, 461.

2. Woodward, *Sea Diary*; Palou, *Historical Memoirs*.

3. Tapis, "Biennial Mission Reports."

4. Augustias de la Guerra Ord, in Bancroft, *History of California*, vol. 5, 47–49.

5. Alta Calfornia corresponds to today's state of California.

6. The four missions that had accompanying presidios in Alta California were San Diego, Santa Barbara, Monterey, and San Francisco.

7. George Tays, "Captain Andres Castillero, Diplomat: An Account from Unpublished Sources of His Services to Mexico in the Alvarado Revolution of 1836–38," *California Historical Quarterly* 14, no. 3 (September 1935): 230–38.

8. *Thomas Wallace More v. M.J. Box*, November 9 1857.

9. May 25, 1858, *Daily Alta California*. This ad ran for several weeks: "Island for sheep raising. For sale—an island containing about 60,000 acres of land, well-watered, and abounding in small valleys of the best pasturage for sheep. There are no wild animals on it that would interfere with the stock. There is a good harbor and safe anchorage. The owner is now in the city, and if a party should desire to place stock on it, an arrangement may be made to do so, by putting the island, to a certain extent, against the stock furnished. There are about fifty sheep now upon the island. Apply at 119 Sansome Street."

10. It seems likely that James Barron Shaw was a relative of William Barron, as Shaw is noted in Ida Storke's early history of the area as visiting relatives in Mexico.

11. Marla Daily, "California Channel Islands Encyclopedia (Islapedia)," begun 1973, Santa Cruz Island Foundation Archives, reports this: James Barron Shaw (1814–1902), son of a Scottish father and an English mother and graduate of the University of Glasgow (1836) and the Royal College of Surgeons, made three trips around the world, serving as ship's surgeon on a variety of sailing vessels, before arriving in Santa Barbara on January 6, 1850. He practiced medicine and became the first president of the Santa Barbara County Medical Society. In 1851 he began paying the taxes on Santa Cruz Island on behalf of island grantee Andres Castillero. In May 1852 Shaw traveled to Tepic, Mexico, to visit friends and relatives. When he returned a year later, Shaw began managing Santa Cruz Island for Castillero. Shaw continued as manager after the island was sold to William Barron in 1857, staying on for twelve years, until its sale to the Santa Cruz Island Company in 1869. Shaw was one of the investors in Santa Barbara's first wharf, built at the foot of Chapala Street, prior to the construction of Stearn's Wharf. He also invested in a number of ranches, including Los Alamos, La Laguna de San Francisco, La Patera, and the Ortega Ranch in Montecito. In

Santa Barbara, Shaw built a large mansion near the northwest corner of State and Montecito Streets. On May 16, 1861, in San Francisco, Shaw married Helen Augusta Green. William Barron, owner of Santa Cruz Island, served as best man. The Shaws had four sons, only one of whom survived to adulthood, James Barron Shaw, Jr. (1862–1935), godson of William Barron. James B. Shaw, Jr., married Alice Teresa Perkins in Santa Barbara on March 29, 1886. They had three children, all of whom married but none of whom had children. James Barron Shaw died on January 6, 1902, at eighty-eight years of age, and he is buried in Santa Barbara Cemetery, along with his wife and namesake son.

12. *New York Times,* January 24, 1874, cited in Livingston, "Study," 484.

13. George M. Wheeler, "Report upon the United States Geological Surveys West of the One-Hundredth Meridian, in Charge of Capt. George M. Wheeler, Corps of Engineers, U.S. Army, vol. 1, Geographical Report, Washington, 1889," cited in Livingston, "Study," 485.

14. Cleland, *Cattle on a Thousand Hills,* 209.

15. Marla Daily, "California Channel Islands Encyclopedia (Islapedia)," reports this: Gustave Mahé (1831–78) was president of the French Mutual Benefit Society in San Francisco as well as director general of the French Savings and Loan Society, La Societe Française d'Espargnes et de Prevoyance Mutuelle. Along with fourteen other founding French and Italian shareholders, he established the Buenaventura Mining Company in 1863, a venture with interests in gold and coal mines. Justinian Caire was its president and Nicholas Larco its secretary. In 1869, Mahé, along with Caire, Larco, and seven others, founded the Santa Cruz Island Company. On September 17, 1878, Mahé committed suicide by pistol when his bank in San Francisco failed as a result of his embezzlement of bank funds.

16. Marla Daily, "California Channel Islands Encyclopedia (Islapedia)," reports this: On March 29, 1869, the deed to Santa Cruz Island was conveyed from William Barron to the Santa Cruz island Company and its ten stockholders: Pablo Baca, Justinian Caire, Giovanni Battista Cerruti, Thomas J. Gallagher, Adrien Gensoul, Nicolas Larco, Gustave Mahé, Camilo Martin, T. Lemmen Meyer, and Alexander Weill. At the time, each owned one-tenth of the capital stock of the company (a total of six hundred shares valued at $500 each for a total of $300,000). They acquired the island as a basis for sheep and livestock operations. These men were also the directors of the French Savings Bank in San Francisco. At the time of the company's formation, there was widespread cooperation between the French and Italian communities of San Francisco, particularly among powerful businessmen. In 1873 the company reorganized and changed its capital stock to a total of one hundred shares valued at a total of $500,000. Under the reorganization, the number of stockholders decreased

from ten to nine: Baca, Gallagher, and Larco dropped out of the company, and Henry Ohlmeyer and J. V. Delaveaga were added as stockholders. Gustave Mahé owned two-tenths of the stock, with one-tenth each owned by Caire, Cerruti, Delaveaga, Gensoul, Martin, Meyer, Ohlmeyer and Weill. The company had no debts or liabilities. After the suicide of Mahé and the failure of the French Savings Bank, Caire began acquiring additional company stock, and by 1878 he owned seventeen of the one hundred shares. Although transfer records and other corporate papers were destroyed in the 1906 San Francisco earthquake, it is known that by about 1880 Caire had become the majority shareholder of the stock of the Santa Cruz island Company, though there is evidence that A. P. More, owner of neighboring Santa Rosa Island, held 30 percent interest in the island at some point in the early 1880s. Before he died in December 1897, Caire transferred the entire capital stock of the Santa Cruz Island Company to his wife, Albina Cristina Sara Molfino Caire, who would outlived her husband by twenty-seven years.

17. Delphine A. Caire, Journal, vol. 3.

18. For a more detailed discussion of these trends, see Cleland, *Cattle on a Thousand Hills*, chap. 8; and Starr, *Inventing the Dream* , 21–30.

19. Marla Daily and Carey Stanton, "Historical Highlights of Santa Cruz Island," in Daily, ed., *Santa Cruz Island Anthology*.

20. Livingston, "Study," 504–505, amalgamates accounts from various sources, including Marla Daily and Carey Stanton, "Santa Cruz Island, A Brief History of Its Buildings," typescript, 1981.

21. Charles Holder, *The Channel Islands*, 260–61, cited by Livingston, "Study," 509.

22. Livingston, "Study," 549–55.

23. Livingston, "Study," 559–62. He cites an interview conducted with Vivienne Caire Chiles.

24. Helen Caire, *Santa Cruz Island*, 72.

25. Ibid., 68.

26. Santa Cruz Island Company correspondence, December 4, 1884.

27. The subject of the island wine is discussed in detail in Pinney, *The Wine of Santa Cruz Island*.

28. Livingston, "Study," 563, citing a memo from Jeanne Caire.

29. Pinney, *Wine of Santa Cruz Island*, 33.

30. Letter dated January 18, 1912, Correspondence of Ciocca-Lombardi Wine Company; Pinney, *Wine of Santa Cruz Island*, 66.

31. Santa Cruz Island Company Payroll Book, 1889–1893, cited in Livingston, "Study," 616–20.

32. Letter from Superintendent Joyaux to Justinian Caire, January 20, 1880, Santa Cruz Island Company Records.

33. February 1882, Joyaux Memorandum from Santa Cruz Island, Santa Cruz Island Company Records.

34. Santa Cruz Island Company, Wool Clip Records, Shearing Records, Ledger, breaks down the different types of sheep sheared and where they were rounded up on the island. Santa Cruz Island Company, D 1890, 296, Santa Cruz Island Foundation, cited in Livingston, "Study," 581.

35. *Potrero* was the word used on the island to denote a field or area that was used for grazing livestock. This distinguished it from a *campo*, a field that was devoted to raising crops such as wheat or alfalfa.

36. Santa Cruz Island Company Ledger, 285–94, 300–301, Santa Cruz Island Foundation, cited in Livingston, "Study," 580. The fall shearing for 1909 showed that the "Scorpion district" produced more wool than the Main Ranch.

37. Livingston, "Study," 570.

38. *San Francisco Call*, December 10, 1897.

39. Arthur Caire, memorandum, ca. 1932.

40. Will of Justinian Caire, January 24 1889; codicil to will of Justinian Caire, January 28, 1889, Alameda County Superior Court, Case No. 5540.

41. Ibid.

42. Edmund Rossi, University of California Oral History Project Interview, 1969, 33–34; Journal of Delphine Caire, vol. 3.

43. Journal of Delphine Caire, vol. 3.

44. Arthur Caire, memorandum, ca. 1931.

45. Albina left an equal number of shares to each of her children (ten shares each in Justinian Caire Company and seven shares each in the Santa Cruz Island Company), but they were endorsed back to her, and she retained ownership of all but four shares of each company. These were the two shares she had given each of her sons before she left for Italy in 1905, in recognition of the amount of their salaries that they had contributed to her upkeep since her husband's death in 1897.

46. Letter from Rossi to Capuccio, August 30, 1906, written on Italian Swiss Colony stationery, cited by John Gherini, *Santa Cruz Island*, 123. The italics are mine.

47. Giustiniano Molfino, letter to Delphine Caire, April 1917.

48. Diary of Arthur Caire, July 28, 1911, December 12, 1911.

49. Santa Cruz Island Company, Secretary's Report 1906.

50. Santa Cruz Island Company, Secretary's Report 1907.

51. Santa Cruz Island Company, Secretary's Report 1908. For example, Amelie Rossi and Aglae Capuccio each received dividends of $1,750 [$42,000 in 2011 equivalent].

52. Santa Cruz Island Company, Secretary's Report 1910.

53. Symmes & Associates, Report on Santa Cruz Island, Section 2, Inventory, Santa Barbara, 1922, sheet 1.

54. Ibid., sheet 2.

55. Symmes & Associates, Report on Santa Cruz Island, 16.

56. Transcript on appeal in *Rossi v. Caire*, SF 7101 (174 Cal. 74), pp. 110–12, cited in Gherini, *Santa Cruz Island*, 238.

57. Arthur Caire, memorandum, "Ownership of Stock," ca. 1932, 92.

58. Arthur Caire, memorandum, ca. 1931, 19.

59. Arthur Caire, memorandum notebook, ca. 1931, 27.

60. *Edmund A. Rossi v. Arthur Caire, et al.*, San Francisco Superior Court, no. 43295.

61. Symmes & Associates, Report on Santa Cruz Island, Section 2, Inventory, Santa Barbara, 1922, sheet 1; Shareholders Report, Santa Cruz Island Company, 1912.

62. Diary of Arthur Caire. Note from his personal diary kept between 1911–30, "Mismanagement," 119.

63. *Rossi v. Caire* (1916) 174 Cal. 74, 161 1161.

64. Gherini, *Santa Cruz Island*, 133.

65. Diary of Arthur Caire, 1920, 99–100, 115–16.

66. Unpublished memo of Ambrose Gherini, 1937, 3–4, cited in Gherini, *Santa Cruz Island*, 133.

67. *Rossi v. Caire* (1916) 174 Cal. 74, 83.

68. *Capuccio v. Caire* (1922) 189 Cal. 514 at 524–25.

69. 1922 Deering memo, cited in Gherini, *Santa Cruz Island*, 146.

70. Memorandum of agreements, January 28, 1921, cited in Gherini, *Santa Cruz Island*, 157.

71. Eaton, *Diary of a Sea Captain's Wife*, 222–23.

72. Santa Cruz Island Company, Shareholders Report, 1920.

73. F. F. Caire, letter to Col. Edward Wentworth, Armour Livestock Bureau, March 13, 1940; McElrath, *On Santa Cruz Island*, 33–48.

74. Company records show that the clip in the 1880s averaged eight hundred sacks per year.

75. Eaton, *Diary of a Sea Captain's Wife*, 212–18, 233–34.

76. A report commissioned for the National Park Service in 1933 stated, "The owners of Santa Cruz Island place a valuation [$4 million] far in excess of its assessed valuation. The Island does not produce a very substantial revenue and in some years it is said to show a loss, but taxes are low and the owners have been able to hold it for a possible future sale." The author suggested an offer of $1.5 to $2 million or a sale of parts of the island with scenic values but no value for agriculture. This report was not acted upon. Cited in Livingston, "Study," 645.

77. Warren, "Agriculture of the Channel Islands," 34, cited in Livingston, "Study," 644.

78. Pinney, *Wine of Santa Cruz Island*, 92–93.

79. *Cappucio v. Caire* (1932) 215 Cal. 518, 529, 11p.2d 1097.

80. *Santa Barbara Press*, July 28, 1925.

81. Gherini, *Santa Cruz Island*, 182–83; National Trading Company, Financial Report of Scorpion Ranch Operations, 1926–1927, cited by Livingston, "Study," 674. Aimee Rossi's interest had already been purchased by her sister when Aimee entered the Sacred Heart Order.

82. *Santa Barbara Press*, July 28, 1925.

83. Gherini, *Santa Cruz Island*, 182–83; National Trading Company, Financial Report of Scorpion Ranch Operations, 1926–1927, cited by Livingston, "Study," 674.

84. National Trading Company, President's Reports of Scorpion Ranch Operations for the year 1928, 1929, cited by Livingston, "Study," 675, 677.

85. Gherini, *Santa Cruz Island*, 184.

86. Gherini, *Santa Cruz Island*, 185.

87. Balance Sheets, Scorpion Ranch, 1927–1944, cited by Livingston, "Study," 677.

88. Gherini, *Santa Cruz Island*, 185–86.

89. Ambrose Gherini to Pier Gherini, June 13, 1951, and Pier Gherini to Ambrose Gherini, June 22, 1951; Earl Warren, "The Agriculture of Santa Cruz Island," cited by Livingston, "Study," 679–81.

90. Gherini, *Santa Cruz Island*, 1997, 193–200.

91. Livingston, "Study," 681–83.

92. Gherini, *Santa Cruz Island*, 202–203.

93. Gherini, *Santa Cruz Island*, 213.

94. Cited in Livingston, "Study," 716.

95. *Santa Barbara News Press*, April 22, 1937.

96. *Santa Barbara News Press*, October 13, 1937.

97. Jeanne Caire, memorandum, March 6, 1978.

98. Inverview with Red Craine by John Gherini September 13, 1983, cited by Livingston, "Study," 722.

99. Coldwell Banker listing, March 1950.

100. Daily and Stanton, *Santa Cruz Island*, 21, cited by Livingston, "Study."

101. Stanton, *An Island Memoir*.

102. Marla Daily, "Chapel of the Holy Cross," Occasional Paper, no. 5, Santa Cruz Island Foundation, 1991.

103. Recollection of Jane Rich Mueller, cited in Livingston, "Study," 745.

104. *Edwin L. Stanton III v. Santa Cruz Island Company, et al.*, Los Angeles Superior Court No. C180228.

105. Marla Daily, cited by Gherini, *Santa Cruz Island*, 168–71.

106. Livingston, "Study," 747–48; Gherini, *Santa Cruz Island*, 172–77.

107. "California: Protecting the Golden State," Nature Conservancy, www.nature
.org/wherewework/northamerica/states/california/preserves.

CHAPTER 6. ANACAPA ISLAND

1. M. Kinsell, "The Santa Barbara Islands," *Overland Monthly* 18 (December
    1891): 617–31, cited in Doran, *Pieces of Eight Channel Islands*, 124.

2. Livingston, "Study," 783.

3. Schoenherr, Feldmeth, and Emerson, *Natural History*, 305. Various details of the
    flora and fauna of Anacapa in this chapter have been identified from this source.

4. J. Southworth, *Santa Barbara and Montecito, Past and Present* (Santa Barbara,
    1920), cited in Doran, *Pieces of Eight Channel Islands*, 123.

5. Channel Islands National Marine Sanctuary, *Winfield Scott*, vessel history,
    2006, www.channelislands.noaa.gov (page discontinued April 15, 2014); "Win-
    field Scott Shipwreck," in *Explore the Channel Islands*, Camp Internet, http://
    www.rain.org/campinternet/channelhistory/expedition2/shipwrecks/ship
    wreckwinfieldscott.html; *Gold Rush Shipwrecks* (Washington, D.C.: Minerals
    Management Service, 2006).

6. Karen Jones Dowty, "Frenchie," *Ventura County Historical Society Quarterly* 23,
    no. 3 (Spring 1978): 25–26, cited in Livingston, "Study," 793.

7. Sidney E. Lang, "The Frenchman of Anacapa Island," cited in Livingston,
    "Study," 794.

8. Ralph and Lisa Shanks, "Anacapa Light Station," unpublished manuscript,
    cited in Livingston, "Study," 803.

9. Livingston, "Study," 806.

10. Shanks, "Anacapa Light Station," *Santa Barbara News Press*, July 16, 1951, cited
    in Livingston, "Study," 806.

11. "Anacapa Light Station," National Park Service, www.nps.gov/chis/history
    culture/anacapalight.htm.

12. Livingston, "Study," 809, cites various relevant memos and agreements.

CHAPTER 7. SANTA BARBARA ISLAND

1. For a contemporary description of the island, see Schoenherr, Feldmeth, and
    Emerson, *Natural History*, 346–57. For descriptions from nineteenth-century
    visitors, see Doran, *Pieces of Eight*.

2. J. R. Britton, "Our Summer Isles," *Sunshine: A Magazine of California and the
    Southwest* 7, no. 5 (October 1897): 192–94, cited in Livingston, "Study," 840;
    Doran, *Pieces of Eight*, 113.

3. Cited in Livingston, "Study," 850. Other details of the Hyder tenure are found in Daily, *California Channel Islands*, 64–70.

4. Cal Reynolds, oral history interview March 1, 1979, Ron Morgan SBMNH #1761, cited in Livingston, "Study," 858.

5. Sumner quoted in memorandum from Victor Cahalane, acting chief, Wildlife Division, to Dr. Russell, et al., August 14, 1939, RG 79, Central Decimal Site Files 1932–53, Box 14, File 201, NA (SB), cited in Livingston, "Study," 863.

CHAPTER 8. SAN NICOLAS ISLAND

1. Various details of geology, flora and fauna are based on Schoenherr, Feldmeth, and Emerson, *Natural History*, 333–46. Other details come from Daily, *California's Channel Islands*, 129–41.

2. The following account is based on William H. Ellison, ed., *The Life and Adventures of George Nidever (1802–1883): The Life Story of a Remarkable Pioneer Told in His Own Words, and None Wasted* (Berkeley: University of California Press, 1937); reproductions of articles in Doran, *Pieces of Eight Channel Islands*, 39–43; Maynard Geiger, *Juana María: The Lone Original Accounts of the Lone Woman of San Nicolas Island* (Ramona, Calif.: Ballena Press, n.d.), reprinted from Reports of the University of California Archaeological Survey No. 55, Berkeley (1961); Robert F. Heizer and Elbert B. Elsasser, eds., *The Lost Woman of San Nicolas Island, 1835–1853* (Santa Barbara: The Serra Shop, Old Mission Santa Barbara, 1976).

3. Paul Schumacher, "Some Remains of a Former People," *Overland Monthly* 15, no. 4 (1875): 374–79, cited in Doran, *Pieces of Eight*, 24–29.

4. Daily, *California's Channel Islands*, 138–40.

5. Schoenherr, Feldmeth, and Emerson, *Natural History*, 41.

6. Daily, *California's Channel Islands*, 146.

7. Ibid., 147.

8. Schoenherr, Feldmeth, and Emerson, *Natural History*, 338–39.

9. M. L. Shettle, Jr., "Naval Auxiliary Air Station, San Nicolas Island: History," California State Military Museum, www.militarymuseum.org/NAASSan-NicolasIsland.html.

10. Doran, *Pieces of Eight*, 24.

11. Schoenherr, Feldmeth, and Emerson, *Natural History*, 345.

12. Steve Chawkins, "Complex Effort to Rid San Nicolas Island of Cats Declared a Success," *Los Angeles Times*, February 26, 2012, 2; Patty McCormac, "Island's Feral Cats Get Home at Rehab Center," *San Diego Union-Tribune*, December 24, 2009.

CHAPTER 9. SANTA CATALINA ISLAND

1. Schoenherr, Feldmeth, and Emerson, *Natural History*, 147–49; Daily, *California's Channel Islands, 1001 Questions Answered*. The section on Santa Catalina Island contains many reference facts cited in this chapter.

2. Martin, *Santa Catalina Island*, 8–10.

3. Dana, *Two Years before the Mast*, 336.

4. White and Tice, *Santa Catalina Island*, 11; Doran, *Pieces of Eight*, 84.

5. Schoenherr, Feldmeth, and Emerson, *Natural History*, 177–82.

6. Schoenherr, Feldmeth, and Emerson, *Natural History*, 154, cites a list compiled by Gary Wallace in 1985.

7. Martin, *Santa Catalina Island*, 11–17.

8. Schoenherr, Feldmeth, and Emerson, *Natural History*, 191.

9. Schoenherr, Feldmeth, and Emerson, *Natural History*, 192.

10. Bruce Coblentz in Dennis Power, *The California Islands*, 167; Schoenherr, Feldmeth, and Emerson, *Natural History*, 157.

11. Martin, *Santa Catalina Island*, 32–34.

12. Schoenherr, Feldmeth, and Emerson, *Natural History*, 150.

13. Martin, *Santa Catalina Island*, 36; Schoenherr, Feldmeth, and Emerson, *Natural History*, 150.

14. Cited by White and Tice, *Santa Catalina Island*, 17.

15. Martin, *Santa Catalina Island*, 32.

16. Eugene Duflot de Mofras, *Travels on the Pacific Coast*, translated and edited by Marguerite Eyer Wilbur (Santa Barbara: Narratives Press, 2004); Dana, *Two Years before the Mast*; Andrew Rolle, *An American in California: The Biography of William Heath Davis, 1822–1909* (San Marino, Calif.: Huntington Library, 1956).

17. Martin, *Santa Catalina Island*, 38.

18. Samuel H. Williamson, "Seven Ways to Compute the Relative Value of a U.S. Dollar Amount: 1774 to present," *MeasuringWorth*, March 2011, www.measuringworth.com.

19. Daily, *California's Channel Islands*, 199–201.

20. Schoenherr, Feldmeth, and Emerson, *Natural History*, 149; White and Tice, *Santa Catalina Island*, 26ff.

21. Starr, *Inventing the Dream*, 66.

22. Doran, *Pieces of Eight*, 97.

23. Sitton, *Grand Ventures*, 213–28.

24. White and Tice, *Santa Catalina Island*, 45–54.

25. Ibid., 52; Doran, *Pieces of Eight*, 100.

26. White and Tice, *Santa Catalina Island*, 57, 148; Sidney Redner, "Population History of Los Angeles," Boston University Physics Department, http://physics.bu.edu/~redner/projects/population/cities/la.html.

27. Daily, *California's Channel Islands*, 184; White and Tice, *Santa Catalina Island*, 201–202.

28. White and Tice, *Santa Catalina Island*, 53.

29. Ernest Windle, quoted in White and Tice, *Santa Catalina Island*, 55.

30. Mallan, *Guide to Catalina*, 56.

31. White and Tice, *Santa Catalina Island*, 129–30.

32. Ibid., 131–39.

33. Ibid., 151.

34. Newmark, Marco, "Early California Resorts," *Los Angeles, Southern California Historical Society Quarterly* 35, no. 2 (1953): 129–52, cited in Doran, *Pieces of Eight*, 291.

35. Interview with Geoff Rusack, executive chairman, Santa Catalina Island Company, Wrigley family member, April 13, 2013; interview with Randy Herrel, CEO, Catalina Island Company, May 4, 2013.

CHAPTER 10. SAN CLEMENTE ISLAND

1. Schoenherr, Feldmeth, and Emerson, *Natural History*, 314ff. Many of this chapter's details on San Clemente Island's flora, fauna, and geology are drawn from this work.

2. Raab et al., *California Maritime Archaeology*, xv–xvii.

3. Rosanna Welch, "A Brief History of the Tongva Tribe," Ph.D. dissertation, Claremont University, 2006, 3–4. Welch discusses the Tongva peoples and their interaction with the explorers.

4. Raab et al., *California Maritime Archaeology*, 145–62.

5. Ibid., 24, 34–35.

6. Ibid., 163–66.

7. Ibid., 178.

8. Ibid., 64. Raab et al. cite R. Cleveland, *Voyages and Commercial Enterprises of the Sons of New England* (New York: Leavitt and Allen, 1885).

9. Ibid.

10. "1935 and 1936 Photos of Gray Whales Slaughtered in the Bay Are on Exhibit," *Argonaut Online*, January 5, 2006, http://argonautnews.com/; a wider discussion of the whaling trade along the Pacific coast can be found in Webb, *On the Northwest*.

11. Schoenherr, Feldmeth, and Emerson, *Natural History*, 318.

12. Daily, *California's Channel Islands*, 169–72.

13. Ibid., 172.

14. Schoenherr, Feldmeth, and Emerson, *Natural History*, 317–18.

15. Ibid., 326–27.

16. Ibid., 327.

17. M. L. Shettle, Jr., "Naval Auxiliary Air Station, San Clemente Island," in San Clemente Island Range Complex, California State Military Museum, www .militarymuseum.org/NAASSanClemente.

18. Raab et al., *California Maritime Archaeology*, 239; Rick C. Torben, Jon M. Erlandson, Rene L. Vellanoweth, and Todd J. Braje, "From Pleistocene Mariners to Complex Hunter-Gatherers: The Archaeology of the California Channel Islands," *Journal of World Prehistory* 19 (2005): 169–228.

Selected Bibliography

ARCHIVAL AND MANUSCRIPT COLLECTIONS

Diaries of Arthur Caire, 1911–1940. In the possession of Justinian Caire III.

Caire Family Archive. In the author's possession.

Journal of Delphine A. Caire, volumes 1–4. In the author's possession.

Justinian Caire Company Journals, 1906–1912, and Justinian Caire Company Records. In the author's possession.

Santa Bárbara Mission Archive-Library, Santa Barbara, California.

Santa Cruz Island Company Records. In the author's possession.

Santa Cruz Island Foundation Archives. Carpinteria, California.

COURT CASES

Capuccio v. Caire, 189 Ca1. 514 (1922) (action began March 1913).

Edwin L. Stanton III v. Santa Cruz Island Company, et al., Los Angeles Superior Court No. C180228, filed January 2, 1976.

Rossi v. Caire, 174 Cal. 74, 161 Pac. 1161. S.F. 7101 (1916) (action begun 1912).

Thomas Wallace More v. M.J. Box, Santa Barbara County District court, 2nd Judicial District, November 9, 1857.

PUBLISHED WORKS

Allen, Kerry Blankenship. *Island of the Cowboys: Santa Rosa Island*. Santa Barbara: Santa Cruz Island Foundation, 1996.

Ascensión, Antonio de la. "Father Ascensión's Account of the Voyage of Sebastian Vizcaino." Translated by Henry R. Wagner. *California Historical Society Quarterly* 7, no. 4 (1928): 345–46.

———. "Spanish Voyages to the Northwest Coast in the 16th Century." Translated by Henry R. Wagner. *California Historical Society Quarterly* 7, no. 4 (1928): 295–394.

Bancroft, Hubert H. *History of California*. 7 vols. Berkeley, Calif.: Bancroft Library, 1886–1890.

———. *The Native Races*. 5 vols. Berkeley, Calif.: Bancroft Library, 1874–1875.

Bown, Stephen R. *A Most Damnable Invention: Dynamite, Nitrates, and the Making of the Modern World*. New York: St. Martin's Press, 2005.

Caire, Helen. "A Brief History of Santa Cruz Island from 1869 to 1937." *Ventura County Historical Society Quarterly* 27, no. 4 (Summer 1982): 3–33.

———. *Santa Cruz Island: A History and Recollections of an Old California Rancho*. Spokane, Wash.: Arthur H. Clark, 1993.

Caire, L. A. Jeanne. "In Memoriam: Delphine A. Caire." *California Historical Society Quarterly* 24 (1949): 81–83.

Camp, Charles L. "The Chronicles of George C. Yount, California Pioneer 1826." *California Historical Quarterly* 2 (April 1923): 2–3.

———, ed. *George C. Yount and His Chronicles of the West*. Denver: Old West, 1966.

Chiles, Frederic Caire. *Justinian Caire and Santa Cruz Island: The Rise and Fall of a California Dynasty*. Norman, Okla.: Arthur H. Clark, 2011.

Cleland, Robert Glass. *The Cattle on a Thousand Hills*. San Marino, Calif.: Huntington Library, 1951.

Cleveland, Richard J. *Voyages and Commercial Enterprises of the Sons of New England*. New York: Leavitt and Allen, 1885.

Crespi, Juan. *A Description of Distant Roads: Original Journals of the First Expedition into California, 1769–1770*. Edited by Alan Brown. San Diego: San Diego State University Press, 2001.

Daily, Marla. *California's Channel Islands: 1001 Questions Answered*. Santa Barbara: Shoreline Press, 1997.

———, ed. *Northern Channel Islands Anthology*. Santa Barbara: Santa Cruz Island Foundation, 1989.

———, ed. *Santa Cruz Island Anthology*. Occasional Paper 1. Santa Barbara: Santa Cruz Island Foundation, 1989.

———, ed. "A Step Back in Time: Unpublished Channel Islands Diaries." Occasional Paper 4. San Louis Obispo: Santa Cruz Island Foundation, 1990.

Daily, Marla, and Santa Cruz Island Foundation. *The California Channel Islands*. Images of America Series. Charleston, S.C.: Arcadia Publishing, 2012.

Dana, Richard Henry. *Two Years before the Mast*. Boston: Houghton Mifflin, 1911.

Doran, Adelaide. *Pieces of Eight Channel Islands: Bibliographical Guide and Source Book*. Glendale, Calif.: Arthur H. Clark, 1980.

Eaton, Margaret Holden. *Diary of a Sea Captain's Wife*. Santa Barbara: McNally and Loftin, 1980.

Fagan, Brian. *Before California*. Lanham, Md.: Rowman and Littlefield, 2003.

Gamble, Lynn. *The Chumash World at European Contact.* Berkeley: University of California Press, 2008.

Gherini, John. *Santa Cruz Island.* Spokane: Arthur H. Clark, 1997.

Gleason, Duncan. *The Islands and Ports of California.* New York: Devin-Adair, 1958.

Guthrie, Daniel A., Howell W. Thomas, and George L. Kennedy. "A New Species of Extinct Late Pleistocene Puffin (*Aves: alcidae*) from the Southern California Channel Islands." In *Proceedings of the Fifth California Islands Symposium,* U.S. Dept. of Interior, Minerals Management Service, Pacific OCS Region, 1999, 525–30.

Hillinger, Charles. *Channel Islands.* Santa Barbara: Santa Cruz Island Foundation, 1998.

Holder, Charles F. *The Channel Islands of California.* Chicago: A. C. McClurg, 1910.

Holland, Francis. "Santa Rosa Island: An Archeological and Historical Study." *Los Angeles, Journal of the West* 1, no. 1 (July 1962): 45–62.

Jones, Terry L., and Kathryn A. Klar, eds. *California Prehistory: Colonization, Culture, and Complexity.* Lanham, Md.: Rowman & Littlefield, 2007.

Kelsey, Harry. *Juan Rodríguez Cabrillo.* San Marino, Calif.: Huntington Library Press, 1986.

Kroeber, A. L. *Handbook of the Indians of California.* Berkeley: California Book Company, 1953.

Lester, Elizabeth. *The Legendary King of San Miguel: Island Life in the Santa Barbara Channel.* Santa Barbara: McNally and Loftin, 1974.

Livingston, Dewey S. "Draft Historic Resource Study Channel Islands National Park." Unpublished manuscript, National Park Service, Department of the Interior, 2006. In collection of the Channel Islands National Park.

Mallan, Chicki. *Guide to Catalina.* Paradise, Calif.: Pine Press, 1996.

Martin, Terrence. *Santa Catalina Island: The Story behind the Scenery.* Las Vegas, Nev.: KC Publications, 1993.

McElrath, Clifford. *On Santa Cruz Island.* Santa Barbara: Santa Barbara Historical Society, 1967.

Miller, Bruce. *The Gabrielino.* Los Osos, Calif.: Sand River Press, 1991.

Nicolson, Adam. *Sea Room: An Island Life in the Hebrides.* New York: Farrar, Straus and Giroux, 2002.

Nidever, George. *The Life and Adventures of George Nidever.* Edited by William Henry Ellison. Berkeley: University of California Press, 1937.

O'Dell, Scott. *Island of the Blue Dolphins.* Boston: Houghton Mifflin, 1960.

Palou, Francisco. *Historical Memoirs of New California.* Edited by Herbert Eugene Bolton. 4 vols. Berkeley: University of California Press, 1926.

———. *Spanish Exploration in the Southwest, 1542–1706.* Edited by Herbert E. Bolton. New York: Charles Scribner's Sons, 1916.

Pinney, Thomas. *The Wine of Santa Cruz Island*. Santa Barbara: Santa Cruz Island Foundation, 1994.

Power, Dennis, ed. *The California Islands: Proceedings of a Multidisciplinary Symposium*. Santa Barbara: Santa Barbara Museum of Natural History, 1978.

Raab, L. Mark, Jim Cassidy, Andrew Yatsko, and William J. Howard. *California Maritime Archaeology: A San Clemente Island Perspective*. Lanham, Md.: Alta Mira Press, 2009.

Roberti, Betsy. *San Miguel Island: My Childhood Memoir, 1930–1942*. Santa Barbara: Santa Cruz Island Foundation, 2008.

Roberts, Lois. *San Miguel Island*. Carmel, Calif.: Cal Rim Books, 1991.

Schoenherr, Alan A., C. Robert Feldmeth, and Michael J. Emerson. *Natural History of the Islands of California*. Berkeley: University of California Press, 1999.

Sitton, Tom. *Grand Ventures: The Banning Family and the Shaping of Southern California*. San Marino, Calif.: Huntington Library, 2010.

Smith, William Sidney. *The Geology of Santa Catalina Island*. San Francisco: California Academy of Sciences, 1897.

Stanton, Carey. *An Island Memoir*. Los Angeles: Zamorano Club, 1984.

Starr, Kevin. *Inventing the Dream: California through the Progressive Era*. New York: Oxford University Press, 1985.

Tays, George. "Captain Andres Castillero, Diplomat: An Account from Unpublished Sources of His Services to Mexico in the Alvarado Revolution of 1836–38." *California Historical Quarterly* 14, no. 3 (September 1935): 230–38.

Torben, C. Rick, Jon M. Erlandson, and René L. Vellanoweth. "Paleocoastal Marine Fishing on the Pacific Coast of the Americas: Perspectives from Daisy Cave, California." *American Antiquity* 66, no. 4. (October 2001): 595–613.

Vail, Edward R. "Diary of a Desert Trail." *Arizona Daily Star*, March 9, 1922.

Wagner, Henry R. "Juan Rodriguez Cabrillo: Discoverer of the Coast of California." *California Historical Society Quarterly* 7 (March 1928): 20–77.

Webb, Robert. *On the Northwest: Commercial Whaling in the Pacific Northwest, 1790–1967*. Vancouver: University of British Columbia Press, 1988.

White, William, and Steven Tice. *Santa Catalina Island: Its Magic, People and History*. Glendora, Calif.: White Limited Editions, 1997.

Woodward, Arthur. *The Sea Diary of Fr. Juan Vizcaino to Alta California 1769*. Los Angeles: Glen Dawson, 1959.

Index

Italics indicate pages with illustrations.